FEAR *and the* FIRST AMENDMENT

RHETORIC, LAW, AND THE HUMANITIES

Series Editor

Clarke Rountree

Editorial Advisory Board

Elizabeth C. Britt
A. Cheree Carlson
Kirsten K. Davis
Marouf Hasian Jr.
Catherine L. Langford
Francis J. Mootz III
Sean Patrick O'Rourke
Trevor Parry-Giles
Eileen A. Scallen
Edward Schiappa
Colin Starger
Omar Swartz
Gerald B. Wetlaufer
David Zarefsky

FEAR *and the* FIRST AMENDMENT

Controversial Cases of the Roberts Court

KEVIN A. JOHNSON AND CRAIG R. SMITH

THE UNIVERSITY OF ALABAMA PRESS

Tuscaloosa

The University of Alabama Press
Tuscaloosa, Alabama 35487-0380
uapress.ua.edu

Copyright © 2024 by the University of Alabama Press
All rights reserved.

Inquiries about reproducing material from this work should
be addressed to the University of Alabama Press.

Typeface: Adobe Jenson Pro

Cover design: Lori Lynch

Cataloging-in-Publication data is available from the Library of Congress.
ISBN: 978-0-8173-2196-3 (cloth)
ISBN: 978-0-8173-6145-7 (paper)
E-ISBN: 978-0-8173-9499-8

Contents

CHAPTER 1   Fear as a Recurring Theme in First Amendment Conflicts   1

CHAPTER 2   Fear and Student Speech: *Morse v. Frederick*   29

CHAPTER 3   Fear and Unlimited Spending in Election Campaigns: *Citizens United v. Federal Elections Commission*   51

CHAPTER 4   Fear and Religious Freedom: *Christian Legal Society v. Martinez, Burwell v. Hobby Lobby,* and *Kennedy v. Bremerton School District*   84

CHAPTER 5   Fear at the Burial of a Soldier: *Snyder v. Phelps*   113

CHAPTER 6   Fear and Protecting Depictions of Violence in Video Games: *Brown v. Entertainment Merchants Association*   130

CHAPTER 7   Fear and Indecent, Obscene, and Graphic Speech: *FCC v. Fox Television Stations, Ashcroft v. American Civil Liberties Union,* and *United States v. Stevens*   151

CHAPTER 8   Themes and Implications of Fear and the First Amendment   175

                    Notes   195

                    Bibliography   221

                    Index   237

FEAR *and the* FIRST AMENDMENT

1

Fear as a Recurring Theme in First Amendment Conflicts

ON FEBRUARY 13, 2021, fifty-seven senators, including seven Republicans, voted to convict ex-President Donald Trump on one article of impeachment. That number was ten shy of the number needed for a conviction on the charge of incitement to insurrection. However, the impeachment trial left us with several questions: What led the House of Representatives to interpret the president's words as incitement? Can other legal entities prosecute the president for incitement?

By the time all the votes were counted in the 2020 presidential election, it was clear that this had been an election like no other. Former vice president Joe Biden received more votes than any presidential candidate in history. However, President Trump received the second most votes of any candidate in history. The fact that Trump ran about seven million votes ahead of his 2016 vote count and still lost led Trump followers to believe that the election had been rigged. This conspiracy theory was promoted by Trump, with help from some social media outlets and even some cable commentary programs. More responsible elements in the media referred to Trump's claims as "the big lie."

On the day before Congress was to convene to certify the results of the electoral college, security forces in Washington, DC, alerted Mark Meadows, the president's chief of staff, that right-wing groups were

CHAPTER I

planning to mass at the Capitol. According to the June 28, 2022, testimony of Meadows aide Cassidy Hutchinson to the House Committee investigating the events of January 6, 2021, she accompanied Trump, Meadows, and the then head of security Anthony Ornato to a rally on the ellipse across from the back of the White House. For security reasons, anyone entering the rally site had to pass through magnetometers. Some entering the area surrendered weapons; others refused to enter, evidently not wishing to surrender weapons.

According to Hutchinson, when Trump surveyed the rally, he asked for an explanation as to why it was so small. He was told about the deterrent effect of the "mags." He immediately ordered the screening to stop and to let all comers in. He was overruled by security forces and became irate. Once he calmed down, he led a delegation onstage to speak to those in attendance. Addressing demonstrators, Rudy Giuliani and Donald Trump Jr. preceded the president, firing up the mob and thus establishing a context for the president's remarks. A short film was screened; it purported to identify the enemies of the president (Joe Biden, Nancy Pelosi, and Chuck Schumer), touted the Lost Cause, and then filled the screen with one word: "FEAR." Trump then emerged and urged his followers to march on the Capitol "peaceably." According to Hutchinson, Trump insisted on being taken to the Capitol. Ornato told him it was too dangerous. The House committee heard Washington, DC, police radios describing armed demonstrators, some with AR-15s. Once in his secure SUV, Trump again insisted on going to the Capitol. Hutchinson testified that Ornato told her that Trump grabbed the wheel of the SUV but was disengaged from it by Secret Service agent Bobby Engel. Trump then lunged at Engel.[1] What is clear is that Trump knew at that juncture that a dangerous demonstration was underway and that he wanted to attend it.

In the meantime, demonstrators already at the Capitol were joined by the mob from the rally. They viciously attacked the small band of Capitol police who were protecting the building. They broke through the police lines, smashing windows and doors, and broke into the Capitol itself. It was the worst attack on the Capitol since the British invasion of 1814. Five people died, including a Capitol police officer, and many were injured in the melee that followed. Trump's followers trashed the building, some urinating in its hallways. They began to chant "Hang Mike Pence,"

2

and the vice president, in a secure location, was notified of the danger. Trump tweeted his indifference to Pence's plight.

The floors of the House and Senate and many congressional offices were attacked in the midst of the insurrection. One demonstrator made his way into Speaker Pelosi's office, sat in her chair, and put his feet on her desk. He left a note behind: "We will never back down." Another took her podium and paraded with it through the Capitol rotunda. Many demonstrators claimed to be following orders of the president. Other demonstrators were heard to yell "Where's Nancy?" and others continued to rant "Hang Mike Pence!" The nation was shocked. Despite pleas from his staff and family, Trump did nothing. Emails and texts sent to Meadows from Fox News contacts, among others, urged him to get the president to call off the demonstration. Trump still did nothing.

Eventually, order was restored, and Congress certified the election over the objections of 140 House Republicans and several Senate Republicans. Over the course of the next week, President Trump was impeached, this time for inciting an insurrection. Incitement to violence is a crime in many states and with the federal government. The federal statute reads: "Whoever incites, sets on foot, assists, or engages in any rebellion or insurrection against the authority of the United States or the laws thereof, or gives aid or comfort thereto, shall be fined under this title or imprisoned not more than ten years, or both; and shall be incapable of holding any office under the United States."[2] But what is the actual definition of incitement? What is the burden of proof that a prosecutor must meet to prove incitement?

Supreme Court Justice Oliver Wendell Holmes argued that for speech to be proscribed, that is, to lose First Amendment protection, it must be a "true threat," which he defined as presenting "a clear and present danger."[3] However, in his dissent in *Abrams*, Holmes condemned the government's "attempts to check the expression of opinions that we loathe and believe to be fraught with death, unless they so imminently threaten immediate interference with the lawful and pressing purposes of the law that an immediate check is required to save the country."[4] That same year, Holmes developed his test with a powerful metaphor in the *Schenk* ruling when he argued that "falsely shouting fire in a theater and causing a panic" was not protected by the First Amendment.[5] Such speech presented a true threat. Thus, Holmes used context to establish

CHAPTER I

when protected ideological speech becomes prosecutable action. What emerges from these opinions is a dialectic between the fear of imminent danger and the fear of quashing legitimate protest.

The next step in the development of the true threats doctrine came in a case that reinforced the use of context to determine whether words could be seen as actions. In this case, the fear of a threat won out over the fear of censorship. During World War II, a pamphleteer named Chaplinsky was stopped from distributing pamphlets by a local constable. Chaplinsky called the officer a "god damned Nazi"; the officer then struck Chaplinsky. The Supreme Court ruled that in the context of the war with Nazis, Chaplinsky's words were tantamount to throwing the first punch and, thus, a true threat to the sheriff, an action not protected by the First Amendment. *In context*, Chaplinsky had uttered "fighting words."[6]

But after the war, the pendulum began to swing back in favor of protecting legitimate protest. In its 1949 ruling in *Terminiello v. The City of Chicago*, the Supreme Court held that even anti-Semitic diatribes were protected speech because they represented an ideological point of view. The speaker, who had been convicted of disorderly conduct, had condemned, among others, "atheistic, communistic Jewish or Zionist Jews."[7] The instructions of the sitting judge are relevant in the case of Trump. The judge instructed the jury that the prosecutor need only prove that the speech "stirs the public to anger, invites disputes, brings about conditions of unrest, or creates a disturbance."[8] Writing for the majority and overriding the judge when the case reached the Supreme Court, Justice William O. Douglas argued that controversial, viewpoint speech often contributes to reform and is therefore protected: "It may indeed best serve its high purpose when it induces a condition of unrest, creates dissatisfaction with conditions . . . or even stirs people to anger. Speech is often provocative and challenging. It may strike at prejudices and preconceptions and have profound unsettling effects as it presses for acceptance of an idea."[9] Douglas set a high bar for conviction.

In 1969, the Supreme Court went even further when it returned to the question of incitement and issued a definitive ruling in the case of *Brandenburg v. Ohio*. Clarence Brandenburg advocated violence against Black people and Jewish people at an Ohio gathering of the Ku Klux Klan, of which he was an official. Standing by a burning cross, he said, "If our president, our Congress, our Supreme Court, continues to suppress

4

the white, Caucasian race, it's possible that there might have to be some revengeance taken. . . . Personally, I believe the n****r should be returned to Africa, the Jew returned to Israel."[10] In this often-cited precedent, the Supreme Court operationalized "true threat" concept. The communication must cause endangerment against *specific* person(s), be "directed to inciting or producing *imminent* lawless action and [be] likely to produce such action."[11] Again, the Supreme Court feared suppressing an ideological point of view that was not imminent enough or specific enough to be deemed criminal action.[12]

And that brings us back to the case of Trump. First, in his context, the president was more specific in singling out targets than was Brandenburg. He mentioned Republicans in Congress and the vice president. Trump warned his vice president to do the right thing. The context was reinforced when Donald Trump Jr. said they were "coming for" those members of Congress who would vote to uphold the electoral college. Second, the action urged was clearly feasible and imminent. The Capitol was just blocks away, and the mob was clearly capable of storming it. When he spoke, President Trump encouraged the demonstrators to march on the Capitol: "We are going to walk down Pennsylvania Avenue. . . . We will never give up. We will never concede. It will never happen. You don't concede when there's theft involved. Our country has had enough. We will not take it anymore." Third, the action that resulted was illegal. The mob was clearly capable of disorderly conduct and posing a threat. But is that what Trump advocated for in his remarks? They can be read in the context of Giuliani's call for "trial by combat." Furthermore, Trump urged his followers to "fight like hell." While the rioting took place, many members of Congress literally feared for their lives.

During the second trial to remove Trump from office, the US Senate was free to assess whether Trump violated the *Brandenburg* standard. Did Trump's words constitute a "true threat," or were they merely protected ideological speech? As we have seen, not enough senators voted for removal of the president from office in the short time he had left, even though a majority believed he was guilty. If the deaths at the Capitol and the damage done to the premises are interpreted in their context to result directly from Trump's words, a jury might be more likely to find him guilty of insurrection. Support for such a charge might emerge from the trials of the more than five hundred people indicted for insurrection at the Capitol.

CHAPTER I

The opportunity for such action developed over the next few months. Attorney General Racine of the District of Columbia looked into charging Trump under the DC statute that carries a sentence of six months in jail. A Mississippi congressman in league with NAACP asked that Trump be charged with violating the 1871 Ku Klux Klan Act, which makes it a crime to conspire to commit an illegal act. And as we have seen, the House committee investigating the events of January 6, 2020, amassed evidence that built a case for indicting Trump for insurrection and incitement.

But can a former president be charged for crimes he committed while president? Most legal scholars agree that he can. In fact, President Ford pardoned former president Nixon in 1974 explicitly so that Nixon could not be prosecuted for obstruction of justice among other infractions. The determining factor in any cases that are brought forward will be whether the jury is allowed to consider whether context creates meaning, thus converting protected speech into a true threat to the nation. Thus, the dialectic of fear that we pursue in this study was readily apparent in the case of President Trump. Many of his supporters feared that conviction would chill ideological speech; many of his prosecutors feared the lack of a conviction would encourage more insurrection or weaken insurrection statutes. The tension between these two fears will surface at the Supreme Court level if the president, his son, and/or his lawyer are convicted of inciting insurrection and one of them appeals his conviction. The intensity of this moment is just one of the reasons we examine how fear functions in the decision-making of the Supreme Court.

The case of President Trump provides a preview of two of this book's goals. First, we examine what fears motivated the parties involved in the cases we examine. Second, we examine how these fears operated dialectically to open these cases to various appeals. To accomplish the first goal, we need to examine how fear has surfaced during various crises and then move on to operationalize fear on the phenomenological level, two tasks to which this chapter now turns.

FEAR AS A THEME

Fear is a persistent theme in the history of the First Amendment. At a basic level, advocates of the Bill of Rights of the United States (US) Constitution were fearful of government intrusion into the lives of its citizens. Motivated in large part by the fear of tyrannical rule, the First Amendment of the US Constitution places four specific restrictions on government intrusion into the lives of Americans and affords US citizens the right to petition the government for the redress of grievances. The freedom to practice one's religion is a response to fears of religious persecution. The freedom to speak is a response to fears that opposing viewpoints will be silenced—a fundamental element of the most tyrannical governments throughout history. The freedom of the press is a response to the fear of government manipulation of its citizens and the right of those citizens to receive information. The right of the people to peaceably assemble is a response to the fear that government will restrict contact between its citizens. Taken together, the First Amendment and the rest of the Bill of Rights are statements against our collective fear that the government will become too involved in regulating our lives. They reflect the enlightened position of Jean-Jacques Rousseau that government should serve the people, not the other way around.

However, we are quick to note that fear may also work in the other direction, to inhibit certain types of expressive freedom. Laws against depicting nude minors stem at least in part from the fear that such depictions will sexually stimulate or motivate adults to act in sexual ways with minors or that the photographer of a nude child will have erotic feelings toward his or her subject. Laws against the burning of crosses stem, in large part, from the way burning crosses have been used to inspire fear of bodily harm in the history of white supremacist violence against Black people. Burning crosses have led to lynchings. Laws against slander and libel are partially rooted in the fear that words will damage a person's reputation. Defamation means to lose face, to de-fame. Laws against untruthful commercial speech are partially motivated by the fear that businesses will value profits over the health and safety of their customers. In short, a whole host of fears motivates calls to restrict individual expression.

Fears are sometimes well grounded, and sometimes they are not. The relationship between fear and the First Amendment persists at the boundary between the present and the future and in the relationship between the self, others, and our government. Fear is persistent in First Amendment controversies: What happens in the future if we don't act now to curb harmful speech? What happens if we do not set a precedent

CHAPTER I

against harmful speech? What happens if, in our quest to protect ourselves against harmful speech, we end up stifling beneficial speech or chill the free marketplace of ideas? What happens if, in calling for the government to suppress others' speech, we empower the government to silence our own expression? The First Amendment can be scary. Limitations on the First Amendment can be scary. The absence of the First Amendment can be scary.

This book discusses the role of fear in contemporary American First Amendment cases that have made their way to the Supreme Court. From the fear that violent video games will encourage our children to behave in aggressive ways toward other people, that unlimited union and corporate contributions to election campaigns will cripple democratic elections, and that pro-drug speech at school events will encourage students to use illegal drugs through to the fear that allowing expletives to air on network television will encourage youth to be vulgar and that allowing protests at military funerals will harm the reputation and emotional stability of family members of the deceased and will destroy the sanctity of a proper burial, Americans have confronted the Roberts Court with a host of challenges that lie at the intersection of fear and the First Amendment.

As figured in historical and recent First Amendment controversies and jurisprudence, fear is at times vague, ambiguous, contested, and multifaceted. Fear is both explicitly articulated and implicitly felt, and sometimes the way fear is articulated and felt is less than clearly expressed or expressible. Yet, fear is persistent in First Amendment history and in so many cases that have appeared before the Roberts Court. If fear is ambiguous, it is not because we have made it so. Rather, this book identifies the way cases in the Supreme Court have rendered fear as ambiguous and hence rhetorical. The meaning of "fear" has been contested such that fear has become important to the various parties in a given case. For the purposes of this book, therefore, whether a given "fear" is valid or not is less important than its persistence as a factor in First Amendment cases. What is more important for our purposes is that the perspectives that lead to the language of "fear" become the basis, and sometimes the foundational basis, for many First Amendment conflicts. Sometimes those perspectives are logical and rational and sometimes they are illogical and irrational. That in so many cases they are *serious* and/or *prevalent*,

8

regardless of how logical and rational they are, is one of the central contributions of this book.

The ambiguity of the term "fear," of course, is rooted in different perceived experiences that lead people to apply "fear" to their interpretation of events; one person might use "fear" to denote being "unsettled," while another uses "fear" to mean they are "terrified." The word "fear" may be used as a motivational tool to get people to take an issue seriously and do something about it or it may be used more loosely as "just an expression." From a rhetorical perspective, it is significant to note that the language of fear is persistent and prevalent in First Amendment cases, both because it explains the nature and scope of the language of fear and because such an understanding is necessary to developing ways to talk about and strategize around fear in future First Amendment conflicts.

A clash of fears may produce a conflict no matter what the *actual* level of fear *is*. In other words, one person may sue another because they are "unsettled," and the other may defend themselves in court because they are "terrified," even though both use the word "fear" to express their emotional states. Discerning who feels more fear in a particular case is less important to this project than the way parties express fear in their rhetoric. For example, in *Snyder v. Phelps* (discussed in chapter 5), the majority opinion applies a language of "fear" (in the "unsettling" sense) to express their "unsettled" (fearful) idea that churches will be liable to a flood of intentional infliction of emotional distress claims (valid or not), whereas the minority opinion expresses being "terrified" (fearful) because of nightmares and night sweats due to being unable to properly mourn the death of their veteran son in combat (valid or not). One fear operates on the register of being terrified, the other on the register of being unsettled. Regardless, the unsettling version of fear won in that case. From a rhetorical perspective, the validity of these types of fears is less important than the need to take them seriously if they are to be productively managed in future cases. For example, when addressing the Court, it would be unwise to dismiss the Court's "unsettling" fear as invalid, even if we believe it to be so, and wise to use their language of fear as a persuasive resource for future cases relevant to that form of expressed fear.

Our central argument in this book is that at times fears are ambiguous (both in their interpretation and expression) and at other times they are clearly known and expressed, even as they are persistent in First

CHAPTER I

Amendment cases that have appeared before the Roberts Court. More simply and broadly, fear is significant and *rhetorical* in First Amendment conflicts. We do not maintain that fear motivates every First Amendment decision. Rather we argue that fear surfaces as a theme in several important, controversial cases and opinions that are precedential. Furthermore, critics who study and attend to First Amendment controversies may offer particular insights by examining the role of fear as the reconstituted Roberts Court is confronted with new challenges. Such an examination may also provide advocates before the Supreme Court with a way to frame their arguments more persuasively and to counter fear appeals from the other side more effectively.

Before analyzing the cases in this study, we provide a context for the relationship between fear and the First Amendment. We approach this account in two ways. First, we provide a chronological historical account of the role fear has played in challenges to the First Amendment throughout significant eras in American history. Second, we provide a topical account by examining the role of fear in significant First Amendment issues. After providing context, we advance a framework for understanding the complexities of fear as a philosophical category.

FEAR AND THE FIRST AMENDMENT'S EVOLUTION

Fear is a prominent factor in the evolution of the First Amendment. In the tumultuous ratification debates, Anti-Federalists resisted the adoption of the Constitution without an accompanying bill of rights to limit the federal government's intrusion into the lives of its citizens. At the heart of this resistance was the fear that government would inhibit the creative thinking and speaking of its citizens. The Anti-Federalists feared that without liberated and educated citizens, everything they had fought for in the American Revolution would collapse. As the colonies declared themselves states, their declarations and constitutions were filled with various rights, including freedom of conscience, assembly, press, and speech. In reaction to the fear that these rights would be rolled back, Anti-Federalists demanded that these specific freedoms to be guaranteed to all US citizens through an amended constitution. For example, George Mason stated that he "would sooner chop off his right hand than put it to the Constitution as [it stood without a bill of rights]."[13] Fearing government invasion into the thoughts, speech, and writing of its citizens, Thomas Jefferson premised his support for the Constitution on a bill of rights. He wrote, "I am one of those who think it a defect that the important rights, not placed in security by the frame of the constitution itself, were not explicitly secured by a supplementary declaration. There are rights which it is useless to surrender to the government, and which yet, governments have always been fond to invade. These are the rights of thinking and publishing our thoughts by speaking or writing."[14]

Since its ratification, the First Amendment has faced significant challenges related to a variety of fears, which vary in terms of their intensity. During the alien and sedition crisis, fears about national security grew more intense as the United States faced the threat of war with France. By June 1797, the French had seized or sunk more than three hundred American ships in the Atlantic Ocean and the Gulf of Mexico. As the American government strategized against the French threat, Federalists feared disaffected aliens would try to destabilize that national government bringing the French Revolution to our shores. Congressman Robert Harper of South Carolina advocated passage of his Sedition Bill of 1798 based on the fear of French Jacobin *philosophes* in America. He stated that such philosophers were "in every country, were paving the way for Jacobins who followed closely in their wake, bent on seizing power by violent means—means that had been used during the reign of terror in France."[15] This fear led to the passage of the Sedition Act, which restricted speech that is disloyal, profane, scurrilous, or abusive about the federal government, its flag, or its armed forces and speech that would cause others to view the American government or its institutions with contempt. The First Amendment survived the alien and sedition crisis as lame-duck president John Adams negotiated the Treaty of Mortefontaine in 1801, and the Sedition Act expired by its own terms on March 3, 1801, the day before Jefferson's inaugural.

Fearing the dissolution of the Union in 1861, President Lincoln gave authorization to suspend the writ of habeas corpus in order to censor political speech about whether Maryland should secede. The fear of surrounding the Capitol with secessionist states led to a declaration of martial law in the city of Baltimore on May 13, 1861. The declaration led to several arrests, including the Baltimore marshal of police George Kane, Baltimore mayor William Brown, and, on September 17, nine members

CHAPTER I

of the Maryland legislature and the chief clerk of the Maryland Senate. The fear of dissolution had led to the worse example of the restriction of free speech in the entire Civil War. Duly elected members of a state legislature were prevented from assembling and speaking on a critical issue at the time. Like John Adams during the sedition crisis, Lincoln would save the Union even if it meant trampling on the rights of elected officials. Lincoln's transgressions against the First Amendment would be forgiven because he had worked to create conditions that protected against perhaps the deepest of American fears—the dissolution of the Union.[16]

From at least 1871 to 1910, the government feared that the labor movement was a threat to capital, and the government's opposition to labor earned support from much of the American public, who feared that the labor movement promoted illegitimate violence. During this era, "a violent public image of labor unions, provoked ironically in large part by aggressive suppression, turned public sympathies against labor, legitimated anti-labor legislation, and turned the tide of the labor movement's major mass unions from socialism toward political moderation."[17] As public sympathies turned against the labor movement because of the fear of labor violence after the Haymarket Riot, Congress passed the Sherman Anti-Trust Act of July 2, 1890, and frequently enforced the labor injunction of the act to suppress labor speech and assembly. The government feared that organized labor functioned as a criminal conspiracy to destroy business and that such a conspiracy could lead to the destruction of lawful free enterprise, particularly of small businesses. In short, the public feared a violent labor movement more than it feared government violence, and the government feared labor would threaten capitalism. As a result, "government techniques were immediate, direct, and cumulative. Given the evidence, the post–Civil War alliance between government and business leaders constituted no less than an attack on union speech, press, and assembly."[18]

During World War I, the federal government responded to suffragists by suppressing their First Amendment rights to petition the government, to speak freely, and to assemble peaceably. A matrix of fears about women led to a variety of attempts to inhibit suffragists' freedom of expression—not the least of which included the fear of women's power over men, the fear of women leading the charge for prohibition of alcohol, the fear of electing weak leaders, the fear of feminizing politics,

FEAR AS A RECURRING THEME

and the fear of irrational decision-making. This matrix of fears led to a variety of assaults on the First Amendment rights of suffragists. Actively, many government officials refused to issue permits for demonstrations or parades, and they arrested picketers as they held signs in front of the White House. Once in jail, many women, including Alice Paul and Lucy Burns, were forced to eat food infested with worms and insects, and several women were attacked by prison guards, beaten, pushed, and dragged into cells. Passively, the government did nothing to discourage members of the public from spitting on, beating, and throwing burning cigars at women as they marched for the right to vote in Washington, DC. Fear had not only motivated the assault on suffragists, but violence was also deployed as a tactic to silence their expression.[19]

At the same time, the success of the Communist Revolution in Russia led to a fear of worldwide Marxist activity. Throughout the time of America's direct intervention into World War I and its attempt to prop up the White Russians after the war, President Wilson and his administration conducted an unremitting campaign of suppression of free speech at home. Once war was declared on Germany, Congress passed the Espionage Act of 1917 and strengthened it in 1918. Section 3 of the act was an outright assault on the First Amendment. One could be arrested for uttering, printing, writing, or publishing "any disloyal, profane, scurrilous, or abusive language about the form of government of the United States, or the Constitution of the United States, or the uniform of the Army or Navy . . . in contempt, scorn, contumely or disrepute."[20] Fines of up to $10,000 could be imposed along with prison sentences of up to twenty years. Fears of communism in the world would arise again in the McCarthy era and the Vietnam War. The Espionage Act remains in effect today and, in January 2012, former CIA officer John Kiriakou was charged under the act with leaking information to journalists about the identity of undercover agents.

The horrific attacks of September 11, 2001, caused intense fear in America that continues to challenge First Amendment rights. Most notably, the fear of increased terrorist tactics against America led to the passage of the USA PATRIOT (Uniting and Strengthening America by Providing Appropriate Tools Required to Intercept and Obstruct Terrorism) Act to afford law enforcement officials greater authority to conduct surveillance for terrorist activities. While many of the objections to

13

CHAPTER I

the act are rooted in other amendments (e.g., the Fourth Amendment's right to privacy), the First Amendment is clearly implicated. For example, the PATRIOT Act makes it a crime to provide material support to any organization designated as a terrorist group by the secretary of state; this includes providing advice to such an organization on how to resolve disputes peaceably or training them on how to make human rights claims before the United Nations. In *Holder v. Humanitarian Law Project*, the Supreme Court ruled that the PATRIOT Act constitutionally prohibited peace-training speech that engages with terrorist groups. Despite the protest of prominent figures such as former president Jimmy Carter, who argued that the decision threatens the work of peacemakers who must interact directly with groups who have engaged in violence, the decision remains law to this day.

FEAR AND FIRST AMENDMENT ISSUES

Fear is more than just a recurring theme in significant eras of American history; it continues to circulate in the most pervasive First Amendment controversies in American life. As we have seen, on one side of the dialectic is from fear of threats, and on the other is the fear of chilling the right to freedom of expression. The chilling effect on expression refers to the form of self-censorship whereby people remain silent because of a fear of governmental and/or other repercussions. The First Amendment is intended to prevent expression itself from being illegal. Out of the fear that the government may encourage people to self-censor, the void-for-vagueness doctrine became embedded in American jurisprudence. Justice Thurgood Marshall wrote in *Grayned v. City of Rockford* that where "a vague statute 'abut[s] upon sensitive areas of basic First Amendment freedoms,' it 'operates to inhibit the exercise of [those] freedoms.' Uncertain meanings inevitably lead citizens to 'steer far wider of the unlawful zone ... than if the boundaries of the forbidden areas were clearly marked.'"[21] Thus, the Court has expressed the fear that government may intimidate its citizens into not exercising their right to free expression and, in many cases, has protected its citizens from laws that are written in a manner that make it difficult to discern what exactly we can and cannot say.

Fear is also a factor in public safety exceptions to First Amendment freedoms. From the sanitation concerns that arise when people assemble

FEAR AS A RECURRING THEME

and occupy public spaces for some time to the concerns that speech will incite violent behavior in people, advocates who seek government regulation of speech have feared the effects that assembly and speech may have on the population as a whole or on specific groups or persons. Perhaps the best example of the fear of the First Amendment's effect on public safety is found in the "incitement to violence" case law. As we have seen, fearing that Ku Klux Klan member Clarence Brandenburg's advocacy of violence would result in actual violence against racial minorities, authorities arrested Brandenburg for violating Ohio's criminal syndicalism statute, which had outlawed the advocacy of violence as a means of accomplishing reform. The Supreme Court ruled that Ohio's statute was unconstitutional and that Brandenburg's speech deserved First Amendment protection because the government cannot restrict the advocacy of violence unless "such advocacy is directed to inciting or producing imminent lawless action and is likely to incite or produce such action."

The meaning of *Brandenburg v. Ohio's* "incitement to violence" standard has been contested in several cases in the lower courts. Whether it's the reenactment of scenes from the film *Natural Born Killers*, which were believed by some to result in several murders in the United States; the violence enacted in real life to imitate the lyrics found in heavy metal and gangsta rap; the notion that rape scenes depicted in films such as *Born Innocent* allegedly led to real-life rapes; a young boy who hung himself while arguably attempting a magic trick he witnessed on *The Tonight Show*; a boy who end up being blinded while attempting to follow the instructions of how to create a sound effect with a BB pellet; a woman dying as a result of attempting to follow the instructions of a diet book; or the implicit threat to abortion doctors and clinics listed in "the Nuremberg Files," many cases involve fears about the safety of members of the public and provide advocates with support for attempting to allow government to restrict public expression.[22]

Fear also operates in the service of restricting freedom of expression when it comes to the security and sanctity of the American nation. American jurisprudence is ripe with examples of the Supreme Court permitting the restriction of freedom of expression when such expression provokes the fear of America's demise. For example, although much of the precedent has been undermined by *Brandenburg*, we have seen that *Schenck v. United States* ruled that citizens cannot advocate against the

15

CHAPTER I

draft because doing so would hinder the efforts of the United States to defend itself against enemy forces during a state of war. Such advocacy, in the Court's opinion, constituted a "clear and present danger" to the United States. Similarly, although the Court in *New York Times v. United States* ruled that the *New York Times* had the right to publish classified Pentagon papers, it also maintained that the freedom of the press was limited if the government were to demonstrate that publication would cause a "grave and irreparable" danger to the United States. Fear of the pending collapse of America as a result of compromised national security is a prevailing fear embedded in the restriction of First Amendment freedoms.

National security need not be at stake for people to fear speech that is critical of America. At a more subtle level than direct threats to national security, some people fear that attacking the sanctity of the United States may be a threat to the nation. In *Texas v. Johnson*, the Supreme Court ruled that burning an American flag in protest of American policies is protected First Amendment expression. However, those who opposed the ruling feared that allowing the flag to be burned would desecrate a sacred object of American civil religion, antagonize people, and encourage a decline in the belief in American governance. For example, Chief Justice Rehnquist in his dissent expressed his fear of allowing antagonizing speech: flag burning is "the equivalent of an inarticulate grunt or roar that, it seems fair to say, is most likely to be indulged in not to express any particular idea, but to antagonize others." Justice Stevens expressed concern in his dissenting opinion that the flag is a vital symbol whose value "cannot be measured," that it is "an important national asset," and that allowing it to be desecrated is an attack on the American values it symbolizes.

Moreover, American fears frequently surface in cases involving fighting words. As we have seen, the Supreme Court invented the fighting words doctrine in the case of *Chaplinksy v. New Hampshire* out of the fear that allowing a person to "address any offensive, derisive or annoying word to any other person who is lawfully in any street or other public place" would create and/or encourage societal disorder and immorality.[23] Justice Murphy wrote in the unanimous decision of the Court, "the insulting or 'fighting' words—those which by their very utterance inflict injury or tend to incite an immediate breach of the peace" are "no essential

16

FEAR AS A RECURRING THEME

part of any exposition of ideas, and are of such slight social value as a step to truth that any benefit that may be derived from them is clearly outweighed by the social interest in order and morality."[24] Embedded in fighting words ordinances, therefore, is the fear of disorder and immorality as the result of shouting matches in public spaces and the fear of confronting verbal assaults from others.

Several cases also express fears that stem from a free press. For example, the case of *Near v. Minnesota* involved a constitutional challenge to a law that some Minneapolis newspapers helped draft because they feared other news outlets would damage the institutional credibility of newspapers in general. The law specifically made it illegal to publish any "malicious, scandalous and defamatory newspaper, magazine or other periodical."[25] In 1927, Jay Near and Howard Guilford launched the *Saturday Press* and published stories that alleged that Jewish gangsters were responsible for bootlegging, gambling, and racketeering in Minneapolis and that certain law enforcement officials were letting the gangsters get away with their illegal behavior.

Fear that these types of stories would encourage muckraking led to the enforcement of the Minnesota law when a restraining order was placed on Near and Guilford to prevent them from publishing the *Saturday Press* or anything similar to it. Near sued Minnesota and argued that the restraining order violated his First Amendment freedom of the press. Chief Justice Hughes wrote the majority opinion and reaffirmed the fear of tyrannical government involvement in the affairs of the press: "The conception of liberty of the press in this country had broadened with the exigencies of the colonial period and with the efforts to secure freedom from oppressive administration. That liberty was especially cherished for the immunity it afforded from previous restraint of the publication of censure of public officers and charges of official misconduct." Fear of tyrannical rule over the press outweighed the fear of delegitimizing the credibility of the newspaper industry.[26]

Fear of reputational damage is not limited to the press. The fear is also manifest in several other Supreme Court precedents. For example, the fear of ongoing reputational attacks targeting prominent Christian leaders led to a clash in the case of *Hustler Magazine v. Falwell*. Larry Flynt had a long history of loathing Christian leaders, especially the likes of Jerry Falwell.[27] Flynt feared that the brand of Christianity espoused

CHAPTER I

by such leaders was dangerous because it represented an assault on the civil liberties of American people in general and his type of publication in particular. When Flynt published a Campari advertisement in *Hustler Magazine* that, among other things, parodied Falwell by imagining sexual encounters between a young Falwell and his mother, Falwell drew the line and filed suit for libel, invasion of privacy, and intentional infliction of emotional distress (IIED). Again, as in *Near*, the Supreme Court affirmed its fear that were Falwell's claims to be granted, the First Amendment freedom of speech and press would be hindered, as people would self-censor for fear of high punitive damage awards in defamation and IIED claims.[28] In this dialectical confrontation, the fear of future censorship outweighed the fear of defamation and IIED.

Moreover, fear of the effects of free expression on our children is manifest in considerations of student expression and obscenity/indecency laws. Ever since the Supreme Court ruled in *Tinker v. Des Moines* that students do not shed their constitutional rights to freedom of expression at the schoolhouse gates, courts have nevertheless found that this freedom is not absolute. Fearing that certain types of clothing may encourage illegal behavior, schools have instituted constitutionally permissible dress codes for students.[29] Fearing that veiled references to sexual conduct among students is a disruption to "school affairs," the Supreme Court ruled in *Bethel School District v. Fraser* that students do not have the right to express sexuality through innuendo if it leads to disorder at a school event. Fear of the consequences of granting students the freedom to express themselves in school newspapers led the Supreme Court to rule in *Hazelwood School District v. Kuhlmeier* that teachers and principals may maintain editorial discretion to prohibit any student publication that bears the imprimatur of the school.

Fear of the effects of obscene and indecent expression on our children has led to a host of legislation and litigation. Fearing obscene images and their impact on children, the Supreme Court has consistently held that obscenity is outside the scope of First Amendment protection. From the Supreme Court's reliance on the English common law case of *Regina v. Hicklin* to its more recent decisions in *Roth v. United States*, *Miller v. California*, *United States v. Playboy Entertainment Group, Inc.*, and *Ashcroft v. Free Speech Coalition*, the fear that obscene pornographic expression has detrimental effects on our children has endured. Fearing the effects of indecent speech on our children, the Supreme Court decided in *Pacifica v. Federal Communications Commission* that broadcasters needed to create a safe harbor for indecent material away from the time children might be exposed to speech that depicts sexual or excretory activities and organs in a patently offensive manner.[30]

While these fears pertain to the First Amendment freedoms of assembly, speech, and press, there are also fears embedded in many of the controversies over the separation between church and state. Indeed, there are many American fears about the intrusion of religion into the affairs of American democracy and vice versa. Some fear that religious groups, their creeds, and/or their hierarchical structures threaten American democratic inclusiveness. Others fear that without religious morals in government, American democracy will decay in the face of moral decadence. Some point to the historical relationship between the Catholic Church and European countries to call out the worst excesses of church involvement in the affairs of the state and fear the same fate if religion is involved in American government. Others fear that separating church and state puts the souls of the state's citizens in jeopardy. Most recently during the pandemic, government restrictions on religious assembly have been struck down as too burdensome on practitioners. At a basic level, defenders of the First Amendment largely fear that if the Jefferson wall of separation is not maintained, one religion will be able to exercise its privilege in a manner that condones state-sponsored religious persecution.[31]

In sum, fear has been instrumental in the history and evolution of the First Amendment. Fear has played a significant role in various eras of American history—from the ratification debates, the alien and sedition crisis, and presidents' suspensions of the writ of habeas corpus to the suppression of labor movement speech, the American government's response to suffragists, the fear of the spread of communism throughout the world, and the fear of terrorism. Significant fears are bound up in our willingness to defend and suspend First Amendment principles with regard to issues in American life. Whether it is fear that compels the chilling of expression, fear for the physical safety of the public, fear of copycats who view violent material, the fear of racist death threats, fear of attacks by American enemies both foreign and domestic, fear of declining American patriotism, fear of verbal assaults in public, fear of losing one's reputation, fear of the press, fear of the effects of expressive material on

CHAPTER I

our children, or fears embedded in the relationship between church and state, fear is everywhere when it comes to the First Amendment.

THEORETICAL ORIENTATION TO FEAR AND THE FIRST AMENDMENT

To this point, we have used the concept of fear in a variety of ways, perhaps oversimplifying fear for those who consider it a complicated construct with affective, psychological, and other behavioral manifestations. Indeed, fear as a complex instinct should be analyzed more deeply. Thus, to analyze contemporary First Amendment cases of the Roberts Court in subsequent chapters, we need to articulate a more nuanced view of fear in its multitudinous nature. We begin with the definition set out by Brian Calabrese: "Fear [is] an emotional or psychological effect of the expectation [of] or experiencing or suffering something undesirable or detrimental. Fear has a subject—the person who experiences it. It has an object—that which is undesirable or detrimental. It relates to future time, whether the immediate or distant future. It may be rational or irrational—justified by valid reason . . . or not. [It] may be felt or experienced individually or collectively."[32] Thus, examining First Amendment controversies from the perspective of fear is complicated by a variety of factors, not the least of which is that fear can be the result of our emotions, rather than an actual threat.[33]

Aristotle's theoretical approach to pathos includes the use of fear for motivational purposes. Furthermore, Aristotle held that the intensity of an emotion can be measured on a continuum that runs from that emotion to its counterpart. For example, he pairs fear with confidence: one is not fearful when one is confident, and one is not confident when one is fearful. Aristotle provides us with a useful way of assessing the intensity of fear invoked in an argument. It can range from concern to paralyzing terror. Moreover, for Aristotle, the intensity of an emotion such as fear is largely a function of proximity. Craig Smith explains Aristotle's theorization of emotions: "The intensity of emotions can be described in terms of the nearness or remoteness of the objects that trigger emotions, including the personal relationships that stimulate them. For example, the closer what we fear is in time and space, the more intensely we experience that fear; the more remote the object of the fear, the less intense is the

20

FEAR AS A RECURRING THEME

experience of fear."[34] By defining fear as a response to a known cause, he differentiates it from anxiety, which has no known cause. First Amendment cases confront people with a host of immediate fears—the intensity of emotional experience may stem from factors including the present facts of a case in the space of the courtroom. Thus, to operationalize our examination of fear, we will need to investigate the causes invoked to provoke fear and how close various advocates bring those fears, in time and space, before their audiences.

Moreover, fear is an intensely *personal* experience; indeed, Aristotle held that the intensity of a range of emotions would vary depending on the soul of the listener. Another factor that modulates the intensity of fear is the proxemics brought on by a particular rhetoric. The closer the rhetor and listener brings the cause of fear in terms of time and space, the more intense the feeling of fear becomes. Aristotle's and other theorists' conceptions of fear, as examined in this book, encourage us to seek the range of rhetorical constructions of fear in a particular case and attempt to explain the rhetorical impact of those cases.

Consider, for example, Justice Clarence Thomas's objection, in the oral arguments in *Virginia v. Black*, to the idea that a burning cross might be considered permissible speech: "Now, it's my understanding that we had almost 100 years of lynching and activity in the South by the Knights of Camellia [sic] and the Ku Klux Klan, and this was a reign of terror, and the cross was a symbol of that reign of terror. . . . My fear is that the—there was no other purpose to the cross. There was no communication of a particular message. It was intended to cause fear . . . and to terrorize a population." In this instance, Justice Thomas's fear is not evidentiary or part of the arguments before him, and yet it motivated him to cite evidentiary fear in support of his opinion in the case. Justice Thomas, who is usually silent during oral arguments in the Supreme Court, was compelled to speak when the history of intimidation by way of cross-burning (evidence of fear) was invoked; the case had fused the history of cross-burning with the present situation and brought the spaces of lynching in the South into the space of the Supreme Court, giving them a new proximity.

Aristotle also taught that "emotions do not exist in isolation; they work in concert with other feelings. For example, experiencing fear may cause one to become angry with those who caused the fear. Or one who

CHAPTER I

is angry may evoke fear in another."[35] In any First Amendment controversy, a wide range of emotions present themselves. For example, feeling pride in one's public reputation may lead to feelings of resentment (non-evidentiary) about a newspaper when it publishes something that attacks one's reputation (evidentiary). These feelings may, in turn, lead that person to feel angry about the newspaper and to fear what people might think about her or him in the future (evidentiary fear of defamation) should the newspaper continue its behavior, which may then lead to a lawsuit that results in limiting the freedom of the press such that defamatory speech is constrained. And, of course, further complicating this picture is the possibility that one emotion may not lead, sequentially, to another. Rather, these emotions may be felt simultaneously. Thus, when we talk about fear in relation to First Amendment controversies, we are not suggesting that these controversies can be reduced to fear alone. Rather, fear is one dimension of a complicated affective field.

Other philosophers help us expand on Aristotle's conception of fear by showing how different people experience fear in different ways, for different reasons, and for different purposes. They open us to many non-evidentiary kinds of fears. For example, the existentialist Søren Kierkegaard proposed fear as the basis of moral systems like Christianity.[36] Friedrich Nietzsche agreed when he wrote, "Fear is the mother of morals."[37] He likely meant that fear formed the basis for prescribing good and evil in moral thought. As evidence of Nietzsche's claim, we might highlight that fear is the first emotion found in the Bible. After Adam ate from the Tree of Knowledge and discovered he was naked, fear was the first emotion he felt (followed by shame). Fear has also formed the basis of much of the theology, from Dante's inferno in the early Renaissance to the Westboro Baptist Church in contemporary American Christian thought. Identifying fear as the foundation of a moral system produce an array of views concerning the First Amendment, not the least of which is the establishment clause, which was designed partially to protect against governmental appeal to religious fears in order to control and persecute its citizens.

The fear of God's wrath in Abrahamic religions is both similar to and different from fear as conceptualized by those who feel fear is a fundamental element from which one should be free. For example, much of Buddhist philosophy is rooted in the belief that one should strive to be free from fear. According to Buddha, "The whole secret of existence is

22

FEAR AS A RECURRING THEME

to have no fear. Never fear what will become of you, depend on no one. Only the moment you reject all help are you freed."[38] More specifically, according to Buddhist philosopher Judith Lief, "The essential cause of our suffering and anxiety is ignorance of the nature of reality and craving and clinging to something illusory. That is referred to as ego, and the gasoline in the vehicle of ego is fear. Ego thrives on fear, so unless we figure out the problem of fear, we will never understand or embody any sense of egolessness or selflessness."[39]

This Buddhist orientation toward the goal of being free from fear is consistent with other theoretical orientations that envision freedom from fear as an ontological priority. The existentialist Jean-Paul Sartre diminished the ego as self in order to kill off his fear. He wrote, "Fear? If I have gained anything by damning myself it is that I no longer have anything to fear."[40] Sartre was suspicious of fear and its ties to morality in much the same way as Bertrand Russell resisted superstition. Russell wrote, "Fear is the main source of superstition, and one of the main sources of cruelty. To conquer fear is the beginning of wisdom, in the pursuit of truth as in the endeavor after a worthy manner of life."[41] What many Buddhists have in common with Sartre and Russell is the idea that fear gets in the way of wisdom by paralyzing thought. At the same time, Buddhists' thinking is similar to that of Abrahamic religions in that they begin with fear as an ontological condition, that is, as the basis for a relationship with God, or the human condition that must be overcome if we are to achieve freedom.

The quest for freedom from fear may lead a person to make certain observations about the nature, scope, and functionality of the First Amendment in American life. The freedom from fear orientation may lead a person to defend, resist, or be apathetic to First Amendment principles. A person may argue that the First Amendment is necessary for protecting the freedom of thought about the freedom from fear mentality, that the failure to have a free marketplace of ideas, as guaranteed by the First Amendment, would result in future generations lacking access to the path of freedom as found in critical works of philosophy, theology, and so on. Or a person may argue that the First Amendment is a construct of government, that leaving interpretation open to a Supreme Court is a way of externalizing responsibility and gets in the way of an inward focus on the self. Or a person may be altogether apathetic about the

CHAPTER I

First Amendment, arguing that the amendment is an outward worldly creation with little regard for the path to internal spiritual life and that it exists merely in aesthetic rather than authentic living. In any case, the "freedom from fear" notion is an important dimension that adds complexity to the relationship between fear and the First Amendment.

In addition to experiencing fear in terms of a fear of God and a "freedom from fear," some people experience fear as productive to material existence. Leonardo da Vinci wrote, "Just as courage imperils us, fear protects us." Some evolutionary philosophers see fear as a fundamental condition of our evolutionary success. For example, Lars Svendsen writes in *A Philosophy of Fear*, "a creature without the capacity to feel fear will have a worse chance of surviving and procreating. . . . Fear not only protects us from predatory animals and other dangers that exist in nature but also from many self-initiated dangers, like walking straight out into heavy traffic without looking. Fear contributes to keeping us alive."[42] This idea of fear as a protective mechanism for our physical survival parallels the marketplace of ideas rationale: the strongest ideas are the ones that will endure and the ones that best respond to the fears embedded in the human condition. This connection between fear and survival is productive in an evolutionary sense, because it ensures the safety of society in the long term—even those already-noted conflicts over how to best ensure public safety are *ideas about safety* that must be freely expressed if the best idea is to survive. Put simply, from an evolutionary perspective, the First Amendment might be considered a construct that has its roots in fear cast as a productive mechanism of our material/physical survival.

Regardless of the way fear is experienced or viewed, fear is temporally oriented toward the future even as it may be inspired by experiences in the past or present. Philosopher Martin Heidegger wrote, "Has not fear been justifiably described as the expectation of a coming evil (*malum futurum*)? Is not the primary temporal meaning of fear the future and not at all having-been? Fear is incontestably 'related' not only to 'something futural' in the sense of what first arrives 'in time,' but this relatedness itself is futural in the primordially temporal sense."[43] The "something futural" about fear may be traced, in part, to Platonic and Epicurean fears about the future (fear of the gods and fear of death) as sources that destroy the pursuit of truth and happiness (respectively). Cases about the First Amendment are often not merely about the given case but about

24

FEAR AS A RECURRING THEME

the relationship between that case and our future: the future "life" of the Constitution (whether it be an originalist fear that the Constitution will become "warped" by activist judges, the fear that the Constitution will die if it does not adapt its relevance to the people it governs, or other concerns about the Constitution's [un]importance); the impact of the case on future First Amendment rights (i.e., the precedential nature of ruling in a particular manner in the case); the impact of the case on the future of the legal system (i.e., will deciding the case in a particular way result a flood of litigation that will overburden lower courts and hinder their effectiveness?); and a host of other fears.

Moreover, fear may be experienced not only on an individual level but also as a collective behavior. For example, theorists have advanced collective order as an extension of a fear of other people, natural disasters, and/or existential angst. In Thomas Hobbes's philosophy of overcoming self-interest, individuals fear of each other becomes a resource for establishing a social community.[44] For Giambattista Vico, civilization began with the fear of thunder, to which all individuals were exposed in the same way, and as everyone fled from the thunder together, their shared fear became a reference point for building a sense of community.[45] Kenneth Burke locates cultural formation in existential angst, describing how people came together in nervous loquaciousness at the edge of an "abyss."[46]

What these three perspectives have in common is their emphasis on the development of a collective set of principles that arise from a universally experienced fear. One of the major concerns that arise from collective life is the way collective power may be exerted against certain minority/dissenting perspectives—perspectives the First Amendment is, in part, designed to protect. While people may share similar types of fears (fear of other people, fear of nature, existential fear, etc.), people also have an array of viewpoints about how society ought to be organized in reaction to these fears—viewpoints the First Amendment is arguably designed to protect people's right not only to have but also to express. While the First Amendment has many purposes, one of its most common justifications is that it prevents the "will of the people" (as expressed in their election of Congress) from infringing on the rights of people (regardless of whether those people are in the majority or minority) in the realms of religion, speech, press, and assembly.

25

CHAPTER I

At a more general level, the problem of power, fear, and collective life is certainly no stranger to political theories of governance. Whether it be Xenophon's Socratic-influenced recognition that fear is essential to rule, or Aristotle's observation that tyranny rests on the proliferation of fear and the generation of mutual distrust and diffidence among its citizens, or Cicero's idea that "fear is but a poor safeguard of lasting power; while affection, on the other hand, may be trusted to keep it safe forever," or the Machiavellian philosophy that "it is much safer to be feared than to be loved when one of the two must be lacking," or the Althusserian fear of the repressive state apparatus that reinforces its ideological counterpart, or poet Robert Frost's "There is nothing I'm afraid of like scared people," or the Foucauldian fear of crime as the basis of police states, or Erich Fromm's notion that people choose new government options that promise a sense of security, or Massumi's politics of everyday fear in the affective loci of consumerist logics, fear is a consistent theme in ideas about the organization of political life. And, in America, so is the First Amendment.[47] We would be hard-pressed to find an aspect of American political life that does not relate in some way to the First Amendment. This is largely due to the fact that most of political life begins with ideas and their expression. Thus, as long as power is involved, fear and the First Amendment inevitably and consistently both clash and appear together.

This clash and conjoining of the First Amendment and the politics of fear is far from surprising. Many of the philosophical underpinnings of the First Amendment are rooted in enlightenment philosophy that arose, in part, out of expressed fears. For example, Montesquieu wrote that fear of despotic terror is the most important justification of the principle of the division of powers and the establishment of liberal order. His liberalism lies at the heart of First Amendment principles and the Constitution. James Madison called Montesquieu "the oracle who is always consulted and cited" on questions of the separation of powers.[48] According to Corey Robin, "with the exception of the Bible, Montesquieu was the most invoked authority of the entire founding generation, and probably remains so today."[49] Because both fear and the First Amendment are deeply rooted in the foundations of American democracy, they serve as the basis for examining contemporary First Amendment controversies that have made their way to the Roberts Court.

Each chapter in this book will analyze at least one significant First

Amendment case and a variety of fears—whether evidentiary or not—that pertain to the given case. The chapters proceed through many of the controversial cases and issues of the Roberts Court. Our claims about the role of "fear" in First Amendment cases cannot determine whether it is more or less prevalent in the Roberts Court than in any other era in First Amendment history. We focus solely on cases of the Roberts Court as a way to note a trend and to think about the current context, because the Roberts Court is the current Court. While several of the justices have come and gone during Chief Justice Roberts's tenure, the era is significant, as it has already stretched for about a twenty-year period of time. The cases that have come before the Roberts Court mark a significant influence on the precedents that will be relevant in negotiating the myriad fears that inform future cases.

Chapter 2 begins by examining a range of fears in *Morse v. Frederick*, including the fear that school administrators will lose authority, that high school students will use marijuana, and that students will lose their right to free speech when they challenge the authority of their administrators. The chapter also addresses some of the fears in the recent student rights case of *Mahanoy v. BL*. Chapter 3 analyzes fears involved in the controversy that developed around *Citizens United v. Federal Elections Commission*. Such fears include the fear of corporate influence on electoral politics, the fear of noncitizen influence in American elections, the use of fear appeals in campaign speech within sixty days of a general election and thirty days of a primary election, the fear of chilling the right of the people to obtain useful information, corporate fears of alienating their consumers by backing political candidates, fears of a slippery slope to zero regulations on campaign finance, and fears of corruption. Chapter 4 takes a look at the fears involved in *Christian Legal Society v. Martinez*, including the fear that student organizations will be coopted by outsiders, fear about the future of legal education in America, fear of religious freedom, and fear of homosexuality. Similarly, chapter 5 examines the fears of homosexuality and freedom of religion in *Snyder v. Phelps* while delving into other fears, including the fear of God, the fear of death, the fear of emotional distress, the fear of terrorism, the fear of failing as a parent, and the fear of losing one's reputation. Chapter 6 investigates the role of fear in *Brown v. Entertainment Merchants Association*, including the fear of violent children, the fear of the consequences of

CHAPTER I

a lack of parental involvement in their children's lives, the fear of manipulation and deception by children, the fear of children's imaginations, and the fear of a predatory relationship between corporations and children. Chapter 7 examines the role of fear in indecent, obscene, and graphic communication, including the fear of damaging children's psyches and encouraging poor behaviors, the fear of the "decline of civilization," the fear of chilling valuable speech as a cost of regulating graphic speech, the fear of economic consequences of a given legislative restriction and/or lawsuits, the fears at the heart of moral panics, the fear of parental failure, the fear of crimes such as credit card fraud and identity theft, the fears that give rise to particular fetishes, and the fear of animal cruelty. Finally, chapter 8 draws some conclusions about the relationship between fear and the First Amendment by interrogating the complicated "fear lines" that are drawn in Supreme Court precedents of the Roberts Court.

Fear is complicated, because we experience fear in both similar and different ways and because the cause of a fear can be admitted as evidentiary or excluded as non-evidentiary. To share similar senses of fear is to form an identification with each other. To run up against different senses of fear is to form a wedge in political life. Fears are made manifest by individuals and collectives as we mediate between present experiences and future expectations. Consequently, how we relate to both our own fears and the fears of others, and how we determine which fears are evidentiary and which are not, will determine the fate of the First Amendment. Justice Brandeis wrote in *Whitney v. California*, "Those who won our independence by revolution were not cowards. They did not fear political change. They did not exalt order at the cost of liberty." Corey Robin reminds us, "it is far easier to believe in cruelty and fear than in freedom and equality. But it is freedom and equality that inspire us to oppose political fear, and it is freedom and equality that underwrite our struggle against it. Fear, in other words, does not come first. Fear is an obstacle and a stumbling block, but it is not, and cannot be, a foundation for politics."[50] Our contention in this book is that contemporary First Amendment controversies confront us with their invocation of many fears. How we answer fear's call will dictate whether First Amendment freedoms will endure.

2

Fear and Student Speech

Morse v. Frederick

In 1969, the Supreme Court ruled in *Tinker v. Des Moines* that students and teachers do not "shed their constitutional rights to freedom of expression at the schoolhouse gate."[1] *Tinker* was more than just a case about First Amendment rights. It was about a deep fear of student disruption in America's educational institutions. Fearing the disruption of the learning environment, school administrators suspended five students who symbolically protested the Vietnam War by wearing black armbands to school. In the majority opinion of the Court, Justice Abe Fortas wrote that "undifferentiated fear or apprehension of disturbance is not enough to overcome the right to freedom of expression." He noted that even though the school may be a site of many fears, the mere possibility of disturbance should not give way to inhibiting the freedom of expression: "Any variation from the majority's opinion may inspire fear. Any word spoken, in class, in the lunchroom, or on the campus, that deviates from the views of another person may start an argument or cause a disturbance. But our Constitution says we must take this risk."[2]

That fear and the First Amendment would intersect in our public schools should not be surprising. After all, schools are havens for fear, some admissible as evidence and some not. For example, many students

CHAPTER 2

fear that they will not be socially accepted, that they will fail to make the team, that they will fail to achieve academic success, or that they will be physically assaulted. Many teachers fear that they will not be able to give enough attention to their students as they see class sizes increase, that they will work for administrators who put other interests ahead of the needs of students, or that they will lose control of the classroom. Many administrators fear disorder in the schools, that they will be subject to legal problems, or that they will be faced with a public relations nightmare. Many parents fear that their child will be left behind, that their child will be exposed to irreversible psychological traumas, or that their child will be a "problem child." Most people fear violent outbursts, that we are not doing enough for our children, or that our children will learn bad behaviors they will carry into adulthood to the detriment of society.

With fear so abundant in our classrooms, it is not surprising that many legal cases involve our public schools. One of the most significant cases pertaining to the First Amendment during the Roberts Court is *Morse v. Frederick* (a.k.a., "Bong Hits for Jesus"). In 2002, the United States played host to the Winter Olympics in Salt Lake City, Utah. Just before the games, the Olympic torch relay passed by Juneau-Douglas High School in Alaska. Students at the high school were permitted to leave classes to watch the Olympic Torch pass by. Joseph Frederick, a student at the school, did not check into school before the students were released to watch the relay on the city's streets. He joined his classmates on the sidewalk and unfurled a banner for television cameras reading, "BONG HiTS 4 JESUS." Principal Deborah Morse seized the banner and suspended Frederick on the basis of violating the school district's antidrug policy. Frederick sued the school district, arguing that he had the First Amendment right to unfurl the banner. The case made its way to the Supreme Court. In a 5–4 decision, the Supreme Court ruled in favor of the school district.

While the major fear involved in *Morse* pertained to the promotion of drug use in high schools, an evidentiary issue, a great number of other fears bubbled to the surface. The purpose of this chapter is to analyze the many fears in the case of *Morse v. Frederick*. We argue that *Morse* is an iteration of ongoing fears in our public schools—fears that are rooted in American history and that are unlikely to go away any time soon. Furthermore, fear is a rhetorically contested and significant element in

30

Morse. To explain and defend this argument, we'll first examine the historical context of fear in the history of our public schools. Second, we'll analyze the fears, both implied and expressed, of the parties involved in the case and in the opinions the Court. Finally, we'll conclude this chapter with some of the fears that will undoubtedly clash at the intersection of fear and our public schools in the wake of the *Morse* case.

FEAR IN THE HISTORY OF AMERICAN PUBLIC SCHOOLS

Historically, fear has played an instrumental part in the creation of American schools. The history of thought that influenced the creation of the American educational system may lead us back as far as the medieval period, if not further. As John Pulliam notes, "It is easy enough to mark the founding of English settlements on the American seaboard with Jamestown in 1607 and the first major school law with the 'Old Deluder Satan Act' of Massachusetts Bay Colony in 1647, but it is quite another matter to trace the cultural forces that shaped the minds and deeds of the colonists."[3] While the Puritan ethic of early America has influenced contemporary educational thought and practice in several ways, it is equally true that "the European settlers were influenced by mainstreams of thought going back at least to medieval times."[4] Undoubtedly, there are more deeply historical-ideological fears underpinning the development of American schools that are rooted in the history of Western civilization. However, we will begin with identifying some of the fears surrounding schools that were expressed in early American life.

Early American history was fraught with a variety of fears that contributed to the rise of schools for children. In seventeenth-century colonial America, the Puritans of the Massachusetts Bay Colony were attracted to state-established, public education both as a way to advance the lessons of religious faith and to curb the spread of anarchy and a serious falling away from God. The Puritans embraced the state's function in establishing schools based on their desire to create and sustain a government in the image of their church.[5] In contrast, in the South, there was little interest in the development of public schooling. The strongest educational institution in the South was the education offered by the Anglican Church, but there was little public investment in public schools.

31

CHAPTER 2

According to Pulliam, "Virginia had money earmarked for education as early as 1618, although the revocation of the charter for the Virginia Company seven years later stopped these funds. From that time until 1660 Virginia passed laws which required children to be taught religion, although public financial support was lacking." So, while there was a generalized support for public schooling in the Massachusetts Bay Colony, there was little support for the same in the more rural South. The revolutionary period, however, ushered in a new era of support for publicly funded education.

Even though a few children did attend public schools in the colonial era, the education of youth was still largely the responsibility of parents during the revolutionary period. Few children attended formal schools at the time. For example, Thomas Jefferson received a private education on the Tuckahoe Plantation on the James River. In 1773, Reverend Jonathan Boucher feared that too many parents were failing to adequately educate their children and felt that the least the American public could do was support decent schools and colleges for their children.[6] Even many of the parents who may have been responsible educators for their children began to fear that homeschooling was deficient compared to the education offered in public schools. One of the factors contributing to this fear was the rise of collective pools of resources and, more specifically, the library collections available to students at public schools. According to Lawrence Cremin, "with the proliferation of types of schooling, the concomitant increase in the variety of printed textual materials for instruction and self-instruction, and the development of libraries for the collection and dissemination of such materials, the range of possible life-styles open to a given individual beyond the particular version proffered by his family, his church, or even his neighboring school or surrounding community, was vastly enlarged."[7] In opposition, many parents and churches feared that educating children in a larger public setting would lead them away from familial bonds and religious faith.

There was also the prevailing fear that leaving the responsibility of education to parents would fail to provide adequate training for children in an expanding economy. As the economic demands for different trades increased, so did the training necessary to accomplish the trade work. As trade increased between the colonies, so did the need to be educated about the other colonies. According to Cremin, "in an expanding economy with a persistent labor shortage and a consequent dearth of certificatory requirements for entry into careers, the access to alternative lifestyles provided by education was confirmed by the access to alternative careers afforded by the economy."[8] Schools could provide children with the training necessary for careers that many parents alone could not.

It is important to note that England not only influenced educational thinking in colonial America but also provided material support. The colonies could purchase educational materials from England and trade educational ideas and resources. After the Revolutionary War, the colonies lost these material ties with England. As Pulliam notes, "lack of money and the interruption of the normal economic process made the operation of educational institutions almost impossible [after the war]. Tory and Loyalist teachers were turned out of their schools. Sometimes the schools were burned and libraries scattered or destroyed."[9] In the aftermath of the Revolutionary War period, education was not a high priority. Indeed, there is no direct reference to a right to education in the Constitution (although it is alluded to in places such as the establishment clause, which allows for religious freedom to teach religious belief).

At the same time, several important framers of the Constitution favored public education as a way to ensure good citizenship, national prosperity, and domestic tranquility. John Jay feared that without education, America would risk falling into the hands of "the weak and the wicked": "I consider knowledge to be the soul of a republic; and as the weak and the wicked are generally in alliance, as much care should be taken to diminish the number of the former, as of the latter. Education is the way to do this, and nothing should be left undone to afford all ranks of people the means of obtaining a proper degree of it, at a cheap and easy rate."[10] James Madison feared that without education, people would be ill-equipped to defend or enjoy liberty: "Learned Institutions ought to be favorite objects with every free people. They throw that light over the public mind which is the best security against crafty & dangerous encroachments on the public liberty."[11] George Washington agreed in his eighth annual message to the Senate and House of Representatives: "The assembly to which I address myself is too enlightened not to be fully sensible how much a flourishing state of the arts and sciences contributes to national prosperity and reputation." He continued by making the case for the institutional education of "our youth in the science of government":

CHAPTER 2

"In a republic what species of knowledge can be equally important and what duty more pressing on its legislature than to patronize a plan for communicating it to those who are to be the future guardians of the liberties of the country?"[12]

Thomas Jefferson was perhaps the most instrumental figure in advocating public education in the formative post–Revolutionary War period. For him, education was part of the experiment that was the American republic. Adolphe E. Meyer wrote that, of the Founders, Jefferson's "'cherishment of the people' impelled him to stride further and more boldly than any of them."[13] In his home state of Virginia, "Jefferson sponsored three important bills: one for religious freedom, which finally enjoyed enactment in 1785; another for the creation of free public libraries; and a third for the establishment of free public schools. Put forth in 1779, Jefferson's plan for education divided every Virginia county into school districts. . . . Every district was put upon to maintain a school where every girl and boy was to be introduced to the three Rs at public expense for three years 'and much longer at private expense as parents, guardians, or friends, shall think proper.'"[14] The Jeffersonian model allowed those who continued their education to aspire to join the ranks of an educational elite—a model Jefferson likely borrowed from the French.

Many feared that Jefferson's experiment would have negative consequences. Concerns arose that his plan would "accept the doctrine of an intellectual elite, that it approaches the problem of education in the spirit of charity, that it fails to make school attendance compulsory," and "that it would have naught to do with the useful and practical subjects so necessary for the economic well-being of the masses."[15] While his educational proposals failed to gain enough support to be adopted, he did succeed in advancing the notion of public education in at least two areas. First, he succeeded in garnering enough support for the establishment of the University of Virginia, of which he became the first rector. Second, and more important for our purposes in this chapter, he, along with John Jay, James Madison, John Adams, and others, successfully shifted the national discussion away from *whether* the government should fund public education and toward *what form* the system of education should take. The result of such national attention was a shift toward the states implementing their own approaches to educating the public. The historical development of education from state to state is beyond the scope of this chapter. What is

34

important to this era is the Founders' near unanimity regarding education as a bulwark against the feared collapse of the American republic. Thus, fear played an important role in the development of America's educational institutions.

Regardless of their public or private standing, American schools historically have developed within fear-provoking contexts. On a general philosophical level, educational institutions exist at the intersection of control and chaos; they fundamentally are institutions that encourage disciplinary and orderly practices to guard against a whimsical and disorderly society. While there is certainly disagreement, the disciplinary function of educational institutions is a point on which even George Washington and Michel Foucault could agree. Within the school environment, administrators and teachers seek to instill a sense of order. A number of rules, procedures, and authoritative powers are designed to administer the life of the student, and students are disciplined to ensure proper obedience to the rules and standards of the educational institution. The disciplinary dynamic in the school environment is a double-edged sword when it comes to fear. Administrators and teachers often fear that their credibility will be diminished such that they will fail to get students to internalize their disciplinary ethic—that if students no longer listen to administrators and teachers as sources of authority, the result will be chaos and disorder. Students and parents often fear that administrators and teachers will be given too much authority in instilling discipline (e.g., via corporal punishment).

More specifically, American schools historically have been the site of particular fears, the causes of which can become evidence in court cases; most commonly, these are fears about violence, the encouragement of immoral/unsafe sex, and drug/alcohol use. People's fear of violence in schools is perhaps due to the history of violence that has occurred in the school setting. Horace Mann reported in 1843 that more than four hundred Massachusetts schoolhouses were "broken up" in the early 1800s as a result of general student violence.[16] Moreover, Princeton University had experienced six campus rebellions, and the University of Virginia was the setting of a campus riot. According to Elizabeth Midlarsky and Helen Marie Klain, "in the late eighteenth and early nineteenth centuries, the emerging American nation sought to define its role and identity within the global community. This endeavor may have been expressed in

35

CHAPTER 2

the acts of rebellion and protest evident in both the society at large and, in microcosm, within the American schools."[17] In 1917, the Gary Plan to bring industrial efficiency practices into the education system resulted in rioting in several New York schools, making school operation impossible.[18] Various types of violence have occurred in our schools throughout history—riots in the 1960s and 1970s, fistfights between students, bullying, rubber band fights, hazing rituals, and so on—proving that fear and violence go hand in hand.

A specific fear in contemporary American life concerns gun violence on campuses from both student and nonstudent shooters. Most shootings in schools prior to 1995 involved nonstudent shooters. The first known act of gun violence in American history occurred on July 26, 1764, and involved four Delaware (Lenape) American Indians who, in retaliation for colonization, entered a schoolhouse in the province of Pennsylvania and shot and killed the teacher and nine children.[19] Several incidents of gun violence date to the colonial era, though gun violence escalated in the 1990s. *Morse* came on the heels of the shooting in 1999 at Columbine High School in Columbine, Colorado, in which twelve students and a teacher were murdered before the two student shooters killed themselves. Among the many conversations about the causes of the shootings were the use of pharmaceutical antidepressants by teenagers and several First Amendment–related issues including teenage Internet use and violent video games.

While violence in general, and gun violence in particular, has been a source of fear since schools first formed in America, the fears that concern school administrators have proliferated since the beginning of the second half of the twentieth century. For example, the National Association of Secondary School Principals (NASSP) has a host of issues for principals to think about that were not part of administrator training in the earlier twentieth century. Such materials encourage administrators to consider several community fears, including bullying, teenage sex (specifically, sexually transmitted diseases), gangs, swine flu, sexting, cyberbullying, and food contamination. One of the dominant concerns is the fear of teen drug and alcohol use, which played a unique role in the *Morse* case.

While the history of drug regulation in America is complicated, the fear of drug use led to the enactment of the Drug-Free Schools and Communities Act Amendments of 1986. The amendments required educational institutions "to establish a means of maintaining drug-free campuses, informing students and employees at the beginning of each school year of the penalties for drug use or sale, and providing information on available treatment."[20] School districts across the country began enacting policies to comply with their congressionally mandated obligation. In the 1980s, "public sentiment grew increasingly antidrug" in fear of the most egregiously harmful consequences of drug use.[21] Important in the *Morse* context is Juneau School District's Policy 5520, which specifically prohibits "any assembly or public expression that . . . advocates the use of substances that are illegal to minors."[22] This policy became one of the central foci of the Supreme Court's consideration of whether Principal Morse's interpretation was constitutionally permissible given student constitutional rights established in *Tinker*.

School administrators and teachers are in increasingly difficult positions in relation to the numerous fears that persist in the school environment. On a daily basis, those in positions of authority are charged with increasing responsibility and are required to make grave decisions at a moment's notice. This context is important to understanding the controversy surrounding the *Morse* case. From student Joseph Frederick's perspective, he was simply unfurling a nonsensical banner reading, "BONG HiTS 4 JESUS." From Principal Morse's perspective, she had to make a quick decision not only because of the sign's content but also because she had to attend to her other responsibilities at the event. Her decision to err on the side of caution in the context of societal fears concerning the school environment in general, and fears about student use of illegal drugs in particular, gave rise to the controversial Supreme Court case.

FEAR IN *MORSE V. FREDERICK*

Several fears persisted in *Morse*. Most prominent was the fear of student drug use. It was central to the majority opinion of the Court. After detailing the health and social consequences of youth drug use, Chief Justice John Roberts concluded, "It was reasonable for [Morse] to conclude that the banner promoted illegal drug use—in violation of established school policy—and that failing to act would send a powerful message to the students in her charge, including Frederick, about how serious the school was about the dangers of illegal drug use. The First Amendment does not

CHAPTER 2

require schools to tolerate at school events student expression that contributes to those dangers."[23] Justice Anthony Kennedy joined in Justice Samuel Alito's concurring opinion, agreeing with Chief Justice Roberts, "Speech advocating illegal drug use poses a threat to student safety that is just as serious, if not always as immediately obvious. As we have recognized in the past and as the opinion of the Court today details, illegal drug use presents a grave and in many ways unique threat to the physical safety of students."[24] Thus, the fear of condoning and contributing to student drug use by tolerating Frederick's speech became the central focus of the case.

At the same time, a variety of peripheral fears received considerably less attention in the national spotlight. For example, one fear was that local administrators might abuse the "interference in the educational mission" standard affirmed in the majority opinion by using it as a justification to regulate constitutionally protected speech in the school context. Justice Alito and Justice Kennedy made this point clear in their concurring opinion, "The opinion of the Court does not endorse the broad argument advanced by petitioners and the United States that the First Amendment permits public school officials to censor any student speech that interferes with a school's 'educational mission.' . . . This argument can easily be manipulated in dangerous ways, and I would reject it before such abuse occurs." With such a clarification, the Court affirmed the heart of *Tinker* while allowing for the very narrow regulation of speech that may be interpreted as speech condoning illegal drug use.

Justice Clarence Thomas added the fear that First Amendment rights in the context of the school environment may result in a collapse of expert authority and the rise of populist reasoning. Relying on the precept of "original meaning," Justice Thomas's concurring opinion described in great detail the learning environment of the early American public schools, wherein "teachers taught, and students listened."[25] He expressed a fear that *Tinker* undermined teachers' authority to instill knowledge and values. Justice Thomas's statement seems consistent with a "banking" model of education, defined as "an act of depositing, in which the students are the depositories, and the teacher is the depositor. Instead of communicating, the teacher issues communiqués and makes deposits which the students patiently receive, memorize, and repeat."[26] In the "banking" model, "knowledge is a gift bestowed by those who consider themselves knowledgeable upon those whom they consider to know nothing."[27] In affirming the education model of the earliest public schools where "teachers taught, and students listened," Justice Thomas appears fearful that student ignorance will override the expertise of the teacher. The fear associated with such a perspective is that the knowledgeable student, who has embraced systematic and disciplined study, will give way to the "misinformed" student—as in the case of so many students who have not thoroughly studied the complications of illegal drug use.

Associated with this fear is the issue of teacher and administrator credibility. Not only is credibility important for "good" teaching, but the fear of a collapse of credibility is related to the fear of disorder in the school environment. Both Justice Thomas and Justice Stephen Breyer agreed on this point. Justice Breyer reasoned, "Although the dissent avoids some of the majority's pitfalls, I fear that, if adopted as law, it would risk significant interference with reasonable school efforts to maintain discipline. . . . And a school official, knowing that adolescents often test the outer boundaries of acceptable behavior, may believe it is important (for the offending student and his classmates) to establish when a student has gone too far." He continued, "Teachers are neither lawyers nor police officers; and the law should not demand that they fully understand the intricacies of our First Amendment jurisprudence. As the majority rightly points out, the circumstances here called for a quick decision."[28] Justice Thomas reasoned that "discipline" was essential: "Teachers commanded, and students obeyed. Teachers did not rely solely on the power of ideas to persuade; they relied on discipline to maintain order."

Principal Morse expressed her evidentiary fear of losing administrative credibility, especially when it came to the message the school district was trying so desperately to enforce concerning illegal drug use. In her report of the events, Elizabeth Pawelczyk explains, "Morse justified her actions by stating that she feared that if she failed 'to respond when Frederick held up his banner . . . [it] could create the impression that the district approved, or at least tolerated, student's use of illegal drugs.'"[29] Thus, Principal Morse was concerned that if she did not act, then she would be perceived as condoning the use of illegal drugs. The majority accepted her argument.

Importantly, related to the fear of losing order and discipline is the fear that set in after Columbine. For example, Gene Policinski reported,

CHAPTER 2

"For their part, groups lining up behind the school system say that to permit Frederick's prank is to weaken the ability of educators to maintain order, educate and protect students in a post-Columbine-shooting era."[30] The larger stakes embedded here are the fear that gun violence may be the result of a collapse of discipline and order. So, even though there were no objective threats of gun violence in this case, parents and groups expressed the larger value associated with discipline and order that is a precondition for creating an environment that, in their view, will help curb the possibility of gun violence in the future.

Not unrelated to the fear of disorder and encouraging illegal drug use is the fear of impending lawsuits and negative publicity. On the one hand, an administrator can easily imagine the angry parent of a student who is punished by a school for illegal drug use suing the school district for negligence in enforcing its anti–illegal drug policies. If such a parent were to sue, then Frederick's sign could be used as evidence that administrators have sent mixed signals about illegal drug use and therefore should be held responsible for their child's illegal drug use. On the other hand, an administrator may, as happened in Frederick's case, be sued by Frederick for violating First Amendment rights and be threatened with personal financial liability for such a violation. Administrators are thus caught in the middle of potential conflicts over risks of litigation versus risks of acting or failing to act in a given situation.

The fear that administrators will be held personally financially liable and the attendant fear that this liability will decrease the incentive for good administrators to take the job led many groups to back the Juneau School District. Carol Comeau, Anchorage School superintendent, articulated a collective fear of administrators of being held personally financial liable: "The one part—we absolutely disagreed with Joe [in] that we did not believe the principal should have been sued personally. . . . That part of the lawsuit—I was furious when I saw it. Why would anyone want to be a principal or an educator, if [it] ends up that they are personally liable for doing their job? So, we felt really strongly about that."[31] Policinski's own analysis of Morse's expressed fear is the context of personal liability (e.g., Morse potentially losing her house): "And because Frederick is seeking monetary damages, saying Morse should have known she was violating his basic constitutional rights, the argument is made that every school authority will be fearful of taking action against

40

STUDENT SPEECH

a disruptive student because of personal liability."[32] This is the fear that Justice Breyer shared in his partial concurrence with the majority opinion where he defended his granting Morse qualified immunity, finding her to be far from "plainly incompetent," and expressed the need for administrators to be unfearful of personal financial loss when acting quickly in difficult situations.[33]

In addition to lawsuits, administrators commonly fear negative publicity. The fear of negative publicity was manifest in this case because of the attention the torch relay had promised to bring to the town of Juneau. James C. Foster explained, "Fueling Juneau's civic leaders' dismay was their embarrassment—and their annoyance. . . . Juneau's municipal elites were mightily displeased that an initially intrusive 'nasty little nuisance' threatened to swallow it and supersede the main event. More was at risk than Juneau's image as an Olympic torch relay host city, however. The reputations of Juneau's governing officials were on the line."[34] The town was excited to host the Olympic torch relay. That the event would be broadcast on television brought even more excitement among Juneau's citizens and officials, because the torch provided an opportunity to spotlight the city before a world audience. If the portrayal were negative, then local administrators would bear the brunt of the blame, as angry citizens typically blame government officials when these kinds of events go wrong. Thus, when Frederick unfurled his banner, Morse had more at stake than her school—she had the influence and reputations of Juneau's public officials on the line.

Together, the fear of lawsuits and negative publicity may lead to ancillary fears concerning public education. For example, Jay Braiman explains, "It is precisely the fear of lawsuits and negative publicity that motivates school officials to forbear or mitigate disciplinary action, subjectivize academic standards, overturn teachers' assessments of student performance, and otherwise placate students and parents in unreasonable and counterintuitive ways."[35] The fact that a banner being unfurled became a symbol of the feared deterioration of America's public schools demonstrates the fear felt by many that there is too much disorder and chaos in today's school environment. The banner become more than a symbol of illegal drug use; it became a symbol of a deeper fear—the fear that our schools are failing.

Additionally, the fear of lawsuits and negative publicity resulted at

CHAPTER 2

least in part from Morse's fear that students would become increasingly unruly because of the banner, causing things to get out of hand quickly. Charles Chulack calls this an "undifferentiated fear or apprehension of disturbance." He explains, "This fear was caused by the atmosphere present while the students waited for the torch relay to pass. There was a report in the record that not all of the students were waiting patiently. Some of the students began throwing coke bottles and snowballs at each other while others got into fights. This description suggested that the atmosphere at the time was on the threshold of anarchy and the proverbial 'last straw' for Morse was Frederick unfurling his 'Bong HiTS 4 Jesus' banner."[36] One can easily imagine a scene where a teenage crowd is getting more and more rowdy, and administrators are getting more and more fearful that things will get out of hand.

At the same time, if only the administrators had fears in this case, then perhaps nothing would have been made of it. But Frederick and First Amendment advocates experienced a variety of fears other than those the administrators experienced. For example, Frederick feared that if he put down the banner after being asked, then the Constitution would fail him. According to Frederick, the Constitution was designed to protect his speech. Frederick expressed the fear that others had of school authorities and his faith in the Constitution: "A lot of people were just dropping [the banner] when she came over because—I don't know. They didn't have faith in their rights of free speech, I guess, and they were scared because they didn't trust the Constitution to protect them, I guess. But I had faith in it, so I held it."[37] Frederick also expressed his belief in the Constitution when recalling his meeting in the office with Morse. He described the conversation, "They said that I didn't put the banner down at first, and that I was questioning why they were suspending me. And I said, 'How can you all be mad about the banner? It was pure speech, and don't we have the Bill of Rights still?' Mr. Staley said not in school because it doesn't apply. Then I quoted Thomas Jefferson to them in the office, saying that 'Free speech can't be limited without being lost.' They told me to stop arguing because I just got another five days [suspension] right after I quoted Thomas Jefferson."[38] Thus, Frederick's fear was that if free speech were not exercised, then the freedom of speech would mean nothing—that the Constitution would not be needed to protect government (school officials in this case) from censorship if students did it themselves out of fear of intimidation by school administrators.

Moreover, those who interpret Frederick's behavior as disruptive speculate that his acting out was rooted in other fears Frederick had about life in the school environment. Frank Frederick, Joseph Frederick's father, explained that when they lived in the Seattle area, "Joe did not like Thomas Jefferson High School (TJHS), the Federal Way, Washington, school Joe attended his sophomore year. Joe told his dad that his unhappiness resulted from antipathy directed toward him by TJHS boys, who were jealous because Joe's lingering Southern accent made him attractive to TJHS girls, and because Joe had run-ins with what Joe called 'Asian gangbangers.'"[39] After his move to the Juneau high school, Frank explained that his son had a bit of a difficult time: Joe "never told me he'd gotten in any fights at school. But I heard about 'em—it was after he graduated. But he never came home and told me he'd gotten into a fight. . . . I found out later . . . how Joe had to get into fisticuffs with football players that would start pickin' on him, but he wouldn't back down." Thus, Frederick's unfurling the banner may have been, in part, a defensive mechanism that symbolized a way of resisting forces he perceived to be bullying him—he might fight football players with fists and administrators with a banner. Possibly in his thinking, both were similar in terms of their encroachment on his feeling of self-worth and expressive desires.

Regardless of whether there was any deep-seated fear, the fear of losing First Amendment freedoms was the explicit focus of both Frederick and some members of the Supreme Court and the American public. At issue, for example, for Justice John Paul Stevens was that restricting speech that may be regarded as pro–illegal drug speech would stifle democratic conversations about public policies on the issue—speech that is essential for democratic decision-making to work. Justice Stevens wrote, "Among other things, the Court's ham-handed, categorical approach is deaf to the constitutional imperative to permit unfettered debate, even among high-school students, about the wisdom of the war on drugs or of legalizing marijuana for medicinal use."[40] He concluded, "In the national debate about a serious issue, it is the expression of the minority's viewpoint that most demands the protection of the First Amendment. Whatever the better policy may be, a full and frank discussion of the costs and

CHAPTER 2

benefits of the attempt to prohibit the use of marijuana is far wiser than suppression of speech because it is unpopular."[41]

Justice Stevens expressed the views of many groups in America who feared that the case would overreach into other areas of student life. For example, many conservative groups, including the Alliance Defense Fund, the American Center for Law and Justice, and the Christian Legal Society "have been at the forefront of that effort to defend students' free-speech rights. Those groups argue that the *Tinker* precedent must stand, because it gives religious people and groups the right to express their viewpoints on public school campuses without fear of censorship." *Tinker* made *Morse v. Frederick* particularly important because of the fear that censoring speech on a public sidewalk may implicate restrictions on free speech beyond the school context. "Indeed, many free-speech supporters have expressed fear that, if the Supreme Court sides with Morse in the 'Bong Hits' case, speech rights for students could be limited outside the walls of public schools as well as inside. Many supporters have voiced concerns that students could be punished for views they express in outside writing projects, activities, or postings to their personal Web sites or Web logs."[42]

Even when such speech is not punished, there is a prevailing fear that students will not know where they stand in terms of the First Amendment, thus leading them to err on the side of caution and self-censor in the school environment. This chilling effect is feared on two grounds. First, because students have been granted First Amendment rights by *Tinker* but then had them scaled back in a number of significant cases, they might believe that "their exception to *Tinker* is next" and their speech will not be protected. Second, many view the standard set forth in the majority opinion in *Morse v. Frederick* as vague, leading students to remain entirely silent about illegal drugs in the school environment. For example, legal scholar Kellie Nelson explains, "The danger of the confusing Morse decision is its potential to lead school officials to prohibit any message in which drugs form the content." She continues, "Even if school officials do not punish protected speech regarding drugs this decision may create a chilling effect on students. Increasing the possibility of punishment for drug-advocacy may encourage students to steer far clear of any speech about drugs, even constitutionally protected speech, out of fear of punishment. A chilling effect is particularly likely since the Court did not attempt to clarify that political or social speech is protected,

44

despite Justice Alito's attempt to make the limits on this ruling clear."[43]

Taken together, there were a host of fears surrounding the First Amendment controversy in *Morse v. Frederick*, including the fear of speech contributing to student use of illegal drugs, the fear the such drug use will lead students into unpatriotic or tragic lives, the fear that administrators will abuse their authority at the local level, the fear that student opinions will be privileged over expert knowledge, the fear of losing the administrative credibility necessary to ensure discipline and order in the schools, the fear that events would get out of hand and lead to physical violence, the fear that good administrators would take other jobs if they feared personal lawsuits, the fear of litigation over acting on the spot, the fear of negative publicity, the fear that students will not be able to express themselves and learn to be involved in democratic deliberation, and maybe even the fear of losing a sense of self-worth. With all of these fears in circulation, it is no wonder that this case made it to the Supreme Court and resulted in public controversy.

POST-MORSE FEARS AND THE FIRST AMENDMENT IN PUBLIC SCHOOLS

In the post-*Morse* environment, these fears are unlikely to go away. Indeed, a variety of fears will likely lead to a battleground concerning First Amendment rights of students in the public-school context—not the least of which are cases likely to surface because of the Supreme Court's reasoning in *Morse* that Morse had the authority to act on Frederick's banner even though he was both across the street from the school (technically off campus) and did not check into school that morning and was counted as absent. If *Tinker* ruled that students do not shed their constitutionally guaranteed freedom of expression at the schoolhouse gate, then *Morse* ruled not only that students are to be treated differently inside the schoolhouse gate but also that the schoolhouse gate may move beyond the physical space of the school. This argument was tested again in a 2021 case before the Court, *Mahanoy Area School District v. B.L.* A young woman who did not make the cheerleading team posted an expletive-laden rant on Snapchat, attacking the "school," "cheer" leading, and "everyone." Since she was off school property, her case allowed the Court to reexamine the *Morse* standard. In it, the Court addressed the fears of cyberbullying and the fear of bodily injury. The Court upheld the cheerleader's claim on free speech grounds because her speech did not meet the standard set forth in *Tinker* that "undifferentiated fear or apprehension . . . is not enough to overcome the right to freedom of expression."[44] The Court concluded that "sometimes it is necessary to protect the superfluous in order to preserve the necessary."[45]

When the schoolhouse gate is moved beyond the physical place of the school, the gate may also become virtual. The virtual schoolhouse gate demarcates a space outside the traditional physical place of the public school, yet because *Morse* allows administrators to take action outside the physical premises of the school, they may also use *Morse* as a rationale for restricting the speech of students in cyberspace. This simple move is likely to enable a host of other fears to percolate into cases involving cyberspace. Depending on one's fears, this may be a good or a bad thing. Regardless, the virtual schoolhouse gate is one of the new frontiers where fear and the First Amendment collide and where issues will likely continue for the foreseeable future.

On the cyberbullying front, fear associated with speech that bullies students in the cyber medium will continue to spur debate about how best to narrowly tailor ordinances to ensure student safety while protecting student freedom of speech. Naomi Harlin Goodno explained the lack of clarity concerning questions about the scope of governmental authority in regulating cyberbully speech: "Cyberbullying is one of the top challenges facing public schools. . . . Neither the legislatures nor the courts have been able to give public schools clear and consistent guidance on how to answer these questions. Indeed, in a recent Third Circuit opinion, the court was deeply divided on how to decide such issues. There is also a circuit split on these issues making it ripe for the Supreme Court of the United States to resolve. Cyberbullying raises issues that require a fine balance between protecting the constitutional rights of public-school students while also creating a safe learning environment."[46] And, importantly, the Supreme Court upheld the ability of school administrators to regulate cyberbullying in *Mahanoy v. B.L.*, "The school's regulatory interests remain significant in some off-campus circumstances. . . . Several types of off-campus behavior . . . may call for school regulation. These include serious or severe bullying or harassment targeting particular individuals."[47]

There is also the issue of students creating parodies of school

46

STUDENT SPEECH

administrators and sharing such parodies in cyberspace. Administrators have widely expressed a fear that if such speech is permitted, they will lose the credibility that is necessary to maintain respect, order, and discipline in the school environment. This fear came to a head in *Layshock v. Hermitage School District*, when a student created a parody profile of his principal and was punished for violating the school's disciplinary code. The case reached the Third Circuit, which refused to clarify the reach of administrator authority in enforcing school policy in the cyber medium: "We need not now define the precise parameters of when the arm of authority can reach beyond the schoolhouse gate because . . . the district court found that [the student's] conduct did not disrupt the school, and the District does not appeal the finding. Thus, we need only hold that [the student's] use of the District's web site does not constitute entering the school, and that the District is not empowered to punish his out of school conduct under the circumstances here."[48] Whether parody will be a First Amendment right of students, or whether the fear of losing administrative credibility wins the day, is yet to be seen.

The cyber medium has also given rise to fears about the effects of sexting. Legal scholar Jamie Williams examined sexting and cyberbullying as conjoined fears in the school environment: "Sexting and cyberbullying—practices by which teens exchange nude or semi-nude photos with each other or bully fellow teens using technology, respectively—are on the rise, and their rapid growth has both parents and schools up in arms. In response to the public's outcry for action, legislators across the nation are drafting laws that criminalize both sexting and cyberbullying. Many of these laws, however, have been met with opposition because of their infringement of the First Amendment right of minors to exercise freedom of expression and the Fourteenth Amendment right of parents to direct the upbringing of their children."[49]

The virtual schoolhouse gate and the fear of losing administrator credibility and order in the school environment are also at issue in cases where students poke fun at teachers and administrators on social networking sites. A panel in the Third Circuit, for example, ruled in favor of the school district's right to punish such speech in the case of *J. S. v. Blue Mountain School District*. The case involved "an eighth grade student who created a fake MySpace profile of her school principal, [facetiously 'self'-]identified as 'a bisexual Alabama middle school principal named

47

CHAPTER 2

"M-Hoe.'" While J. S. claimed the profile was intended to be a joke between herself and her friends, she created it after the principal had twice disciplined her for dress code violation. The profile was filled with 'crude content and vulgar language,' and was laced with 'profanity and shameful personal attacks aimed at the principal and his family.'"[50] After the initial posting, anyone with access to the Internet could view the material. After several students told J. S. that they found the material to be funny, J. S. marked the content "private," and limited access to students who were her MySpace friends. When the principal viewed a printout provided by a student, the principal suspended J. S. for ten days, citing a violation of the school's disciplinary code. The parents sued, citing First Amendment rights of the student, and the Third Circuit panel ruled in favor of the school. Because the ruling conflicted with another panel the same day, the Third Circuit reheard the case en banc and reversed the panel's decision, ruling in favor of the student.

The feared proliferation of jokes about administrators and teachers has led educators to think about how to best respond. The traditional remedy for the posting of objectionable content is more speech—meaning that teachers may be compelled to respond to students who post material by refuting (at best) or taking revenge (at worst) in the cybersphere. In other words, teachers may be tempted to create what they perceive to be an adequate response or invoke the "two can play that game" mentality. The problem is that many teachers fear losing their jobs by responding—leading to asymmetrical rights in the cybersphere. Emily McNee explains, "a teacher might be less willing to engage in what could be protected speech under the First Amendment, due to concerns about being subject to discipline by the school district or fears of complaints from parents who somehow gain access to the speech. Teachers' fears about discipline for their online activities, coupled with their knowledge that their speech will receive little protection, is likely to cause teachers to self-censor and refrain from engaging in speech on important societal concerns."[51]

Taken together, cyberspace is implicated by the Court's ruling in *Morse* in its blurring of the lines regarding the location of the schoolhouse gate. In addition, schools will be challenged with several other First Amendment considerations in the wake of *Morse*. At least some legal scholars believe that *Morse* was too narrow and leaves administrators

STUDENT SPEECH

wary of disciplining gang communication that may qualify for First Amendment protections. Citing *Morse* as the latest in a string of narrow rulings, legal scholar Keith Collins explains, "the Supreme Court's failure to provide a broad, guiding principle addressing First Amendment rights within the special context of public schools has left administrators hesitant to discipline many forms of cyberbullying and gang activity out of fear of violating students' First Amendment rights. These harmful types of expression, largely unaffected by the narrow rulings in Tinker, Bethel, Hazelwood and Morse, justify a departure from tradition because public schools should be free to enjoin these harmful types of expression without fear of violating the First Amendment."[52] Thus, the fear of violating the First Amendment will continue to bump up against the fear of the perceived negative consequences of speech.

CONCLUSION (WITH A NOTE ON *MAHANOY AREA SCHOOL DISTRICT V. B.L.*)

In sum, fears have pervaded schools since the founding era in America. Many of these fears bubbled to the surface in *Morse v. Frederick*, and will likely persist in the future. This reality is evidenced by the fears expressed in the recent *Mahanoy v. B.L.* decision. A student cheerleader made two posts to her Snapchat, one of which showed a picture of her with two middle fingers and the caption "Fuck school fuck softball fuck cheer fuck everything." In response, she was suspended from the cheerleading team. The school feared that her speech would affect "team morale" and that "there was negativity put out there that could impact students in the school."[53] The Court, however, ruled that this speech constituted an "undifferentiated fear" and thus protected speech. Moreover, supporting the student cheerleader in the case gives voice to the fear that students will choose not to speak at all for fear of punishment—an environment that is antithetical to raising reasoned citizens who are capable of freely communicating with each other. For example, Catherine Kuhlmeier of *Hazelwood v. Kuhlmeier* feared such a slippery slope: "I think if (the court rules) against the student, every high school student's walk is going to become a lot more difficult. . . . You're going to have, essentially, Big Brother looking over your shoulder, whether it's within the walls of the schoolhouse or outside."[54]

CHAPTER 2

One of the common themes running alongside the variety of fears associated with the First Amendment is a fear of youth *becoming* adults. Had the banner in *Morse* been held by a nonstudent adult at the Olympic torch relay, the speech would have been clearly protected by the First Amendment. Students, especially those who are of high school age, face a variety of fears on a consistent basis. In so many ways, the fears that are experienced in the school environment are no different from those experienced by adult Americans, up to and including murders in our schools and in our streets. High schools are a microcosm of society, as they represent the next generation of adults in society.

The way the next generation of adults are treated and educated regarding their freedom of speech may have a lot to do with the way they communicate and participate in democracy upon reaching voting age. This connection has been affirmed by the Court on a number of occasions. In 1943, the Court affirmed the importance of the school as a training ground for citizenship when Justice Robert Jackson wrote, "That [schools] are educating the young for citizenship is reason for scrupulous protection of constitutional freedoms of the individual, if we are not to strangle the free mind at its source and teach youth to discount important principles of our government as mere platitudes."[55] In 1957, Chief Justice Earl Warren wrote in the Court's opinion in *Sweezy v. New Hampshire*, "Teachers and students must always remain free to inquire, to study and to evaluate, to gain new maturity and understanding; otherwise, our civilization will stagnate and die."[56] In 1967, Justice William Brennan further defended the idea for the Court, writing, "The Nation's future depends upon leaders trained through wide exposure to that robust exchange of ideas which discovers truth 'out of a multitude of tongues, [rather] than through any kind of authoritative selection.'"[57] Frederick failed in the First Amendment principle by refusing to engage in conversation about the effects that his "BONG HiTS" speech might have on others, insisting that it was "merely" nonsense speech. Morse failed in the First Amendment principle of being able to use speech to persuade Frederick that his speech may have had harmful effects. Instead, the entire situation succumbed to fears that preceded the event in the public-school context. The First Amendment demands more of all the parties involved in the incident in Juneau, Alaska, and demands more of us as we move forward and face our fears in our public schools.

50

3

Fear and Unlimited Spending
in Election Campaigns

Citizens United v. Federal Elections Commission

A FEW DAYS AFTER THE Supreme Court handed down its decision in *Citizens United v. Federal Elections Commission*, the ruling became more relevant to the public when President Obama expressed the fears about reformers in his State of the Union Address: "With all due deference to the separation of powers, last week the Supreme Court reversed a century of law that I believe will open the floodgates for special interests—*including* foreign corporations—to spend without limit in our elections." Justice Alito could be seen mouthing the words, "That's not true," as he sat before the president in the bay of the House chamber. The attention this ruling has received from all sides certainly makes it worthy of detailed consideration. However, before we consider this controversial ruling in detail, we want to contextualize it in terms of Obama's reference to the "century of law" that was overturned.

In September 1901, at the Pan-American World Exposition in Buffalo, Leon Czolgosz, a communist anarchist, assassinated President William McKinley. The assassin believed McKinley to be the embodiment of corrupt capitalism, because the president had received more corporate

CHAPTER 3

contributions than any presidential candidate to that date. During his presidential campaigns, McKinley's wealthy, longtime friend Mark Hanna personally welcomed corporate heads to McKinley's home in Canton, Ohio. McKinley's first run in 1896 against the Populist Democrat William Jennings Bryan had initiated this "front porch" strategy in part because McKinley's wife, Ida, had petit mal epilepsy and did not travel well. When the strategy proved successful, it was used again in the campaign of 1900; however, the new vice presidential nominee on the ticket, Theodore Roosevelt, decided to go out on the campaign trail against Bryan, who was nominated again by the Democrats.[1] After a rousing campaign, Roosevelt claimed he felt strong as a "bull moose." The McKinley-Roosevelt ticket won an easy victory. At the time, no one knew that the election of Roosevelt as vice president would lead to major campaign reforms.

This chapter examines the myriad fears that lead up to the landmark case of *Citizens United v. Federal Elections Commission*. Between the McKinley-Roosevelt ticket and the case of *Citizens United* during the Obama administration, several fears developed that were then expressed in the landmark case. This chapter examines those fears, arguing that *Citizens United* functions as yet another site for exploring how "fear" became a persistent factor in Roberts-era First Amendment cases. As a general matter, therefore, this chapter functions as further evidence that fear is both rhetorically contested in cases of interpreting the First Amendment in the Court's doctrine and a significant element in First Amendment conflicts. This chapter is organized by first examining the historical context of campaign reform, then examining the fears that developed from the Watergate scandal, then the fears surrounding negative advertising, and finally the extension of those fears as they manifested in *Citizens United* in the context of democratic debate and commercial speech.

THE CONTEXT OF CAMPAIGN REFORM

When the president died of his wounds in 1901, Theodore Roosevelt became president and instantly set about taming the large monopolies that had formed by the end of the nineteenth century. These included the railroad empire of Averell Harriman, the oil monopoly of John D. Rockefeller, the financial empire of J. P. Morgan, and sugar trust of E. C. Knight.

Having seen what corporations could do in an election, Roosevelt feared that unfettered capitalism was contrary to and corrupting of democracy. So he not only restored competition to the marketplace, but when Senator Mark Hanna died in 1904, Roosevelt began coaxing Congress to pass legislation restricting corporations from contributing to federal election campaigns. His first obstacle came in 1905, when the Supreme Court, in a 5–4 ruling in *Lockner v. New York*, claimed that corporations were entities that enjoyed Fourteenth Amendment rights, a claim that would resurface in the *Citizens United* case. Roosevelt went into full battle mode to restore competition to the marketplace. Along the way, he signed the Tillman Act in 1907, written by Populist senator "Pitchfork Ben" Tillman of South Carolina. It was the first campaign reform law since 1867, when Congress prohibited federal candidates from soliciting funds from navy yard workers.

When Roosevelt decided not to seek a third term, his handpicked successor, William Howard Taft, was elected in his place. Taft continued to break up trusts, but he was more business friendly than Roosevelt had been. Capitalist leaders were often seen coming and going from the White House and the offices of cabinet officials. Nonetheless, Taft also feared the influence of big business and signed the Federal Corrupt Practices Act of 1910, which required state political parties to disclose their contributions to campaigns for the House of Representatives. In 1911, this law was extended to Senate campaigns and to the newly emerging primary campaigns, the result of the growing Progressive movement across the country.[2]

However, ten years later, in the *Newbury* ruling, the Supreme Court struck down the 1911 extensions of the law.[3] Coincidentally, the untoward influence of big business was soon revealed to the public in the Teapot Dome scandal. In exchange for corporate money between 1922 and 1923, Secretary of Interior Albert Fall gave cheap leases to naval oil and gas reserves in Wyoming's rich fields on the Teapot Dome. Following well-publicized hearings by Senator Thomas Walsh, Congress passed the Federal Corrupt Practices Act of 1925, which required quarterly reports on contributions of more than $100 to parties that operated in more than one state. However, the law was difficult to enforce and easy to avoid by using single-state parties as vehicles for campaign contributions. The Supreme Court upheld the law in the *Burroughs* ruling of 1934.[4] In

CHAPTER 3

the same year, in an attempt to further level the political playing field, Congress required broadcasters to provide equal time and equal access to all candidates for office. The new provisions were enforced by the recently formed Federal Communications Commission.

The 1925 law was strengthened by the Hatch Act of 1939, which prevented federal employees from participating in political campaigns, and the Smith-Connally Act of 1943, which was passed over President Franklin Roosevelt's veto and prohibited union contributions to federal campaigns. A provision of the Taft-Hartley Act of 1947 reinforced the laws that applied to labor unions and restricted them and corporations from making independent contributions to federal campaigns for the first time. The 1925 law as amended stayed in effect until 1971, when it was replaced by the Federal Election Campaign Act, which strengthened the reporting provisions for federal campaigns. Though Richard Nixon had narrowly won the presidency in 1968, he did not bring his party to power in Congress. The Democrats, upset that Nixon's presidential campaign had received huge amounts of funds from rich donors, set about correcting the precedent by limiting contributions and requiring disclosure of their sources. Instead of allowing unions and corporations to make direct contributions, the law required them to form Political Action Committees (PACs) specifically for the purpose of contributing to federal campaigns. The law also allowed citizens to check a box on their income tax returns that would set aside a dollar for federal funding of campaigns starting in 1976.

FEAR FLOWING FROM THE WATERGATE SCANDAL

On June 17, 1972, five bells sounded on the Associated Press ticker in newsrooms around the world. A group of men, some with connections to the CIA, had been arrested for breaking into the Watergate Hotel in Washington, DC. Specifically, the men had entered the offices of the Democratic National Committee. These burglars were part of a rogue operation started earlier by the White House when Nixon attempted to plug leaks to the press; the "plumbers" were formed to stop the leaks. Among other invasive actions, the "plumbers" then entered the office of the psychiatrist of Daniel Ellsberg, the man who released the Pentagon Papers to the press, hoping to find information to be used against him.

SPENDING IN CAMPAIGNS

Led by former CIA operative Howard Hunt, the "plumbers" exceeded their authority—hence the forced entry into the Democratic offices. Nixon would make the politically fatal decision to cover up his knowledge of the break-in. While Nixon eventually carried forty-nine states in the ensuing election, over the next two years the continuing cover-up would become more egregious than the original crime. In August 1974, the House Judiciary Committee voted to send articles of impeachment to the House floor. Nixon resigned rather than face impeachment.

The investigation of the Watergate scandal revealed how Nixon had conducted his political campaign of 1972. Nixon and many other candidates enjoyed large contributions that were often untraceable. In other cases, such as the donation of $1,000,000 by millionaire Clement Stone, the campaign contribution cast a shadow of undue influence over the administration. In response, Congress began work on a major campaign reform bill. Reformers claimed that monied influences threatened the integrity of the electoral system. That fear justified not only regulating campaign contributions and spending but also curtailing both.

FEAR OF NEGATIVE ADVERTISING

Most of the spending on political campaigns goes to advertising for or against candidates. The more money one has on hand, the more advertising one can place. Political advertisements were first televised in the 1952 presidential campaign; they were amateurish cartoons and short on specifics. In 1964, the first "negative" political advertisement in a presidential campaign was put on the air. It depicted a small girl picking petals from a daisy as the narrator called out a countdown to nuclear war. Run only once because of protests, the advertisement was clearly an attack on the policies of Republican candidate Barry Goldwater by the sitting president Lyndon Johnson. Goldwater had advocated using tactical nuclear weapons in the Vietnam War. Negative or attack advertising has been with us ever since.

Many states now have campaign fair practices commissions that can fine and/or censor candidates for distorting the record or defaming their opponents, among other offenses. Nonetheless, negative or attack advertising is more common than ever, and members of the House and Senate, the most common targets of such advertising, fear its influence and have

CHAPTER 3

attempted to limit its funding, whether the funds come from opponents or advocacy groups.

In the wake of the Watergate scandal, a passel of requirements was added to the Federal Election Campaign Act of 1971. Citing the threat of corruption, the reforms required that any contributor giving $10 or more to a federal campaign had to be included in the campaign's next quarterly report to the Federal Elections Commission (FEC); the name and address of the contributor was required.[5] The new federal rules limited individual contributions to $1,000 per election per candidate, prohibited direct corporate and union contributions, but allowed employees to contribute to a campaign by forming PACs, which could make maximum contributions of $5,000 per candidate per election. No individual would be allowed to give more than $5,000 to a PAC or $25,000 overall to federal candidates during a single election cycle. The new law also carefully monitored and limited what corporations or unions could contribute in kind—equipment, services, travel, and the like. However, for-profit (501c6) and nonprofit (501c4, 501c3) organizations could provide advocacy advertisements favoring or opposing federal candidates or their issue positions as long as such activity was not "coordinated" with that campaign. This provision opened a loophole in the law that allowed religious, environmental, and other groups to campaign against candidates who opposed their agendas. It also allowed for the creation of independent action groups—designated as 527s—which are tax-exempt and can raise unlimited amounts of money for political activity and issue advocacy.

Two of the most infamous of these action groups were the independent group from the 1988 presidential campaign that placed the "Willie Horton" negative advertisement against Michael Dukakis and the "Swiftboat" advocacy group that attacked presidential candidate John Kerry during the 2004 election. The 1988 advertisement was created by Floyd Brown for an independent committee called Americans for Bush, and in 2004, Brown challenged a documentary made by Michael Moore, *Fahrenheit 9/11*.[6] It contained a direct attack on President George W. Bush and cost more than $2 million. In his complaint to the Federal Elections Commission, Brown argued that Moore's documentary was express election communication and therefore, under the law, prohibited from airing on television thirty days before a primary and sixty days before the

56

general election. The FEC disagreed and allowed the documentary to run. Brown was infuriated and formed Citizens United, an independent advocacy group for the 2008 election. Brown with his partner, David Bosse, made the documentary *Hillary: The Movie*, the discourse seeking First Amendment protection in *Citizens United*.

Along with the "Willie Horton" and "Swift Boat" attack ads, many more surfaced in presidential campaigns, creating the fear that rogue independent groups could influence the outcome of elections. This fear would lead to more attempts at reforms, particularly those that forbade "electioneering communication" by independent groups that advocated for the election or defeat of a specific candidate. That would be important to the *Citizens United* case, because if *Hillary: The Movie* was considered entertainment or a documentary by the FEC, it would be protected speech. But if it was considered "electioneering communication," that is, an express advocacy of the defeat of a candidate, it would fall under the rules in place prohibiting such communication thirty days before a primary and sixty days before a general election.

While Citizens United was revving up its operation, the campaign reforms were failing because they were shot through with loopholes. In the first sixteen months of the 1997–98 election cycle, the national Republican and Democratic Parties raised a total of $90 million that they could then pass through to state parties.[7] In 2000, for example, more than $500 million was spent by 130 "independent" groups on campaign-issue commercials.[8] By 2010, American Action Network at $23 million, American Crossroads at $18 million, the Chamber of Commerce at $75 million, the Service Employees International Union at $15 million, and the American Federation of State, County and Municipal Employees at $11 million were heavily involved in campaign spending.[9]

And while the political parties were forced to allocate their contributions based on population formulas, they could provide unlimited money for the purpose of "party building activities" in various states. This provision opened the law to what is called "soft money": unlimited contributions given to the party for grassroots and party-building activities that were allowed under amendments to the Federal Election Campaign Act (FECA) passed in 1979. These activities were not subject to the limitations of the FECA or the regulations of the FEC. Nor were certain activities of corporations and unions, including corporate communication

CHAPTER 3

to stockholders, labor communications to its members or their families, nonpartisan voter registrations and get-out-the-vote activities, and the creation of PACs. Further, the law provided for public financing of presidential nominating conventions and for matching funds to help pay for presidential primary and general election campaigns. In return for accepting matching funds, presidential candidates were limited in how much they could spend overall. If they refused matching funds, they could spend all the money they could raise. Senator Barack Obama chose this latter course in the 2008 presidential campaign, the first major party candidate to take this course since federal funding was made available in 1976. Obama then raised more money from more donors than anyone in history: more than $750 million from more than 3.5 million reported donors.[10]

Senator John McCain accepted federal funding. Thus, following his convention, McCain was limited to spending only the $84.1 million the federal government provided to him, while Obama could spend all he raised and, thus, vastly outspent McCain. Mitt Romney learned from McCain's mistake. Both candidates in 2012 would abjure federal funding in favor of private fundraising. In the end, they raised an astounding amount of money: around $1 billion each.[11]

There were other problems with the law. First, the distribution of federal funds favored the two-party system, thereby quashing the voices of third-party candidates. Full matching funds were provided only to those parties that scored 25 percent of the vote or more in the previous presidential election. Worse yet, the law funded the two parties' primary candidates, conventions, and election campaigns while marginalizing third parties and their candidates. On top of that, by creating joint committees and joint fundraisers, operatives and supporters could raise large sums at various gatherings for campaigns. Prior to the Republican Convention of 2008, the developer Alex Spanos, who owned the San Diego Chargers football team, provided more than $85,000 to the McCain campaign using this tactic. The family of Carl Pohlad, the owner of the Minnesota Twins, provided $170,000 to the Obama campaign under the same scheme.

Second, to require disclosure of the membership in an organization may be a violation of the rights of privacy and assembly.[12] As recently as 1995, the Supreme Court reinforced this right of private assembly and

58

did so in the political context. In *McIntyre v. Ohio Elections Commission*, the Court held in a 6–3 decision that an Ohio law prohibiting the distribution of anonymous tracts was unconstitutional.[13] Mrs. McIntyre had been fined $100 for violating the law; the conviction was upheld by the Ohio Supreme Court, which relied on the disclosure provisions of federal law. However, in his majority opinion, Justice John Paul Stevens referred to the long tradition of anonymous political dissent going back to the American Revolution. For example, in the debate over ratification of the Constitution, Federalists and Anti-Federalists used pseudonyms when publishing their editorials. Stevens claimed that anonymity is a "shield from the tyranny of the majority." This argument clearly implies the right to contribute anonymously to a political campaign. In light of this decision, lower courts have ruled that the FEC overstepped its authority and allowed a loophole that required the disclosure only of those who donated for the explicit purpose of funding television advertising as "express advocacy."

Third, the reform favors incumbents, since they don't need to spend money to attain name identification with voters and their opponents usually do. The less money available to candidates, the more incumbents have an advantage. By equalizing contributions and expenditures through arbitrary limits, the law virtually institutionalizes incumbents and marginalizes their opponents unless independent groups intervene.

APPEALING FOR RELIEF

Loopholes and bad law aside, the Watergate reforms faced other challenges. Fearing a loss of First and Fourth Amendment rights, Senator James L. Buckley, a conservative Republican senator from New York, and Eugene J. McCarthy, a liberal Democrat and former senator from Minnesota, were the first to bring suit against the Watergate reforms. They argued that the rules infringed on freedom of expression because money is tantamount to speech; the more media time a campaign can buy, the more it can communicate its message. Limiting campaign funds limits campaign communication and, thereby, violates the First Amendment. They also argued that campaign contributions were tantamount to symbolic speech, the contributed money being the same as an endorsement. Thus, limiting the collection of funds chilled political speech. And this

CHAPTER 3

was particularly egregious given that the nation's Founders believed political speech had the highest value in a democratic republic. Buckley and McCarthy lost at the appellate level when the court found that preventing the "appearance of corruption" in federal elections was more important than First Amendment concerns. The case went to the District of Columbia Court of Appeals, which affirmed the lower court ruling and added that contributions and spending were conduct, not speech, and therefore were not protected by the First Amendment. This ruling was appealed to the Supreme Court.

The Supreme Court released a curious per curiam ruling in *Buckley v. Valeo*, the most important section of which argued that restrictions on contributions were constitutional but that limitations on campaign spending were not.[14] The former, said the Court, were appropriate ways of controlling undue influence in a campaign; the latter, however, restricted freedom of expression. The majority, which was cobbled together by Justice William Brennan,[15] also used the "undue influence" argument to allow full disclosure of membership in organizations that become involved in political campaigns. The Court upheld the provisions that lead to unfair treatment of third parties, those candidates who were not incumbents, and those candidates running against candidates with larger personal fortunes.

No wonder the majority was so fragmented and fragile. Only Justices William Brennan, Potter Stewart, and Lewis Powell concurred in all parts of the decision; other justices dissented in part and endorsed different sections of the ruling, creating pluralities for one part or another. Basically, the Court was divided between those who feared the influence of money in light of the Watergate scandal and those who feared the loss of First Amendment protection of political speech, including anonymous association. Thus, a plurality claimed that contributions could be restricted, and a different plurality claimed that expenditures should not be restricted. (Money does not equal speech in the former case, but it does equal speech in the latter.)

In his dissent in *Buckely v. Valeo*, Justice Harry Blackmun wrote that the Court could not make a distinction between contributions and expenditures on the basis of which was more vital to freedom of expression. Joined by then Associate Justice William Rehnquist, Chief Justice Burger said in his dissent: "Contributions and expenditures are two sides of the same First Amendment coin."[16] One person's contribution is another person's expenditure. Fearing that they might be harassed or fired by employers of a different political persuasion, Burger strongly objected to disclosing the names of small donors. He opposed the public funding of elections because such funding favors the two major parties and undercuts representative democracy in general and third parties in particular. Joined by Associate Justice Byron White, Burger also argued that the reform favored rich candidates, who could rely on their own funds, over poor candidates, who had no choice but to raise funds from the public in small amounts.

While the *Buckley* decision was widely criticized, the Court did not overturn the decision when it had the chance and often supported the contradictory rulings with contradictory decisions. In *FEC v. Massachusetts Citizens for Life*, for example, the Supreme Court closed down a vital right in any political system. It upheld the rule that the FEC could limit speech by organizations that "expressly" advocated for one candidate or for the defeat of another in federal elections, though these groups were still free to enter into issue advocacy.[17]

In 1987, the Supreme Court denied certiorari in a Ninth Circuit case, *FEC v. Furgatch*, which established a three-part test to determine what constituted legitimate issue advocacy. To fall under the FEC's jurisdiction, the speech must be "unmistakable and unambiguous" in its meaning. Second, it must include a "plea for action" and not be merely informative. Third, the speech must be "express advocacy of the election or defeat of a candidate."[18]

In 1996, the Supreme Court later clarified the *Furgatch* standard in two cases. In *Colorado Republican Committee v. FEC*, the Supreme Court ruled that the First Amendment prohibited the application of any provision of the FECA (1971, as amended 1979) to political party expenditures made independently.[19] The majority argued that party advocacy was a core democratic value.[20] Not surprisingly then, in the first fifteen months of the 1997–1998 cycle, the national Democratic and Republican Parties raised a total of $90 million.[21] In that cycle, because of overseas contributions—some of which were laundered through subsidiaries—the Democrats caught up with the Republicans in terms of fundraising but also faced serious ethical and legal questioning. Thus, in 2001, the Supreme Court took up *FEC v. Colorado Republican Party*, ruling 5–4 to

CHAPTER 3

reaffirm the prohibition on coordination between party organs and campaigns in federal elections.[22]

However, while the Court moved to protect issue advertising, it also gave the states the right to issue the same restrictions the Court had upheld on the federal level with regard to contribution limits. In *Nixon v. Shrink Missouri Government PAC*, the Supreme Court argued that *Buckley* is the authority for comparable state limits on contributions and that those limits need not be pegged to the precise dollar amounts approved in *Buckley*.[23] Justice David Souter, writing for the majority, revived the fear of the appearance of corruption; thus, the state of Missouri had a compelling interest in restricting contributions. In Souter's opinion, that interest, combined with Missouri's right to regulate its own elections, overwhelmed the fear of restricting freedom of speech and association. The decision was a clear endorsement of efforts at reform on the state level, but it also restricted the First Amendment rights of candidates at that level, making the *Buckley* restrictions all the more pervasive.

Buckley v. Valeo and the decisions that followed created many problems. The provisions that were retained often proved unworkable, circumventable, and/or unconstitutional. For example, the contribution limits were not indexed for inflation. One thousand dollars in 2009 would be a lot less than it was in 1975, when the law was passed. Furthermore, with regard to ending or limiting PAC contributions, one could argue that dollars given to political campaigns no longer represent corporations and unions; they represent individuals who associate in campaigns by giving to their favorite candidates through PACs to increase their influence. Thus, while the average contribution to a PAC was only $120 a year in 1996, by combining such contributions in PACs, they gained more clout.[24] Thus, PACs provide a way for citizens to participate in the political process and give clout to that participation by uniting those with similar interests. Millions of people contribute to PACs. As long as contributions must be fully, promptly, and publicly disclosed, as they are now, it seems antidemocratic to limit what they can spend.

Fearing for the funding of their campaigns after the decision in *Buckley*, politicians scrambled for ways by which they could raise money in small amounts but gather enough contributions to meet their campaign needs. The loopholes created by the Supreme Court had several weird consequences, each of which created disparities. First, as we have seen,

62

SPENDING IN CAMPAIGNS

those running for office could spend their own money in unlimited ways, a loophole through which John Connolly, Ross Perot, Steve Forbes, and Donald Trump, among others, have driven their self-funded campaign wagons. As we shall see, those fearing rich candidates having an advantage tried to pass a millionaires' amendment, but it was struck down.

Second, the Republican Party became the party of the small donor by using very sophisticated direct mail campaigns to build long lists of supporters. The result was that in the first eighteen months of the 1986 election cycle, for example, the National Republican Senatorial Committee raised $59.6 million, compared to the $6.8 million raised by its Democratic counterpart. But the Republican donations were much smaller than the Democratic donations.

Third, the "soft money" loophole meant that rich donors, corporations, and unions could give a great deal of money directly to political parties, and with a wink and a nod, it would wind up in the pocket of their preferred candidate. In 1984, the national Republican Party placed money in the coffers of the Colorado Republican Party, which then paid for advertisements attacking the Democratic candidate. As we have seen, this practice was upheld by the courts when the FEC tried to stop it.[25]

The bottom line on the soft money loophole was that it further disempowered third parties, individual voters, and the poor while ratcheting up the influence of big labor and corporations and their PACs. From 1993 to 1997, campaign contributions by the 544 largest public and private companies in America jumped 75 percent, to $129 million.[26] Soft money was the fastest-growing component of this sum. For example, in the 1996 election cycle, Philip Morris contributed $3.9 million, and AT&T contributed $2.2 million in PAC money to the two major parties. From January 1, 1995, to November 25, 1996, the Republican national committees reported raising $141 million in soft money, an increase of 183 percent over the previous cycle. The Democratic national committees raised $122 million, an increase of 237 percent. In the round of "soft money" donations reported by *Time* magazine in September 1999, the Democratic National Party received $525,000 from the Communication Workers of America, $460,000 from the American Federation of State, County and Municipal Employees, $315,000 from commercial realtor Walter H. Shorenstein, $315,000 from Williams Bailey Law Firm, and $305,350 from AT&T. Each of these donors had lobbied extensively for

63

CHAPTER 3

legislation that was then supported by the Democratic Party.[27] For example, Williams Bailey Law Firm opposed personal-injury tort reform; most Democrats supported the firm's position.

The givers in the same period to the national Republican Party were AT&T with $527,000, American Financial Group with $500,000, Philip Morris with $378,467, United Parcel Service with $363,550, and Kojaian Management with $300,000. Again, each of these companies lobbied extensively for legislation that was supported by the Republican Party.[28]

Finally, with regard to soft money, the 2000 presidential campaign led to an influx of foreign money into campaign coffers. While foreigners are prohibited from contributing to federal campaigns, green card holders are not.[29] Furthermore, foreign groups, particularly Asian ones, attempted to circumvent the law by passing money through American citizens or American subsidiaries. Both tactics are illegal if the money is spent directly on candidates; however, if the money is given to parties as soft money, the contribution was allowed. John Huang, a representative of the Indonesian-based Lippo Group, an official at the DNC and the Commerce Department, raised more than $4 million for the Democratic Party primarily from Asian Americans, some of whom were used as conduits for foreign funds.[30] Cheong Am America's $250,000 was returned when it was pointed out to the DNC that the money was from a subsidiary of a South Korean firm that had not yet generated revenues in the United States. Resident aliens Arief and Soroya Wiriadinata donated $452,000 in twenty-three separate contributions to the DNC, of which $320,000 was donated after they returned to Indonesia. Since the couple did not file 1995 income tax returns, the DNC returned the money. Many of the agents involved in these transfers, including Huang, pled guilty to violating the law.

None of these scandals stanched the flow of funds to the coffers of the two major parties. In the 2000 election cycle, the two major parties raised more than half a billion dollars in soft money. No third party raised anywhere close to even 10 percent of that amount. Furthermore, the use of independent groups to carry out separate attack campaigns accelerated. In 2004, the "Swift Boat" ads against candidate John Kerry were made by an independent group. In the same year, liberal philanthropist George Soros donated $27.5 million to independent groups opposing the reelection of President Bush.[31]

SPENDING IN CAMPAIGNS

In the meantime, PACs, through which employees can shift money to campaigns, grew in number to more than four thousand by 1986. By 1996, PAC contributors, including union and corporate members, numbered more than four million, and total donations to House and Senate campaigns reached more than $200 million. Cantor reports that "twenty-nine percent of House and Senate general election candidates' funds came from PACs in 1996, up from less than 20% in 1976."[32]

NEW REFORMS

All of these fears, along with the controversial presidential election of 2000, which was decided by the Supreme Court, generated the introduction in 2001 of more than seventy-two bills to reform the system. These bills were born of many fears, not the least of which were the fear of big money influence peddling, the fear of polluting the free marketplace of ideas, and the fear that the opposition party will raise more funds. These reforms included such unconstitutional content reform proposals as making the openings and closings in federal campaign commercials uniform, requiring candidates to appear in their commercials, and forcing stations that aired "negative ads" to grant free response time to attacked candidates. Emerging from this sea of legislation was a consensus bill, S.25, authored initially by Senators John McCain (R-AZ) and Russell Feingold (D-WI). It became the *Bipartisan Campaign Reform Act* (public law no. 107–55) when signed by President Bush in March 2002.

Like its progenitors, this act contained controversial provisions. For example, it raised contribution limits to only $2,000 per person per candidate and not to exceed $25,000 for all candidates funded during any calendar year, thereby retaining an unrealistically low ceiling on individual contributors, although pegged to inflation.[33] Thus, the average citizen continued to be restricted when it came to expressing enthusiasm for a candidate through the symbolic gesture of giving funds. For example, if you contributed $2,000 to thirteen candidates for any federal offices, you would exceed the federal limits.

Reporting to the FEC was now required of those who financed advertising for elections in excess of $10,000. The law also required that no party organ could solicit funds from or make donations to any organization

65

CHAPTER 3

that holds charitable or nonprofit status. This provision was aimed at preventing further collaboration between nonprofits and party organs.

Other provisions required that no candidate for federal office could receive any funds that did not meet FECA requirements. Accepting funding from foreign nationals was forbidden. "Express advocacy" was redefined as communication that advocates the election or defeat of a candidate by containing the phrase "vote for," "reelect," or words that in context can have no reasonable meaning other than to advocate the election or defeat of a clearly identified candidate. The law mandated that if a broadcast advertisement appears within sixty days of a federal election and refers to a "clearly identified candidate," it is considered an "electioneering communication" and is prohibited because these ads are tantamount to campaign contributions. The law said that union members could not be required to pay full union dues if some of those funds were used for political purposes.

To obtain federal funding, the act compelled candidates to say they approved their own ads. If they did not identify themselves in their advertisements, they would not be allowed to advertise at the medium's lowest unit rate; if candidates admitted that they did "approve" their ads, media were required to offer them the lowest unit rate on advertising.[34] Furthermore, the lowest unit rate was also restricted to positive ads; to receive the rate, the law stated, candidates "shall not make any direct reference to another candidate for the same office." In other words, in such ads, one candidate could not criticize the record of his or her opponent.

The "millionaires' amendment" was included to close a loophole for wealthy candidates. Realizing that the Watergate reform had a huge loophole that allowed the rich to fund their own campaigns at no limit, McCain–Feingold included a provision that allowed candidates who were opposed by self-funded candidates to receive more funds from their party. If your opponent used more than $350,000 of his or her own money in a campaign for a House seat, you could receive more funds from your party. (The threshold for Senate seats was set based on population.) However, when a House candidate challenged this provision of the law in 2007, the Supreme Court struck it down.

Senator Mitch McConnell (R-KY), head of the National Republican Senatorial Campaign Committee, sought to weaken the McCain–Feingold law by arguing that it contained unconstitutional provisions.

66

Nonetheless, the Supreme Court upheld many of the provisions when it took up the law as a whole in *McConnell v. FEC*. The *McConnell* ruling, mainly crafted by Justices John Paul Stevens and Sandra Day O'Connor, was a bare 5–4 decision.[35] The number of concurring comments took the ruling to 275 pages wherein the past arguments regarding *Buckley* again surfaced.[36] In the end, the majority upheld Congress's right to regulate federal elections; the dissenters argued that the First Amendment had been violated and the two parties entrenched because the law disadvantaged third parties via the unrealistic threshold they had to achieve in terms of votes received. They also argued that the limitation on negative advertising worked to the advantage of incumbents, whose lengthy records would not be subject to attack in the last sixty days of a federal campaign.

The ruling allowed Congress to bar the collection of soft money by candidates for federal office and even forbid pre-election campaign broadcast advertising funded by unions or corporations. Later in *FEC v. Wisconsin Right to Life*, the Supreme Court modified this provision by ruling that "core political speech" is protected by the First Amendment and therefore issue ads were permissible inside sixty days of an election.[37] The division was 5–4 on the issue. In his dissent, Justice Souter recognized that the Court had effectively overturned McCain–Feingold. The ruling paved the way for *Citizens United*.

CITIZENS UNITED V. FEC

The foregoing history of attempts at campaign finance reform reveals the fears that motivated both campaign reformers and First Amendment advocates. Reformers feared influence peddling by donors, overwhelming monetary advantages on the campaign playing fields, and the appearance of corruption in the political system. Their opponents feared a closing down of the free marketplace of political ideas due to a constriction of campaign voices, and the denial of the voters' right to hear political messages from multiple sources. This dialectic of fears would be reflected in the opinions of the justices in the *Citizens United* decision.[38]

During the 2008 presidential primary campaigns, *Hillary: The Movie*, a ninety-minute made-for-cable documentary, attacked Democratic candidate Hillary Clinton as a "Machiavellian . . . unfit for public office." One

CHAPTER 3

cable company was offered $1.2 million to play the documentary for free for viewers on its video on demand service.[39] The film was funded by a corporate advocacy group with an $11 million budget known as Citizens United, and because it was going to be shown on on-demand cable within thirty days of various primary elections, injunctions succeeded in stopping the broadcast of the film alleging it violated federal election laws.[40] A three-judge panel of the District of Columbia Court of Appeals upheld the injunctions under the provisions of the Bipartisan Campaign Reform Act, ruling that the film was "electioneering communication" directed against a candidate. The decision was appealed to the Supreme Court.

During the first set of oral arguments in March 2009, Justice Samuel Alito asked the Deputy Solicitor General Malcolm Stewart, who was defending the injunction, if the same rule could be applied to a book that was critical of Clinton and funded by a corporation. Stewart answered in the affirmative, shocking the justices. Alito remarked, "That's pretty incredible. You think that if a book was published, a campaign biography that was the functional equivalent of express advocacy, that could be banned?"

Stewart responded, "I'm not saying it could be banned." But he clearly implied that it could be prohibited thirty days out from a primary.

Justice Anthony Kennedy broke in by asking if such a book were distributed through Amazon's Kindle device, whether it could be banned, and Stewart again answered, "Yes."

Kennedy continued to push: "Your position is that, under the Constitution, the advertising for this book or the sale for the book itself could be prohibited within the sixty- and thirty-day periods?" Stewart reluctantly agreed.

Chief Justice Roberts joined in the same line of questioning: "If it has one name, one use of the candidate's name, it would be covered?"

"That's correct," Stewart answered.

"If it's a five-hundred-page book, and at the end it says, 'And so vote for X,' the government could ban that?" Roberts surmised.

"Well, if it says 'vote for X,' it would be express advocacy and it would be covered by the pre-existing Federal Election Campaign provisions," Stewart affirmed.

Citizens United chief counsel was Ted Olson, who had defended the Bush campaign in the *Bush v. Gore* case. Thinking it was a safe strategy not to ask too much of the Court, he tried to narrow the case to the single

68

SPENDING IN CAMPAIGNS

instance of this documentary. After some back-and-forth among the justices behind the scenes, Justice Souter, who had been disillusioned by the *Bush v. Gore* decision, presented a scathing dissent.[41] Justice Roberts decided the case needed to be reargued and announced on June 29, 2009, the last day of the session, that it would be heard again. The second set of oral arguments was set for September 9, 2009, which would allow time to write a ruling before the 2010 election cycle. By that time, Justice Elena Kagan had replaced Justice Souter.

In oral arguments in September 2009, it became clear that Olson had shifted his position, sensing that he could get a broader ruling on corporate rights than he had believed during the first set of oral arguments. During the reargument, Justice Ruth Bader Ginsburg asked, "Mr. Olson, are you taking the position that there is no difference" between corporate and individual rights? "A corporation, after all, is not endowed by its creator with inalienable rights," Ginsburg said. "So is there any distinction that Congress could draw between corporations and natural human beings for purposes of campaign finance?"

Olson responded, "What the Court has said . . . is that corporations are persons entitled to protection under the First Amendment." Kagan and Stevens then tried to narrow the case back to Olson's original position, and Kagan tried to help Stewart undo his mistake from the first set of arguments. But it was all to no avail, the majority opinion assigned to Justice Anthony Kennedy struck down the ban on independent corporate and union advertisements on January 21, 2010. His most important argument was based on the fear of closing off the public's right to know: "Speech is an essential mechanism of democracy, for it is the means to hold officials accountable to the people. . . . The right of citizens to inquire, to hear, to speak, and to use information to reach consensus is a precondition to enlightened self-government and a necessary means to protect it. . . . The First Amendment protects speech and speaker, and the ideas that flow from each." He clearly sided with those who feared constricting the free marketplace of political ideas.

Inside his 183-page opinion, Kennedy wrote for the 6–3 majority that in light of no compelling government interest, the Court would overturn previous rulings, particularly *Austin v. Michigan Chamber of Commerce*, because Congress could not deprive corporations and unions of First Amendment rights, including the right to participate in political

69

CHAPTER 3

campaigns by making commercials.[42] He claimed that he was opening the free marketplace of ideas to all comers. He rejected the rationale of *Buckley*, which argued that the fear of undue influence over and corruption of the free marketplace and the political system were compelling government interests. In light of fake news, social media, and false advertising, critics of Kennedy claim that the dissenters have been vindicated. But at the time, Justice Kennedy specifically rejected calls by the government to limit the decision to the case at hand and considered the cable documentary an exception, something like a biography of Hillary Clinton.

Previously, as we have seen in *McConnell*, the Supreme Court upheld limits on electioneering communications in a facial challenge, relying on the holding in *Austin* that political speech may be banned based on the speaker's corporate identity. Reversing that position, the majority argued that corporations and unions are composed of citizens who hold First Amendment rights and that corporate and union entities have a presumptive First Amendment right. Beyond speakers themselves, messages are meant to be protected by the First Amendment so that audiences can hear them.

CITIZENS UNITED AS AN EXTENSION OF COMMERCIAL SPEECH FREEDOMS

In reaction to the 1971 campaign reform law, a Richmond, Virginia, lawyer named Lewis F. Powell urged the Chamber of Commerce to fight for corporate First Amendment rights using the courts as a vehicle. A few months later, Powell was nominated to the Supreme Court by President Nixon. Then in 1978, Powell wrote the 5–4 majority opinion in *First National Bank of Boston v. Bellotti*, which struck down a Massachusetts law that prohibited banks and other corporations from spending money to fight ballot measures. Justice Stevens joined Powell in this ruling and so began the unraveling of the restrictions on corporate speech. *Bellotti* was only one step in the de-regulatory process that would culminate in the *Citizens United* ruling.

Bellotti came in the midst of a major shift with regard to the Supreme Court's attitude toward commercial speech, and Justice Stevens was a prime mover in this shift. It began with *Bigelow v. Virginia* when the Supreme Court overturned the conviction of a Virginia newspaper editor who was found guilty of running advertisements for a New York

70

SPENDING IN CAMPAIGNS

abortion referral service at a time when abortions were illegal in Virginia. One reason the Court decided to extend limited protection to these advertisements was that it believed Virginians had a *right to receive* the information contained in them. Justice Stevens concurred in this opinion, which framed the issue around the consumer's right to information as opposed to the low level of protection previously accorded to commercial speech as mere transaction.

Stevens also concurred in the following year in *Virginia State Board of Pharmacy v. Virginia Citizens Consumer Council.* In *Virginia Pharmacy,* the Supreme Court rejected the idea that commercial speech "is wholly outside the protection of the First Amendment."[43] It repudiated "the highly paternalistic view that government has complete power to suppress or regulate commercial speech."[44] Once again, the Court protected the consumers' right to receive commercial information, thus protecting a message as opposed to a speaker: "As to the particular consumer's interest in the free flow of consumer information, that interest may be as keen, if not keener by far, than his interest in the day's most urgent political debate."[45] More than any other, this opinion frames the thinking that would be reflected in the majority opinion in *Citizens United.* Four years after *Virginia Pharmacy,* the Court reaffirmed this line of thought in 1980 in *Central Hudson Gas.* When the majority led by Chief Justice Rehnquist briefly reversed this trend in the *Posadas* ruling of 1986, Stevens dissented bitterly and argued that Rehnquist had come down on the side of patronizing consumers.

Justice Stevens got his revenge a decade later when the Court took up a case regarding the state of Rhode Island's ban on the advertising of beer, wine, and liquor prices. On May 13, 1996, the Supreme Court handed down a *unanimous* ruling on commercial speech in *44 Liquormart, Inc. v. Rhode Island.* Writing for the Court, Stevens claimed that a "complete ban on truthful non-misleading commercial speech" is unconstitutional. He continued, "The First Amendment directs us to be especially skeptical of regulations that seek to keep people in the dark for what government perceives to be their own good."[46] Thus, it was Stevens and Powell who led the Court down the path toward *Citizens United,* though Stevens reframed his vision of corporate speech when it came to political campaigns and shifted to the pro-regulation side.

In his ninety-page dissent in *Citizen United,* the longest he ever wrote,

CHAPTER 3

Justice Stevens spends a good deal of time in part I arguing that the case should never have come before the Supreme Court and that the lower courts had properly applied the law. That aside, Stevens argues in part II of his dissent that the case could have been decided on much "narrower grounds" relieving Citizens United of its burden and certainly without overturning the *Austin* precedent or the one set in *McConnell*. And now Stevens argued that corporations were not persons and therefore should not be afforded the same First Amendment protection as persons. "Unlike our colleagues," Stevens wrote, the Founders "had little trouble distinguishing corporations from human beings." Stevens went back in history to buttress his point, citing the Tillman Act of 1907.

Kennedy did not buy Stevens's argument. First, he rejected the premise that corporate speech is not human speech, which was consistent with past rulings on commercial speech but not on corporate political speech. In part III of his decision in which all of the conservatives concurred, Kennedy argued that "Section 441b's prohibition on corporate independent expenditures is . . . a ban on speech. As a 'restriction on the amount of money a person or group can spend on political communication during a campaign,' that statute 'necessarily reduces the quantity of expression by restricting the number of issues discussed, the depth of their exploration, and the size of the audience reached. Were the Court to uphold these restrictions, the Government could repress speech by silencing certain voices at any of the various points in the speech process."[47]

In the introduction to his dissenting opinion, Justice Stevens attacked Kennedy's premise that the voice of corporations was equivalent to that of citizens: "The conceit that corporations must be treated identically to natural persons in the political sphere is not only inaccurate but also inadequate to justify the Court's disposition of this case. In the context of election to public office, the distinction between corporate and human speakers is significant. Although they make enormous contributions to our society, corporations are not actually members of it. They cannot vote or run for office." In part III of his lengthy dissent, Stevens extended the argument by pointing out that members of a union or corporation and even owners of such entities are free as individuals to place advertisements in the media. Thus, it is clear that the conservatives and the liberals, pragmatic though Stevens may be, were afraid of different outcomes. And those fears lent themselves to different rhetorical frames.

72

SPENDING IN CAMPAIGNS

Another premise that Kennedy rejected was that independent donors, corporations, and unions have undue influence. Following from Stevens's rejection of patronizing the public in past rulings on commercial speech in the 1970s, Kennedy argued that the public had a right to hear corporate and union speech and were capable of deciphering it properly. He argued that open and free speech was essential to Jefferson's dream of an educated public for a properly functioning democracy.

In response to Kennedy's claim, Stevens pointed to the history of regulations placed on corporate speech to prevent it from corrupting the political system or polluting the free marketplace of ideas. He credits Congress with amassing an evidentiary record of corruption that justified the application of McCain–Feingold to the case at bar: "Congress crafted BCRA in response to a virtual mountain of research on the corruption that previous legislation had failed to avert. The Court now negates Congress's efforts without a shred of evidence on how §203 or its state-law counterparts have been affecting any entity other than Citizens United." In part III of his dissent, Stevens extended the argument: "Laws such as §203 target a class of communications that is especially likely to corrupt the political process, that is at least one degree removed from the views of individual citizens, and that may not even reflect the views of those who pay for it. Such laws burden political speech, and that is always a serious matter, demanding careful scrutiny. But the majority's incessant talk of a 'ban' aims at a straw man."

Kennedy rejected the argument that corporations and unions fund advertisements with other people's money and are therefore not protected by the First Amendment. Referring to *Bellotti*, Kennedy wrote, "Prohibited, too, are restrictions distinguishing among different speakers, allowing speech by some but not others. . . . As instruments to censor, these categories are interrelated: Speech restrictions based on the identity of the speaker are all too often simply a means to control content." In his opinion in part III B, Kennedy took considerable time to bury *Austin* as a mistake that "was not well reasoned" because it assumed guilt before a harm was proved and deprived citizens of important campaign speech. Kennedy argued that recent political experience had undermined *Austin's* rationale: "If the First Amendment has any force, it prohibits Congress from fining or jailing citizens, or associations of citizens, for simply engaging in political speech. If [Stevens's] antidistortion rationale were

73

CHAPTER 3

to be accepted, however, it would permit Government to ban political speech simply because the speaker is an association that has taken on the corporate form." Chief Justice Roberts reinforced this position in his concurring opinion, which had the effect of reversing *Austin*.

Relying on such respected historians as Bernard Baylin and Gordon Wood, Kennedy created an argument from original meaning to assert that the Founders placed no limits on the sources of political speech. Returning to the present, Kennedy claimed that the "censorship we now confront is vast in its reach" and that the government had muffled the "voices that best represent significant segments of the economy." He was reinforced by Justice Antonin Scalia, who argued in his concurrence that Justice Stevens's use of "corporation-hating quotations" from the Founders was sophistry and illegitimate. Scalia then provided ample evidence that many corporations existed at the time of the passage of the First Amendment and that they were meant to be protected by the Founders.

One of the overlooked provisions of the McCain–Feingold reform was an exemption for media corporations, ostensibly so they could comment on political campaigns. However, the exemption was put into the law so that Congress could not get into the business of favoring one medium over another, for example, by leveling the playing field between the *Washington Post* and the *Washington Times*. In his majority opinion, in *Citizens United*, Justice Kennedy made clear that such a provision would have forced the courts to decide what was and what was not a media corporation, which is bad law since most media companies are held by other companies. Furthermore, Kennedy wrote, "With the advent of the Internet and the decline of print and broadcast media . . . the line between the media and others who wish to comment on political and social issues becomes far more blurred." Fearing this provision could be applied in an arbitrary way, the majority struck it down.

THE AFTERMATH OF *CITIZENS UNITED*

Obviously, the first impact of *Citizens United* came in the 2010 election. For example, the FEC reports that the US Chamber of Commerce poured $75 million into the midterm election; American Crossroads, advised by Karl Rove, spent $52 million; free market–backer Americans for Prosperity spent $45 million; and the conservative Club for Growth

SPENDING IN CAMPAIGNS

spent $24 million. Other big spenders included American Action Network at $23 million, the Service Employees International Union at $15 million, and the American Federation of State, County and Municipal Employees at $11 million, the latter two focusing on getting Democrats elected.[48]

The imbalance between corporate and other spending was part of the reason the Republicans took control of the legislatures *and* governorships of twenty states, including Wisconsin, Michigan, Ohio, Florida, and Pennsylvania, in 2010. They took control of the legislatures of five more states where they did not occupy the governor's mansion. In many other states, they split the state houses, leaving the Democrats with absolute control of governorships and state houses in only a handful of states, a remarkable reversal from the 2008 results. Thus, the fears of reformers were realized in 2010. The price of an open marketplace of ideas unrestricted as to funding may result in one side overwhelming the voices of the other in a capitalistic republic.

The trend continued in the presidential cycle of 2012. In May 2012, Americans for Prosperity, supported by the oil-rich Koch brothers, spent $6 million dollars in battleground states attacking President Obama. By June 1, 2012, the two Crossroads groups had raised $100 million. Crossroads GPS, a conservative group with 501(c)4 status, spent $25 million in attack ads against President Obama in the summer of 2012 in ten battleground states. Unions, particularly those formed by teachers, planned to fight back, but as of Labor Day 2012 they had not come close to matching the funds of the more conservative groups. From April 1 to September 16, $152 million had been spent by independent groups: $89 million against President Obama; $35 million against former Governor Romney. Overall, pro-Romney independent groups provided funding for *half* of the ads run supporting him.[49] According to the Center for Responsive Politics, independent groups spent more than one billion dollars in the 2012 campaign, more than *three times* what was spent in 2008.

A hefty portion of these funds was spent on down ticket races and ballot propositions.[50] For example, Crossroads GPS placed $850,000 worth of ads in one Iowa district as part of an $8.1 million offensive in just eleven congressional races.[51] In California, an independent group called "America Shining" intervened in a congressional race with $600,000 for the Democrat who was being badly outspent by the incumbent,

75

CHAPTER 3

Congressman Ed Royce.[52] Independent groups poured more than $42 million into California congressional races alone.[53] This downticket spending may help explain why in the face of a Democratic president winning 51.1 percent of the popular vote, Republicans actually increased their majority in the House.

In the 2014 election, more outside money than ever was spent in the midterm elections. New York University's Brennan Center for Justice found that spending from sources outside of the campaigns exploded between 2010, the year of the *Citizens United* ruling, and 2014. Spending by super PACs reached $1 billion, with $600 million coming from only 195 donors. In Senate elections, outside funding more than doubled from 2010 to 2014, reaching half a billion dollars.

By the 2016 presidential cycle, the fine art of campaign contributions had soared to new levels, and candidate super PACs reemerged as a force to be reckoned with. For decades, candidates' former employees have formed super PACs, which can raise unlimited sums of money as long as they do not "coordinate" directly with the candidates' campaigns. The first difficulty with this procedure is that directors of these super PACs could have received instructions as to how to spend their funds before they became their directors. Or they can simply listen to the candidate's news conference to see how he or she would have spent the money were he or she in charge. The money can then be funneled to candidates for lesser office in exchange for their support in primaries or at the convention. The money can also be used for issue advertisements or to support ballot initiatives.

The second difficulty with this procedure is that it allows donors to contribute unlimited amounts of money to the super PACs. For instance, in 2015, Miguel Fernandez, founder of MBF Healthcare, gave $3 million to Jeb Bush's super PAC. Dan and Farris Wilks of Frac Tech gave $15 million to Ted Cruz's super PAC.[54] Haim and Cheryl Saban of the entertainment industry gave $2 million to Hillary Clinton's super PAC.

Another impact of the *Citizens United* ruling concerned how candidates cope with all these rogue independent groups and donors. Many fear that the rhetoric of candidates has been distorted or overwhelmed. First, to gain super PAC and independent group support, candidates must cater to them in some way. However, in doing so, candidates might fear offending independent or moderate voters, because big-time contributors

76

SPENDING IN CAMPAIGNS

tend to be more left or right than the average voter and certainly than the kind of independent voter that is going to decide the election. Second, candidates don't want to say anything that might set a donor off, thus encouraging him or her to contribute to opponents. In this way, major donors have a chilling effect on campaign persuasion.

Third, candidates ostensibly have no control over independent groups and so may lose control of the messages of the campaign. Both the "Willie Horton" and the "Swift Boat" ads were run by independent groups, and these ads muddy waters of campaign persuasion. Fourth, and as a corollary, mainstream news media are being circumvented not only by advertising but by such cable and movie theater documentaries as *Hillary, the Movie*, and *Obama 2016*. This trend will likely further segregate voters into reinforced, divisive voting blocs. Finally, corporations and unions are certainly not always persuasive, and they run the risk of offending their buyers and members. Many union members have protested using their dues for political purposes. And the Chick-fil-A condemnation of same-sex marriage was a public relations disaster. So unions and corporations might be wise to develop a healthy fear of potential backlash against their messages and spending.

Another impact of *Citizens United* has been its progeny. The Supreme Court has issued several rulings to clarify its position. In the first subsequent ruling, the Court reinforced some provisions of the 2002 McCain–Feingold law so as to allay the fear there would be no accountability in campaign contributions. On June 24, 2010, in *Doe et al v. Reed*, the justices voted 8–1 to support the position that the public had a right to know who signed petitions for ballot propositions, in this case in the state of Washington. The majority had ruled in favor of disclosure of whom or what was responsible for advertisements in the *Citizens United* ruling. This declaration comes in part IV of Kennedy's opinion, where he was joined by some liberals and abandoned by Justices Thomas and Scalia. While such a decision adds more transparency to the process, which may be good public policy, it compromises fundamental First Amendment rights that Thomas and Scalia sought to protect. The *Doe et al.* ruling violates the spirit of the secret ballot and, as we have seen, the historic position of the Founders, who often published under assumed names to maintain their secrecy and to avoid retaliation. The decision also overturns precedents set in the 1958 *NAACP v. Alabama*, in which

77

CHAPTER 3

the Warren Court claimed that the right of assembly also meant the right to assemble in secret.[55] (In Alabama, when employees were found to be members of the NAACP, they were often fired. When the state of Alabama sought the NAACP membership lists, the NAACP sued for relief to protect the secrecy of its members. The Supreme Court sided with the NAACP.) More recently, as we have shown, the Court ruled that Congress may not abridge the "right to anonymous speech" based on the "simple interest in providing voters with additional relevant information."[56] That is why Justice Thomas dissented from part IV of the *Citizens United* ruling. Thus, in an attempt to contain the impact of the *Citizens United* ruling, the Supreme Court in Thomas's view damaged prior protections of the right to assemble secretly, a right implied in actions of the Founders and the secret ballot and contained in stare decisis. This issue came before the Supreme Court in April 2021 in *Americans for Prosperity v. Bonta* involving a challenge to the Internal Revenue System's and California's rights to force charities to disclose donors. During oral arguments, Justices Alito and Thomas referred to the Founders' protection of secret societies and the current fear that some donors have of being made victims of threats and other harassment if their names are disclosed.

In a second one-line ruling after *Citizens United*, the Supreme Court upheld the restrictions on corporate and union contributions to party organs. As we have seen, this so-called soft money was often redistributed by the parties to their state affiliates in the name of party building; that money was then often used to advertise for or against candidates in state races. Thus, the Court left the restrictions on political parties' use of corporate and union contributions in place.[57] The bottom line is that corporations and unions can independently advertise for and against candidates, but they cannot give to political parties for registration drives and other party-building functions.

As previously noted, McCain–Feingold's Millionaires' Amendment was struck down. When the state of Arizona passed its own version of this law, the Supreme Court intervened with an emergency order in June 2010, extending its federal 5–4 ruling to the states. Justice Kennedy issued the order, which does not disclose who voted for it, though such an order cannot be issued without the authorization of five members of the Court.

78

SPENDING IN CAMPAIGNS

In another ruling, despite the fact that twenty-two states backed Montana in its attempt to retain its century-old limit on campaign spending by corporations inside that state, the Supreme Court on June 25, 2012, held that the law was invalid. In *American Tradition Partnership v. Bullock*, the Supreme Court ruled 5–4 that Montana could not restrict the private financing of candidates by corporations. The ruling was significant because it marked a reversal of campaign laws that were put into place to curb the corruption that Montana experienced in the era of what some refer to as the "Copper Kings." During the Gilded Age, these "kings" sat on top of an almost-limitless deposit of copper ore that became known as "the richest hill on earth."[58]

Larry Howell fears that overturning Montana campaign laws will lead to the same types of corruption that prompted the laws in the first place. For example, he notes the influence that "copper king" William Andrews Clark had on the political process of electing him to the US Senate: "Clark reportedly was willing to spend as much as a million dollars of his fortune to bribe state legislators, who elected senators until the adoption of the Seventeenth Amendment in 1913, at the rate of up to $10,000 per vote." It would take him even more money because of the many rounds of voting required in the process: "Late in the game he had to raise the amount to as much as $50,000 per legislator. In the end, Clark may have paid more than $430,000 for 47 legislators' votes and reportedly offered another $200,000 to 13 more who refused bribes."[59]

There were several other instances of corruption that occurred in Montana at the time, leading President Theodore Roosevelt to complain about the "Montana Situation."[60] A significant problem was the perceived influence that private interests were having in judicial affairs. F. Augustus "Fritz" Heinze provided significant funds to back the election of two Butte district court judges. These two judges would not only ensure control of the docket by forming the majority ruling for which cases were heard, but they would also assign themselves to the cases involving Heinze. And, in those cases, they consistently ruled in favor of Heinze. As a result, Montana banned the use of private funds in their elections by passing the Corrupt Practices Act of 1912.[61] However, as we have seen, the Supreme Court recently used the *Citizens United* decision as precedent in the *American Tradition Partnership* case to rule the Montana Act unconstitutional. Thus, not only did the Supreme Court overrule a law

79

CHAPTER 3

that had been in effect for a century, but the Supreme Court prompted fears of the return to local and state corruption. Thus, the *Citizens United* rule now applies to the states much in the way *Buckley* does.

Most importantly, on April 2, 2014, the Supreme Court ruled 5–4 again that the limit on how *many* federal campaigns to which a person could contribute was unconstitutional. While the ruling left the $2,000 limit per primary and general campaign and donor identification in place, it removed the limit on the number of campaigns to which one could contribute. Writing for the majority in *McCutcheon v. FEC*, Chief Justice Roberts claimed, "There is no right in our democracy more basic than the right to participate in electing our political leaders." Contributions constituted participation; therefore, restricting them restricts participation.

Justice Breyer, echoing his fears in the *Citizens United* case, wrote that the *McCutcheon* decision opened "the floodgates" of campaign donations from the rich. However, the 2014 ruling had other unforeseen consequences. Donors began to do their own contributing at the expense of PACs, super PACs, and independent committees. For example, Karl Rove's super PACs America Crossroads and Crossroads GPS spent $117 million on campaigns in 2012; in 2014, he could afford to fund no more than 20 percent of that amount.[62] This forced Rove to focus his spending on closely fought races such as those for the Senate in North Carolina and Alaska. However, the Center for Responsive Politics reports that spending in 2014 ran three times as high as it was during the 2012 elections.[63] The center claimed that when all spending was added up, including that by candidates, Republicans spent $1.75 billion and Democrats spent $1.64 billion.[64] While spending on campaigns is up, the sources have shifted somewhat from super PACs to individual giving, and as we know, individuals are less influential than PACs, particularly given that individual can give only $2,000 per elections while independent PACs can supply a lot more in terms of independent media advertising. Just as interesting is that liberal PACs and super PACs have caught up with and surpassed conservative PACs in terms of campaign spending by a margin of $270 million to $181 million in the 2014 cycle. The Center for Responsive Politics reports that the 2014 election cycle was the most expensive of all time at over $4 billion; super PACs constituted only 25 percent of that total.[65] Another reason for super PACs

80

SPENDING IN CAMPAIGNS

retraction is that while super PACs are required to divulge their donors, so-called social independent PACs are not.

CONCLUSION

What is clear from this analysis is that well-intentioned justices are motivated by different fears and different ideologies. The dialectic between originalism and a living constitution results in different opinions about how to reform campaign contributions and spending. Several justices, notably Scalia, Thomas, and Alito, relied on the original meaning of the Founders to buttress their opinions. Stevens and Breyer read the Constitution as being adaptable to the times. These ideological frameworks for reading the Constitution led to a dialectic between the fear of corrupting the marketplace of ideas, and thereby corrupting democracy itself, and the fear of closing down the same marketplace to corporate speakers who may have valuable information to offer the public. On the one side, justices argued that the mere appearance of corruption reduces the credibility of the democracy. Corrupt practices and fallacious arguments are supported by big money, and when the amounts of dollars are introduced as evidence, the fear becomes much more intense. This leads to a second fear that corporate voices will drown out the voices of citizens, and the already-noted evidence of corporate spending only intensifies this fear. Furthermore, some fear that voters are not sophisticated enough to see through the fallacies and smoke screens of some corporate campaign advertising. Anyone familiar with California's system of initiatives and referendums can tell you how incredibly misleading the advertising surrounding them can be and how often voters who think they are affirming a proposition have actually voted against it.

On the other side, advocates fear that unless corporate speech is allowed, citizens will not receive valuable information essential to the political marketplace. Citing previous rulings on freedom of assembly, Justices Scalia and Thomas fear that the disclosure of donor information will lead to intimidation and harassment, a true threat in modern times. They believe that because corporations existed when the First Amendment was adopted, they were meant to have First Amendment protection. They fear that the corporate right of expression will be curtailed by campaign spending laws that overreach. They believe that citizens on

CHAPTER 3

each side of an issue can form or join political action committees that will give their voices more impact.

This dialectic was embodied by the principal speakers for each side in *Citizens United*. Where Kennedy fears restricting participation in the democratic process, Stevens fears quid pro quos that he makes visceral in the evidence he cites. He wrote in part IV of his opinion, "On numerous occasions we have recognized Congress's legitimate interest in preventing the money that is spent on elections from exerting an 'undue influence on an officeholder's judgment' and from creating 'the appearance of such influence,' beyond the sphere of *quid pro quo* relationships."[66] Stevens would defer to Congress on this matter, unlike the majority, which feared that Congress had infringed on the First Amendment and thereby passed unconstitutional measures.

Where Kennedy fears closing down the marketplace of ideas, which is a pathway to the truth, Stevens fears that corporate funds will drown out the voices of other campaigns, let alone citizens, and bury the truth. In other words, where Kennedy fears the government as moderator and endorses the free marketplace instead, Stevens fears that market forces will distort the truth if they are not regulated by the federal government. Kennedy believes that the marketplace functions to scrutinize the government and hold its members accountable; therefore, having the government regulate the marketplace is counterproductive. Kennedy strengthens his argument with the fact that other laws are specifically aimed at quid pro quo influence from or campaign coordination with corporations and unions.

In the process of forming his opinion, Justice Stevens turned away from his previous originalism in commercial speech cases, because he perceived in political advertising a special interest threat to the integrity of the political process and the "faith" of the people in that system. Stevens specifically states in part III of his dissent that political corporate speech is different from other commercial speech precisely because core political communication needs to be regulated to prevent corruption of the system. He claimed he had made that difference between corporate commercial and political advertising clear in his *Bellotti* opinion. In the *Citizens United* case, Stevens prefers a regulatory approach for fear of corporate political speech distorting the truth and marginalizing citizens' voices. In this case, Stevens believed America needed a living Constitution

82

SPENDING IN CAMPAIGNS

that could be interpreted to meet circumstances the Founders could not have foreseen. When Justice Alito openly disagreed with Obama's State of the Union declaration that the *Citizens United* decision would open the floodgates of corporate contributions, Justice Stevens would have been in agreement with Obama on historical and living Constitution grounds.

4

Fear and Religious Freedom

Christian Legal Society v. Martinez, Burwell v. Hobby Lobby, and *Kennedy v. Bremerton School District*

RELIGIOUS PERSECUTION IS A central component of America's founding narrative. Such persecution motivated the founding of several colonies, including Massachusetts, Rhode Island, Maryland, and Pennsylvania. The most common understanding of the Founders' concern with a "separation of church and state" stems from the colonists' reaction to the tight connection between church and state that characterized the European experience. Medieval and renaissance popes acquired large land holdings and called for holy wars. Julius II even took part in battles to secure his beloved Papal States. Martin Luther led the Protestant Reformation of the church but also wrote political tracts and condemned the revolt of the German peasants. Jesuit priests became close advisors to such political leaders as Queen Mary Tudor of England, Queen Isabella of Spain, and King Louis XIV of France. Henry VIII and Oliver Cromwell were both political leaders and heads of their respective religious sects. Taken together, the blending of religion and politics in the American colonies was not a novel or theoretical situation.[1]

The "separation of church and state" emerged in the founding era in response to the way European states handled religious involvement in national governance. The original idea of America's constitutional "separation of church and state" is commonly attributed to Thomas Jefferson. However, as Philip Hamburger points out, the phrase "wall of separation between church and state" may have taken root in the aftermath of the election of 1800 and in Jefferson's letter to the Baptists of Danbury, Connecticut, in 1802, but Jefferson was following a path laid out by his fellow Republicans. Hamburger explains, "Federalist clergymen had preached that Jefferson was an infidel and therefore unworthy to be President, and Republican propagandists responded by arguing that clergymen should keep religion and politics—and even church and state—separate. In effect, these Republicans used a version of the idea of separation to condemn Federalist ministers for speaking about politics."[2] As noted in chapter 1, Montesquieu was "the most invoked authority of the entire founding generation,"[3] and he identified the fear of despotic terror as the most important justification of the principle of division of powers and the establishment of liberal order. Jefferson shared Montesquieu's fear of federal tyranny. According to David Steinberg, "Jefferson eventually endorsed a relationship identical to that described by Montesquieu. Jefferson argued that the federal government had authority to deal with foreign affairs and national security, leaving domestic lawmaking and policy to the state governments,"[4] and specifically "feared centralized control over religion by the federal government."[5] He was at heart a states' rights Republican who insisted on a bill of rights to protect states against the federal government.

In this chapter, we examine several recent cases pertaining to church-state separation and related fears that have evolved from the founding era. Specifically, we examine two recent contemporary controversial cases within this context—*Christian Legal Society v. Martinez* (hereafter *CLS*) and *Burwell v. Hobby Lobby* (hereafter *Hobby Lobby*). Both of these cases involved fears pertaining to the status of religious organizations in relation to the government. More generally, cases involving religious freedom demonstrate this book's ongoing focus on the ambiguous, contested, motivational, and vague nature of fear and its significant in First Amendment cases. To examine the major fears involved in cases of the Roberts Court, we will briefly outline their historical origins and evolution with regard to freedom of religion in America. Then, we will examine the variety of fears involved in *CLS* and *Hobby Lobby*. We conclude with a few of the fears expressed in *Kennedy v. Bremerton School District*.

85

CHAPTER 4

FEAR AND RELIGIOUS FREEDOM
IN THE UNITED STATES

Even though the relationship between church and state grew from the European tradition, what was relatively new to the colonists was the issue of religious tolerance, which was hotly debated. Spanish colonies were Catholic and often intolerantly so; they had been established during the Spanish Inquisition, which had been reasserted by Queen Isabella and King Ferdinand in 1492. In the English colonies, the tradition was different. Virginia was first settled in 1607 by adventurers led by Captain John Smith, following the failed commercial efforts of Sir Walter Raleigh. They were loyal to the English crown but had witnessed changing commitments to various forms of Catholicism and Protestantism over the years. In 1630, John Winthrop, a minister, brought his weary band of Puritans to Massachusetts to escape persecution in England and to found a "shining city upon a hill," amid the Pilgrims that had preceded him. The Calvinist Puritans, however, were an intolerant lot, believing the sin of one to be the sin of all. Conformity was critical if their city was not to lose its luster. Soon Anne Hutchinson left Massachusetts to found Connecticut and Roger Williams left to found Rhode Island; both new colonies were strongly committed to religious freedom, Providence providing the first synagogue in the colonies.

The diversity of beliefs in the colonies was astounding. Quakers founded Pennsylvania; Catholics founded Maryland; prisoners settled Georgia; adventurers and speculators settled Virginia; Pilgrims and then Puritans settled Massachusetts. The leadership in many communities centered on the church, and preachers and priests were not shy about making recommendations on political matters. Those that read Enlightenment thinkers realized that religious freedom necessitated religious tolerance.

The vulnerability of religious groups to state control and regulation led to the expression of many fears in the colonial era. The most central fear leading up to the adoption of the establishment clause was, according to James Madison, the elevation of one religion above all others in the form of a national religion. According to Zachary Somers, Madison's draft of the establishment clause was meant "to prevent the national government from elevating any one church into an exclusive position above all other churches and denominations. As Madison stated, the Amendment was driven by the fear that Congress might 'make laws of such a nature as might . . . establish a national religion.'"[6]

The path toward tolerance is evident in North Carolina's reluctance to ratify the Constitution. North Carolina did not convene for its ratification convention until July 21, 1788—more than a month after New York began its convention. And, in early August, North Carolina voted not to ratify, joining Rhode Island in holding out on ratification. There was lively debate in North Carolina concerning religious freedom and the Constitution. Legal Scholar Carl Esbeck took note of Baptist minister and revolutionary patriot Henry Abbott's explanation that "the people harbor a fear for religious conscience under the new system, and that by the treaty power the central government might 'make a treaty engaging with foreign powers to adopt the Roman Catholic religion in the United States.' He went on to claim that 'many wish to know what religion shall be established. I believe a majority of the community are Presbyterians. I am, for my part, against any exclusive establishment; but if there were any, I would prefer the Episcopal.'"[7]

James Iredell, a leading Federalist in the state, responded by suggesting a spirit of tolerance for all religions. As noted by Carl Esbeck, the response by Iredell addressed the fear of religious establishment "by first extolling the spirit of toleration in the American states and pointing out that the Religious Test Clause was to restrict Congress (not empower it), and thus it promoted religious liberty."[8] Iredell failed to convince North Carolina that the religious test clause was enough to settle the issue of church and state relations, and so North Carolina voted against ratification. However, the success of tolerance as a prevailing viewpoint may be found in the fact that North Carolina recommended amending the Constitution to prohibit the establishment of one religion over all others. While some may interpret the proposed amendment as allowing the possibility of equal congressional support for all religions, Esbeck provides a compelling historical argument to the contrary. He argued that most delegates were opposed to government support of all religious groups "because government involvement in religion had led only to corruption of the church and religious persecution. These sentiments in North Carolina aligned with those who had successfully brought about the Virginia disestablishment in 1784–1786. Thus, in their view, government had no

CHAPTER 4

jurisdiction over organized religion, which is left on its own to find voluntary support."[9]

The clear sentiment from the colonial era was that if one religion was suppressed, then all were vulnerable to the will of the majority.[10] Even though the prevailing belief in Jefferson's "wall of separation between church and state" became fundamental to America's understanding of the establishment clause, the fears of governmental involvement in religious affairs were far from settled. As civil society conflicted with religious practices, the Supreme Court began hearing cases that would test the limits of religious tolerance.

In 1878, the Supreme Court ruled in the case of *Reynolds v. United States* to prohibit bigamy among Mormons despite their plea for free exercise of religious rights. Many fears were expressed in both the events leading up to that case and its aftermath. For example, according to Robert Morris, the Mormon Church's president, John Taylor, "feared all kinds of evils would come to Utah with the advent of the federal regulators who were coming to stamp out Mormon polygamy, and 'sodomy' was one of many items on his list."[11] The passage of federal regulations against polygamy stemmed from the fears of some in the mid-1800s that polygamy would disempower women and lead to "immoral, unhealthy, and ultimately vicious behavior" and "directly but inevitably to widespread unemployment, poverty, disease, and crime"; such fears were in part rooted in attitudes of cultural superiority to people in Asia and Africa.[12] For example, "Francis Lieber, who articulated a position for free exercise exemptions, argued long before the public learned of the Mormon practice of polygamy that polygamy had the inevitable effect of retarding a society's ability to develop."[13] The issues were resolved by the Supreme Court when Chief Justice Waite made a distinction between performance and thought: "Suppose one believed that human sacrifices were a necessary part of a religious worship, would it be seriously contended that the civil government under which he lived could not interfere to prevent a sacrifice?"[14] The Court feared that free exercise would lead to abuse. Thus, only the freedom to believe is absolute, not the freedom to act.

Even though the "freedom to believe" would prevail for more than a hundred years, the 1961 case of *Sherbert v. Verner* would offer a new paradigm for interpreting establishment clause cases by attempting to *balance* the interests of one side against another instead of establishing absolute rules. The resulting *Sherbert* test contained three steps, with "the most important step being a demonstration that . . . [the government] had a compelling interest in controlling specific kinds of behavior."[15] In *Sherbert*, a Jehovah's Witness in South Carolina was denied benefits for refusing to work on Saturday, a Sabbath for that religion. Writing for the majority, Justice William Brennan argued that the state's interest was not compelling enough to justify denying benefits to the woman. Denying her benefits, therefore, infringed on and over-burdened her right to freely express her religion.

    Sherbert resulted in more cases where fear came to the forefront in carving out exemptions. For example, *Wisconsin v. Yoder* concerned the right of Amish parents to refuse to send their children to public schools past the eighth grade. Wisconsin argued against the practice because of "the plausible fear that some Amish children might later choose to leave the Amish community and would be 'ill-equipped for life' without a high school education."[16] The Court disagreed, rejecting the "fear as 'speculative,' demanding specific evidence both that Amish adherents were leaving their community and that they were 'doomed' to become burdens on society."[17] The Court furthermore shared the fears of *Yoder* regarding indoctrination by public schools. Specifically, "the Court granted the exemption in recognition of the feared impact that compulsory high school attendance would have on Amish communities, namely, by corrupting Amish children through exposure to worldly influences 'at the crucial adolescent stage of development.'"[18]

    The cases of the *Sherbert* era are known as "the Sherbert line, or the Sherbert-Yoder line" and together "established that even generally applicable health, welfare, and safety regulations could be struck down if their burden on religious practice, however accidental, did not meet certain constitutional requirements," including the burden on the state to demonstrate a "compelling state interest."[19] However, the *Sherbert* decision would eventually be overruled in *Employment Division v. Smith*, which concerned the question of whether a state could deny unemployment benefits to a person who had been fired for using peyote, despite the drug being used as part of a religious ritual. The Court ruled that states are not required to accommodate illegal acts in pursuit of religious beliefs. Furthermore, the Court ruled against the burden imposed on the

CHAPTER 4

state. The Court "found that the compelling interest test was an impermissibly strict constitutional bar for the state to meet should any law incidentally burden an individual's religious practice."[20] The Court ruled that "accidental interferences with religion posed no Free Exercise problem and that the state was not required to meet strict scrutiny, and any level of scrutiny for that matter."[21]

Smith involved several expressed fears. Aside from the underlying fear of drug use in America as outlined in our previous chapter on *Morse v. Frederick*, this case also involved the fear of anarchy by encouraging everyone to have their own set of religious laws that trump civil society. Jonathan C. Lipson has suggested that the Court's free exercise clause jurisprudence is rooted in struggle with this fear and is reflected in the *Smith* ruling beginning with "the fear expressed by Justice Scalia in *Employment Division v. Smith*, that broad religious liberty exemptions would court anarchy by permitting individuals to become laws 'unto themselves.'"[22]

Religious groups began to fear that the Court's ruling in *Smith* would open the door to restricting parts of their religious ceremonies. For example, if peyote could not be used in a religious ceremony because it was illegal, then what about communion wine given to Catholics who were under the legal drinking age? Bonnie Robin-Vergeer explains, "Religious groups and federal legislators feared the matter would only get worse. *Smith* raised the specter that neutral laws could prohibit the sacramental consumption of wine by underage Catholic or Jewish children, could force the Catholic Church to ordain female priests and could outlaw conscientious objection, Jewish circumcision, kosher slaughter and a host of other religious practices—all without meaningful recourse to the courts."[23] Thus, as a result of the fear that many religious practices would be threatened with *Smith*, Congress acted in 1993 by passing the Religious Freedom Restoration Act (RFRA).[24]

The RFRA's stated purposes were "(1) to restore the compelling interest test set forth in *Sherbert v. Verner* and *Wisconsin v. Yoder* and to guarantee its application in all cases where free exercise of religion is substantially burdened; and (2) to provide a claim or defense to persons whose religious exercise is substantially burdened by government."[25] In debates about the RFRA, people have expressed a number of fears about its implications. For example, Wendy Whitbeck highlighted that "some feared that the RFRA would allow challenges to the participation

RELIGIOUS FREEDOM

of religious organizations in public programs, or it would expand standing to challenge an organization's tax-exempt status."[26] Eric Shumsky explains that many who opposed RFRA feared the act's consequences for prisons and children: "Prison administrators feared the disruption of prisons. State officials claimed that 'prisoners could . . . , in the name of religious freedom, compel authorities to supply them with chateaubriand and sherry and even with civilian clothing that would make it easier for them to escape.' Children's advocacy groups hinted that religious exemptions under RFRA would mean the end of state protections—and the beginning of wicked consequences—for children."[27]

In 1997, the Supreme Court ruled in *City of Boerne v. Flores* that RFRA violated states' rights and thus Congress had overreached in its enforcement power. In her dissenting opinion, Justice Sandra Day O'Connor desired to overturn *Smith* and uphold the constitutionality of RFRA. Her rationale was rooted in her agreement with expressed fears of the founding era. She cited two conflicting fears regarding religious liberty in the debate over whether it should be included in the Constitution. On the one hand, she wrote, Federalists "feared that guaranteeing certain civil liberties might backfire, since the express mention of some freedoms might imply that others were not protected. According to Alexander Hamilton, a Bill of Rights would even be dangerous, in that by specifying 'various exceptions to powers' not granted, it 'would afford a colorable pretext to claim more than were granted.'"[28] On the other hand, Justice O'Connor concluded by arguing in favor of RFRA's constitutionality with evidence that the framers voted to prevent states from interfering in religious matters. She wrote, "Baptist and other Protestant dissenters feared for their religious liberty under the new Federal Government and called for an amendment guaranteeing religious freedom. In the end, legislators acceded to these demands" by passing the Bill of Rights to include religious freedom.[29] As noted in our discussion of the colonial era, this fear is rooted in the real fear that government involvement in the affairs of religion would allow small, unpopular, and/or weak or minority religions to be regulated/oppressed by the government. The Court recognized this fear when it ruled in *Gonzales v. O Centro Espirita* that RFRA was constitutional for federal law, and thus the federal government could not restrict the use of hallucinogenic tea in religious ceremonies.

91

CHAPTER 4

The current status of the establishment clause is tenuous. The RFRA remains in effect for federal laws, and a few states have passed laws that are similar to state-level RFRAs. The Roberts Court has navigated a few important cases that reflect many of the fears in the evolution of church-state relations. We are currently at the tip of the establishment clause's constitutional iceberg, with the Roberts Court uniquely situated to shape our understanding of it. As L. Darnell Weeden notes, "current Establishment Clause law is unquestionably indecisive and could be presented with significant changes during the time of the Roberts Court. A person reviewing the current religion opinions of the Supreme Court will not find a single approach to First Amendment law as open to radical revolution as those cases construing the Establishment Clause."[30] Thus far, we have seen a few cases in the Roberts era involving the expression of similar recurring fears.

For example, *Hein v. Freedom from Religion Foundation* involved a challenge to President George W. Bush's initiative to allocate federal funds for financial aid to faith-based community groups. Those challenging President Bush's initiative reiterated "that one of the specific evils the drafters of the Establishment Clause feared was the government's abuse of its taxing and spending powers 'to aid one religion over another or to aid religion in general.'"[31] Similarly, *Pleasant Grove City v. Summum* involved whether the government is allowed to display a privately donated religious monument bearing the Ten Commandments while denying public space to other religious monuments. While the Court ruled in favor of the government's right to allow the monument to the Ten Commandments without allowing other religious monuments, the ruling resulted in the expression of a familiar fear—namely, the fear expressed in the founding era that aiding or elevating to privileged positions certain religions would spell the beginning of suppressing the freedoms of minority religions.

While these cases seem to revolve around similar fears that have been expressed in the historical progression of establishment clause cases, two cases stand out as particular to the contemporary evolution of establishment clause fears because they have required balancing equal protection and privacy considerations with establishment clause considerations. These two cases are *Christian Legal Society v. Martinez* and *Burwell v. Hobby Lobby*, each of which we examine in detail.

RELIGIOUS FREEDOM

CHRISTIAN LEGAL SOCIETY V. MARTINEZ

During the 2004–2005 academic year at Hastings Law School in San Francisco, leaders of an existing Christian registered student organization (RSO) formed the Christian Legal Society (CLS) by affiliating with a national Christian association, which required the CLS members and officers to sign a "Statement of Faith."[32] The statement included the beliefs that sexual activity should not occur outside of marriage and that marriage by definition was between a man and a woman. CLS interprets its bylaws to exclude students from membership in their society if they engage in "unrepentant homosexual conduct" or if they hold religious convictions different from those in the Statement of Faith. Hastings rejected CLS's application for RSO status because the law school believed the Statement of Faith violated the school's nondiscrimination policy. CLS filed suit against Leo Martinez (dean of Hastings Law School), alleging that Hastings's refusal to grant the group RSO status violated their First and Fourteenth Amendment rights to free speech, expressive association, and free exercise of religion. In a narrow 5–4 decision, the Court ruled that "the all-comers policy is a reasonable, viewpoint-neutral condition on access to the RSO forum; it therefore does not transgress First Amendment limitations."[33] The Court furthermore ruled that "Hastings' all-comers policy is viewpoint neutral. . . . The policy draws no distinction between groups based on their message or perspective; its requirement that *all* student groups accept *all* comers is textbook viewpoint neutral."[34]

In addition to the Court's finding that the "accept all-comers" policy is viewpoint neutral, they added two significant rationales for upholding the policy: one on equal protection grounds, and the other on First Amendment grounds. In the majority opinion, Justice Ruth Bader Ginsburg stressed the importance of the all-comers policy in securing equal protection against discrimination. She wrote, "How should the Law School go about determining whether a student organization cloaked prohibited status exclusion in belief-based garb? If a hypothetical Male-Superiority Club barred a female student from running for its presidency, for example, how could the Law School tell whether the group rejected her bid because of her sex or because, by seeking to lead the club, she manifested a lack of belief in its fundamental philosophy?"[35] Thus,

93

CHAPTER 4

she concluded that Hastings Law School had created the all-comers policy as an adequate protection against the discrimination against "gay persons as a class."[36]

Siding with the majority, Justice Anthony Kennedy provided the important swing vote.[37] In his concurrence, he added a First Amendment rationale rooted in the marketplace of ideas in the law school environment: "Objectives may be better achieved if students can act cooperatively to learn from and teach each other through interactions in social and intellectual contexts. A vibrant dialogue is not possible if students wall themselves off from opposing points of view."[38] The rationale of encouraging "vibrant dialogue" by supporting encounters with "opposing points of view" is importantly distinct from a rationale rooted in equal protection—important because the former treats homosexuality as an idea rather than as something intrinsic to a person (if intrinsic to the person, then equal treatment of that person is a Fourteenth Amendment issue).[39]

Regardless, there were a variety of fears expressed in the case. Most notably, Justice Samuel Alito wrote a strongly worded dissent to express his fear of group speech being silenced. He wrote, "I do not think it is an exaggeration to say that today's decision is a serious setback for freedom of expression in this country."[40] Using "fear" as a synonym for "concern," he wrote, "I fear that the Court's decision marks a turn in [the wrong] direction. Even those who find CLS's views objectionable should be concerned about the way the group has been treated—by Hastings, the Court of Appeals, and now this Court. I can only hope that this decision will turn out to be an aberration."[41] According to Justice Alito, Christian Legal Society is more than an assembly of people that are gathered together for religious purposes. To him, they are a group that represents an idea among other groups in a public forum, and to require that the group change its beliefs in order to gain RSO status is to prevent those left behind beliefs from being expressed in such a forum; the free exercise of religion includes the freedom to express the group's ideas in public. In other words, Justice Alito's fear is that forcing the group to change its beliefs in order to gain access to public law school forums means eliminating the belief in the public marketplace of group ideas.

Justice Alito thus identified with CLS's fear that if they had to accept all comers into their group, then their ideas would be under the threat of

RELIGIOUS FREEDOM

those who might join the group and elect to change the group's beliefs. Hastings Law School disagreed, arguing that "the Society's fear that their opponents might take over the group's leadership positions is at best hypothetical and is not supported by concrete examples of similar incidents at Hastings or other schools."[42] The fear that CLS would be taken over and forced to change its beliefs parallels fears from the founding era regarding the European tradition of persecuting minority religious beliefs.

Justice Ginsburg addressed such a fear in her majority opinion on at least two grounds. First, she dismissed the fear as merely a hypothetical. Justice Ginsburg wrote, "CLS also assails the reasonableness of the all-comers policy in light of the RSO forum's function by forecasting that the policy will facilitate hostile takeovers; if organizations must open their arms to all, CLS contends, saboteurs will infiltrate groups to subvert their mission and message. This supposition strikes us as more hypothetical than real. CLS points to no history or prospect of RSO-hijackings at Hastings."[43] Justice Ginsburg continued, "Students tend to self-sort and presumably will not endeavor en masse to join . . . groups pursuing missions wholly at odds with their personal beliefs."[44] Second, Justice Ginsburg explained that there were content neutral requirements that discourage such a takeover. Justice Ginsburg explained how RSOs "may condition eligibility for membership and leadership on attendance, the payment of dues, or other neutral requirements designed to ensure that students join because of their commitment to a group's vitality, not its demise."[45]

Aside from the fears expressed by the parties in the case, and the Supreme Court opinions, there were additional fears expressed in the public sphere. Echoing Justice Alito's dissenting opinion, some commentators feared that the Court's opinion meant the destruction of CLS. For example, John Inazu reflected on both Justice Antonin Scalia's oral argument and Justice Alito's dissenting opinion. He wrote, "During oral argument in this case, Justice Antonin Scalia reflected on the alternative: 'To require this Christian society to allow atheists not just to join, but to conduct Bible classes, right? That's crazy.' And that is where the court has left us today."[46] He continued, "Justice Alito's dissent warns that Monday's decision 'is a serious setback for freedom of expression in this country.' But I fear worse. Expression presupposes existence. And the Court's decision doesn't silence CLS—it destroys it."[47] This fear is grounded in the transformative effect that accepting all comers would have on CLS.

CHAPTER 4

Arguably, the fear also reflects a lack of confidence that such ideas will prevail out of Justice Kennedy's "vibrant dialogue." Thus, collapsing the "wall of separation" between students in the law school environment may be ineffective.

Furthermore, fears pertaining to the role of free speech within groups came to a head in the public sphere. On the one hand, some argued that students should be able to join an unpopular group without fear of reprisals, and that also means protecting an entity that is organized around an unpopular idea. For example, Erica Goldberg cited *Brown v. Socialist Workers '74 Campaign Comm.* and *NAACP v. Alabama* to argue that *CLS v. Martinez* should be amended to protect expressive association as an independent right in a limited public forum. She argued, "These cases protect the individual's ability to join an unpopular organization without fear of 'threats, harassment, and reprisals' but also protect the organization as an entity, as disclosure requirements can 'cripple a minor party's ability to operate effectively.'"[48] In other words, the fear is that *CLS v. Martinez* may spell the beginning of the end for groups who are as unpopular as the NAACP was in 1958.

On the other hand, some expressed the fear that if group ideas garnered protection, then speech may be chilled out of the fear that a vague code of conduct would discourage students for speaking their minds. John K. Wilson explains, "The CLS decision didn't diminish First Amendment rights for students; it expanded them. . . . It guaranteed the right of students to elect their own leaders rather than having them banned by vague 'codes of conduct.' And it guaranteed the right of students to be able to speak freely without fear of being published by banishment from a student group for their opinions. This is a total victory for student rights and the First Amendment."[49] Taken together, the Court's decision spoke indirectly to the question of whether there was a safe haven for students in CLS to express unpopular views, or whether students may be afraid to voice unpopular views for fear of being kicked out. The result of the Court's decision is that students do not need to fear being kicked out of a student group for expressing unpopular views within the group. However, one could argue that such a rule is tantamount to compelled speech, forcing CLS members to accept messages contrary to their ideology, a practice that runs contrary to the rulings in *Hurley* (1995) and *Miami Herald* (1975).

One of the more interesting issues involving fear in the wake of *CLS v. Martinez* is whether students will fear forming groups that differ in beliefs from those of the administrators at their school. Peter Bozzo, for example, expressed his concern that the case may set a bad standard for universities that, in his opinion, have an interest in promoting plurality of student groups even if those groups "fail to uphold internal standards of plurality with regard to membership policies."[50] Allowing a plurality of groups to take a variety of forms is, according to this reasoning, in the interest of universities because "students should not have to fear whether their group's beliefs conflict with those of administrators at their school."[51]

The idea that students may fear administrators who hold beliefs different from their own is consistent with Justice Alito's observation that the UC College of the Law, San Francisco (formerly known as Hastings Law School) singled out the Christian Legal Society. Justice Alito quoted Hastings's statement concerning its nondiscrimination policy: "As Hastings stated in its answer, the Nondiscrimination Policy 'permit[ted] political, social, and cultural student organizations to select officers and members who are dedicated to a particular set of ideals of beliefs.'"[52] Justice Alito reacted to this statement by noting that Hastings had "singled out" the Christian Legal Society: "But the policy singled out one category of expressive associations for disfavored treatment: groups formed to express a religious message. Only religious groups were required to admit students who did not share their views. An environmentalist group was not required to admit students who rejected global warming. An animal rights group was not obligated to accept students who supported the use of animals to test cosmetics. But the CLS was required to admit avowed atheists."[53] Particularly troubling to Justice Alito was that "Hastings currently has more than 60 registered groups and, in all its history, has denied registration to exactly one: The Christian Legal Society (CLS)."[54] This argument provides a context, therefore, for rationalizing Bozzo's fear that students will fear forming groups that run counter to administrator beliefs, the exceptional treatment of CLS producing the feeling of being singled out by administrators in positions of power.

The nexus, however, is whether CLS was treated exceptionally with regard to their belief that runs counter to the nondiscrimination policy or whether they were treated exceptionally because they were the only group claiming exception to the nondiscrimination policy. The Court

CHAPTER 4

ruled in favor of the latter, opining that CLS was treated exceptionally because they were the exception, since they were the only group claiming they should be exempted from the nondiscrimination policy. The Court's majority, in other words, did not fear that the nondiscrimination policy jeopardized CLS's beliefs, though they appear open to reconsidering CLS's claim should its fear of hijacking materialize, with "outsiders" taking over other groups in the Hastings Law School.

In sum, *CLS v. Martinez* brought many of the fears regarding the church-state relationship that have persisted throughout history into conflict with the equal protection clause of the Fourteenth Amendment. On the church-state front, fears included the fear that public funding of a religious group would increase meddling in religious affairs, which the Founders rejected based on their experiences with the European tradition; the fear that religious groups would be denied a voice in public forums to express their group's opinions; and the fear that religious groups will be taken over by outside interests that could inhibit the freedom of religious association for like-minded believers. On the equal protection front, fears included the fear that religious exemptions would be used to authorize discrimination against classes of people; the fear that allowing students to separate themselves from each other would result in viewpoint discrimination whereby certain ideas were not allowed within student groups; and the fear that conduct may supersede status in considerations of identity. Undergirding CLS's rhetoric of fear is the fear of God's wrath against homosexuality—that accepting homosexuality as a behavior would mean spiting God, sinning, and risking being condemned to hell. These issues are far from resolved, and many of them resurfaced in the case of *Burwell v. Hobby Lobby*.

BURWELL V. HOBBY LOBBY

Burwell v. Hobby Lobby involved a conflict between the Religious Freedom Restoration Act of 1993 (RFRA) and President Obama's signature legislation, the Patient Protection and Affordable Care Act of 2010 (ACA). The ACA authorized the Department of Health and Human Services (HHS) to decide the meaning of the ACA provision requiring "specified employers' group health plans to furnish 'preventive care and screenings' for women without 'any cost sharing requirement.'"[55] HHS interpreted the "preventative care and screenings" to require nonexempt employers "to provide coverage for the 20 contraceptive methods approved by the Food and Drug Administration, including the 4 that may have the effect of preventing an already fertilized egg from developing any further by inhibiting its attachment to the uterus."[56]

The *Hobby Lobby* case involved the owners of Conestoga Wood, Hobby Lobby, and Mardel—each of them being closely held, for-profit corporations. The owners opposed the four contraceptive methods capable of "preventing an already fertilized egg from developing any further" because they hold "sincere Christian beliefs that life begins at conception" and it "would violate their religion to facilitate access to contraceptive drugs or devices that operate after that point."[57] They filed suit on grounds that requiring the corporations to provide these four types of contraception violates the freedom Congress had envisioned when it passed RFRA in response to the *Smith* precedent (mentioned earlier in this chapter). HHS argued, "The connection between what the objecting parties must do and the end that they find to be morally wrong is too attenuated because it is the employee who will choose the coverage and contraceptive method she uses."[58] HHS argued further that "the owners of the companies forfeited all RFRA protection when they decided to organize their businesses as corporations rather than sole proprietorships or general partnerships."[59]

In a 5–4 ruling, the Court decided in favor of the three corporations and the RFRA. In rejecting HHS arguments, Justice Samuel Alito wrote the opinion of the Court upholding the RFRA to protect owners of for-profit corporations: "The plain terms of RFRA make it perfectly clear that Congress did not discriminate in this way against men and women who wish to run their businesses as for-profit corporations in the manner required by their religious beliefs."[60] The Court advanced two central arguments. First, the Court reasoned that the price the corporations would have to pay for refusing to comply with the contraceptives mandate was substantial and burdensome. Justice Alito explained that if the owners did not comply with the HHS mandate because they believe it will facilitate abortions, "they will pay a very heavy price—as much as $1.3 million per day, or about $475 million per year, in the case of one of the companies. If these consequences do not amount to a substantial burden, it is hard to see what would."[61]

CHAPTER 4

Second, the Court argued that HHS could have met the requirement to provide contraceptives coverage with less restrictive means. Justice Alito explained, "There are other ways in which Congress or HHS could equally ensure that every woman has cost-free access to the particular contraceptives at issue here and, indeed, to all FDA-approved contraceptives." The Court reasoned that if nonprofits can be religiously exempt while still providing access to all FDA-approved contraceptives, then it *is* possible for HHS to allow a less restrictive means while also complying with the preventative care requirement in the ACA. Justice Alito noted that HHS had already designed such a plan "to respect the religious liberty of religious nonprofit corporations while ensuring that the employees of these entities have precisely the same access to all FDA-approved contraceptives as employees of companies whose owners have no religious objections to providing such coverage." He continued, "HHS has provided no reason why the same system cannot be made available when the owners of for-profit corporations have similar religious objections."[62]

Justice Ruth Bader Ginsburg wrote a dissenting opinion that was joined by Justices Sonia Sotomayor, Steven Breyer, and Elena Kagan: "In a decision of startling breadth, the Court holds that commercial enterprises, including corporations, along with partnerships and sole proprietorships, can opt out of any law (saving only tax laws) they judge incompatible with their sincerely held religious beliefs."[63] Justice Alito addressed this point specifically by clarifying that the Court's ruling is "very specific" to this case and that the Court does not rule to allow for-profit corporations to "opt out of any law."[64] Despite Justice Alito's attempt to clarify, the fears surrounding the *Hobby Lobby* decision are many.

To begin with, Justice Ginsburg expressed fear of the fallout from *Hobby Lobby*. In perhaps her most famous passage from her dissent, she wrote that the Court has an "overriding interest" in "keeping the courts 'out of the business of evaluating the relative merits of differing religious claims,' . . . or the sincerity with which an asserted religious belief is held."[65] She then explained her belief that equal protection is embedded in the Establishment Clause by noting the potential inequality that may privilege one religious belief over others. She wrote, "approving some religious claims while deeming others unworthy of accommodation could be 'perceived as favoring one religion over another,' the very 'risk the Establishment Clause was designed to preclude.' The Court, I fear,

RELIGIOUS FREEDOM

has ventured into a minefield."[66] Justice Ginsburg's fear, more a concern than an emotive appeal, is grounded in the potential *perception* that the Court's decision privileges some religious beliefs over others.

Justice Sotomayor argued that this fear was realized in the recent case involving Wheaton College (a Christian school). Wheaton was eligible for religious exemption even prior to *Hobby Lobby*. Their religious status allowed them to claim a religious exemption and then to turn all of their contraceptive coverage over to their insurance company. However, Wheaton believed they should not have to fill out a form to turn the contraceptive coverage over to their employer. Sam Baker explained Wheaton's objection, "Signing the form to claim a religious exemption means that the college is complicit in making contraception available, albeit from someone else, and so [the college] objects to filling out the form."[67] The Supreme Court had the opportunity to require Wheaton to fill out the form, but they did not. Going beyond mere concern, Justice Sotomayor wrote of the Court's refusal, "After expressly relying on the religious non-profit accommodation . . . the court now, as the dissent in Hobby Lobby feared it might, retreats from that position."[68] Thus, Justice Sotomayor believed *Wheaton* to be the beginning of the Court's complacency regarding more and more employers claiming religious exemption as a way of denying accommodations to meet the contraceptives mandate.

Perhaps because of *Hobby Lobby*'s visibility, legal scholars and members of the public have expressed several fears. One prevalent fear among supporters of the ACA is that *Hobby Lobby* will be used as a rationale for securing exemptions from other areas of the ACA, beyond contraceptives. Ashley Young reported on the "fear [that] other companies will use the exemption to opt out of paying for other medical medicines and procedures," which she described as a "slippery slope": "For example, Jehovah's Witnesses refuse blood transfusions due to a moral code. According to the US National Library of Medicine, blood transfusions on average cost $343 per session. What if an individual has severe anemia and their company refuses to allow coverage because the owners are Jehovah's Witnesses?"[69]

Of course, the Court has attempted to ease the fear that other areas of the ACA will be exempted. Darcie Falsioni and Jeffrey Tanenbaum explain, "The Court attempted to ease these fears by noting this opinion does not mean that all mandates will fail. Each challenge must separately

CHAPTER 4

consider the government's compelling interest and whether the least restrictive means in achieving that interest has been applied."[70] The Court's least-restrictive-means standard might mean that if there are no other means to treat the severe anemia than transfusion, then the hypothetical Jehovah's Witness owner would have to provide the care. There are no other less restrictive means to provide care. In other words, the Court believes the critical difference in contraceptives coverage is that the HHS had infringed on religious freedoms unnecessarily since the four types of contraceptives (which the Hobby Lobby side characterized as abortifacients) are not necessary to provide for the "preventative care" required by the ACA, since there were sixteen other such means to provide the same care.

At the same time, some fear that the least-restrictive-means standard will be less important to those eager to emphasize the Court's application of RFRA to for-profit corporations in order to claim exemption from more general laws. This fear came to fruition in a Utah case concerning child labor laws. Shadee Ashtari reported that "less than three months after [Justice Ginsburg] warned about the widespread repercussions of the Supreme Court's majority decision . . . , a federal judge in Utah has cited the controversial ruling in his decision to excuse a member of the Fundamentalist Church of Jesus Christ of Latter-Day Saints from testifying in a child labor investigation."[71] The ruling comes on the heels of a Department of Labor investigation over allegations that church leaders ordered children out of school to harvest pecans on a private ranch, without pay, for up to eight hours a day. Erwin Chemerinsky echoed the fear of the dissenters in *Hobby Lobby*; he "fear[s] it is just the start of cases of people claiming religious exemptions from general laws."[72]

In addition to the fears that religious exemptions will be granted from general laws, there are the specific fears that RFRA will undermine efforts to preserve equal protection and antidiscrimination laws. The fear is most common in those battles whereby religious beliefs have been used to counter civil rights efforts. Pema Levy, for example, reported, "Many people fear the opinion could have wide-ranging effects that will once again allow discrimination in public accommodations and hiring."[73]

The fear that religion could be used to reverse the gains of equal protection is rooted in confrontations with such reasoning in movements

102

for equal rights. For example, the famous Supreme Court case of *Loving v. Virginia* provided equal protection for the right of couples to interracially marry that had previously been denied on religious grounds. Prior to the Court's ruling, the lower court used religion as a basis for exempting the legal protection of marriage for interracial couples. In ordering the Lovings (an interracial couple) to either serve a year in jail or leave the State of Virginia for at least twenty-five years, the lower court judge used a religious rationale to exempt equal protection for interracial couples to marry, stating, "Almighty God created the races white, black, yellow, malay and red, and he placed them on separate continents. . . . The fact that he separated the races shows that he did not intend for the races to mix."[74] Thus, the religious exemption of RFRA (and RFRA-like laws at the state level) reopens the wounds of those affected by the use of religious reasons for denying people equal protection under the law.

Hobby Lobby raises fears about using the religious exemption to erode equal protection rights based not so much on race as on equal protection for LGBT people and women. For LGBT people, the *Hobby Lobby* decision raises at least two fears. One fear pertains to a rationale whereby employers feel justified in discriminating against LGBT in hiring, firing, and promotion decisions. Jonathan Capehart explained this fear about *Hobby Lobby*: "Many folks always seem to invoke their religious beliefs when talking about and expressing their opposition to issues related to abortion or the lesbian, gay, bisexual and transgender (LGBT) community. So, it wasn't a far leap to fear that bosses would try to apply the same rationale to thinning their ranks of gay employees."[75] In other words, some fear that religious freedom advocates will use *Hobby Lobby* to legalize LGBT discrimination through RFRA's. This threat to LGBT people has come to fruition in states like Indiana, where religious freedom advocates have introduced legislation that LGBT advocates feared.

From an LGBT movement perspective, the battle pitting religious freedom advocates against LGBT rights advocates could divide religious allies from the LGBT movement—hurting both religious allies and LGBT people in the process. Molly Ball notes that the "major conflict that has erupted in the wake of [*Hobby Lobby*] has been between religious freedom and gay rights. The resulting controversy has split gay-rights and faith groups on the left, with wide-ranging political fallout that some now fear could hurt both causes."[76] The fear stems from both

CHAPTER 4

LGBT rights rhetoric that fuels anti-religious sentiments and religious freedom rhetoric that fuels anti-LGBT sentiments. Ball continues, "Name calling, advocates fear, could alienate allies that have been tremendously important to the cause of gay rights. The larger fear is that such splits could bring back the bad old days when gay rights and religious rights were seen as irreconcilable—and liberals suffered politically for the image that they were alienated from religious values."[77]

The more specific issue for LGBT people in the context of ACA is that the religious exemption may be used to deny important health services. Capehart wrote that it was not "unwise to fear that employers would try to deny LGBT workers coverage for, say, HIV medication or hormone replacement therapy for transgender men and women. Alito was clear on that last point when he wrote that the majority opinion 'is concerned solely with the contraceptive mandate.' But that's cold comfort."[78] Perhaps the reason for Alito's statement being cold comfort is that even though the *Hobby Lobby* case applied only to the contraceptive mandate, it could be extended to the ACA in general by exempting a type of coverage mandated in the act. LGBT advocates, therefore, fear that even though *Hobby Lobby* was concerned with only the contraceptive mandate, this did not explicitly preclude future cases from testing the limits of how many other mandates the Court would be willing to exempt. In such circumstances, the least-restrictive-means standard may become the most significant point of contention.

The *Hobby Lobby* decision also raised fears about the equal protection of women. One advocate explained, "Women, for whom their reproductive system is even more critical than a mans [*sic*] in terms of magnitude of impact it has on their everyday health (our hormones fluctuate more, affect more systems in more overt ways), are treated differently. Not only do employers apparently feel that they are entitled to object to certain treatments which 'may' have the effects the employer doesn't like (it 'may' cause a miscarriage/abortion), they feel that they can apply this fear to every woman, no matter the circumstance." And the circumstances are significant. One is that contraceptives are a tool women use to control their reproductive systems—control that is necessary if women are to receive equal treatment to men.

A related circumstance that women's rights advocates fear is the Court foreclosing consideration of the impacts that may be felt for women—specifically, those women who would benefit from the four types of contraceptives at issue. Compounding the unequal treatment are those women who are denied the four contraceptives but may never experience a miscarriage/abortion from using those contraceptives (e.g., those who are not sexually active but may use the contraceptives for other health-care purposes). In short, treating all women as though they are sexually active preconditions the unequal treatment of women who are not sexually active—non-sexually active women are disparately impacted by being denied access to the four types of contraceptives based on the false presumption that they are engaging in sexual activity. The Court's refusal to allow even some women (i.e., those who are not sexually active) to have the four types of contraceptives covered by their insurance may be rooted in a more general fear about women's sexuality.

Importantly, pro-choice advocates have pointed to the fear of women's sexuality/promiscuity as the basis of most, and maybe all, cases concerning contraceptives. Jessica Valenti, board member of the National Association for the Repeal of Abortion Laws, tweeted that *Hobby Lobby* is "really about a fear of women's sexuality."[79] In a separate article, she explained that the case is part of a long history wherein "legal decisions about contraception have always been based, at least in part, on concerns about women's potential promiscuity."[80] Valenti cited the Court's 1972 decision in *Eisenstadt v. Baird* that gave unmarried Americans the right to procure birth control—the case "was sparked by the arrest of William Baird after he handed a condom to an unmarried woman at a lecture he was giving about birth control at Boston University. At the time, his action violated Massachusetts law on 'crimes against chastity.'"[81] Given the efforts of the women's rights movement to combat fears of women's sexuality in the history of cases concerning contraception, the fear that the *Hobby Lobby* decision is the beginning of a return to the *Eisenstadt* era is unsurprising. For the women's rights movement and its fight for equal protection, the decision may be impossible to separate from that context.

Moreover, some advocates have given voice in their reactions to *Hobby Lobby* to the unequal fears that men and women feel about getting pregnant. Randall Winn commented, "What is it about sex that has you all worried? Sex is normal activity, and men can have it all we want without fear of pregnancy. Why shouldn't women have the same freedom?

Why should women pay extra?"[82] This statement may be hyperbolic in the sense that it implies that men do not fear getting a woman pregnant. What Winn is expressing, though, are fears about getting pregnant, including what pregnancy does to a woman's body, and fears about being a single parent—both of which uniquely impact the lives of women.

One of the most popular women to express fears about what pregnancy does to a woman's body is celebrity trainer Jillian Michaels, who, because she "fears pregnancy will 'ruin' her body, plans to adopt."[83] Fears about pregnancy's effects on the body are rooted in the medical scientific findings about the physical changes and discomforts women experience during and after pregnancy. According to the United States Department of Health and Human Service's Office on Women's Health, pregnancy may result in a variety of bodily changes, including "body aches, breast changes, constipation, dizziness, fatigue, sleep problems, heartburn and indigestion, hemorrhoids, itching, leg cramps, morning sickness, nasal problems, numb or tingling hands, stretch marks, skin changes, swelling, urinary frequency and leaking, [and] varicose veins."[84] These do not include the possible complications during childbirth, the variety of bodily changes that occur after giving birth to a child, and the fears about the child's health (e.g., being responsible for the health of the infant both before birth and after). For some women, pregnancy is indeed a fearful endeavor, as certain health conditions make being pregnant a life threatening condition.

The other fear related to becoming pregnant is the fear of hardship associated with being the head of a single parent household. Single mother heads of the household are far more common than single father heads of the household. Even though the number of single father heads of the household has increased in recent years, their numbers still fall well short of the number of households headed by single mothers. According to the Pew Research Center's documentation of social and demographic trends, despite a nine-fold increase in single father heads of the household since the 1960s, in 2011, there were still more than three times as many single mother heads of households than men (8.6 million women compared to 2.6 million men).[85] The Pew Research Center also found notable differences between single mothers and single fathers: "Single fathers are more likely than single mothers to be living with a cohabiting partner (41% versus 16%). Single fathers, on average, have

RELIGIOUS FREEDOM

higher incomes than single mothers and are far less likely to be living at or below the poverty line—24% versus 43%."[86]

These equal protection clause fears intersect with the fears of some religious organizations, especially those that have a "fear of God." David Trindel, for example, explained that his disappointment was "that the Supreme Court ever had to hear the case, not in their decision." He is "seriously concerned that people expect the Government to make God fearing Americans put aside their faith."[87] *Hobby Lobby*, therefore, is bound up in a plethora of fears that have collided at the intersection of the religious freedom and equal protection clauses.

In addition, at least two more fears circulate in the *Hobby Lobby* decision that are not directly bound up in the tension between equal protection and religious freedom. First, among those who advocate a single-payer health care system, some have suggested that the ACA and employer provided health originated in a fear of centralized power in the first place. Louis Johnston argues that the *Hobby Lobby* "decision makes it clear that America's experiment with employer-provided health care is a failure and that we need to move to either a single-payer system or a voucher system and remove employers from the health-insurance business."[88] He continues, "How did we get in this mess to begin with? As usual in American public policy, it's a combination of historical accident and a chronic fear of centralized power."[89] The fear of centralized power, of course, is deeply rooted in American politics dating back to the Federalists and Anti-Federalists.

The second fear worth noting is the strictly economic fear of going out business that incentivizes some companies to claim a religious exemption. This fear has manifested itself in the wake of *Hobby Lobby* in a case involving the Christian Brothers Employee Benefit Trust (CBEBT). CBEBT has developed a market in providing health benefits to Catholic nonprofit organizations that want to be confident the health insurance they are providing is consistent with Catholic teachings. The CBEBT has filed a class action lawsuit with other similar nonprofit religious organizations that do not meet the definition of religious employers. W. David Koenninger notes that the lawsuit comes in the wake of *Hobby Lobby* because "the real fear of the [CBEBT] appears to be not that it will be forced to comply with the contraception mandate, but rather that implementation of the ACA's mandate will put it out of business."[90] He

107

CHAPTER 4

continues, "If the contraception mandate is upheld because of the accommodation for non-profit religious organizations, there would no longer be a market for the Trust's services."[91] Indeed, the fear that the ACA may cause some struggling companies to go out of business took hold in the political/economic context leading up to *Hobby Lobby*. In short, not only are all the equal protection and religious freedom fears apparent in the *Hobby Lobby* ruling, the fear of business collapse that surrounds the ACA is also brought to the forefront.

In sum, *Hobby Lobby* is more than a case about Obamacare; it is a case that reflects a plethora of fears that circulate in American life. From the fear of "stepping into a minefield" of privileging some religious organizations over others, the fear that religious corporations will use *Hobby Lobby* to sidestep labor and other laws, and the equal protection fears rooted in the religious rationales used to legalize discrimination in history to the fear of LGBT rights advocates and harming important alliances with religious people, the fears involved in the history of the women's rights movement and its quest for equal protection, including fears about women's sexuality and the everyday health and well-being of women, the fear of centralized governmental power, the fear of God, and the fear of going out of business, *Hobby Lobby* condenses some of the most politically charged fears in our country into one single case.

These fears may actually be just the beginning, as there is much in the decision that has received little or no attention. For example, an interesting rhetorical shift pertaining to corporate personhood occurred in *Hobby Lobby*. Specifically, the Court's opinion explained, "An established body of law specifies the rights and obligations of the *people* (including shareholders, officers, and employees) who are associated with a corporation in one way or another. When rights, whether constitutional or statutory, are extended to corporations, the purpose is to protect the rights of these people."[92] The Court continued by reasoning how prior decisions extended rights to corporations to protect all who are included in the definition of "people" in corporate personhood (i.e., shareholders, officers, *and* employees). The Court used both the Fourth Amendment and property seizures as examples: "For example, extending Fourth Amendment protection to corporations protects the privacy interests of employees and others associated with the company. Protecting corporations from government seizure of their property without just compensation protects all those who have a stake in the corporations' financial well-being."[93] Those examples are significant because in the sentence that follows these examples, the Court reasons that *Hobby Lobby* does the same thing: "And protecting the free-exercise rights of corporations like Hobby Lobby, Conestoga, and Mardel protects the religious liberty of the humans who own and control those companies."[94]

The rhetorical shift, therefore, in *Hobby Lobby* is that while prior decisions pertaining to the rights of corporations were designed to protect the interests of shareholders, officers, *and* employees, *Hobby Lobby* protects only the rights of the owners. In the Court's reasoning, when corporations are given Fourth Amendment rights, those rights protect all involved in the corporation (i.e., the privacy of shareholders, officers, and employees), and when corporations are protected from government seizure of property, all those involved are at least arguably somewhat protected (i.e., if property is seized, then shareholders, officers, and employees suffer, whereas just compensation might allow the corporation the resources to continue functioning for shareholders, officers, and employees). This rationale is a further extension of the majority's view in *Citizens United*, where the Court ruled that the expressive rights of a corporation in an election is in the interest of all those involved in the corporation (i.e., when a corporation backs a politician, it advances the interests of that corporation as an organization. See chapter three.). What makes *Hobby Lobby* different is that it does not protect all parties involved in the corporation, as has previously been the rationale. In other words, *Hobby Lobby* potentially changes the corporate personhood standard from "and" to "or." Now a corporation's rights are determined by the rights of shareholders, officers, *or* employees, with priority given to owners, who now stand as synonymous with the corporate person. It is a synecdochic rhetorical move whereby the owner-person comes to mean the corporate person and which will likely be significant for the fear of corporate power.

KENNEDY V. BREMERTON SCHOOL DISTRICT

The recent case of *Kennedy v. Bremerton School District* demonstrates how fear continues to be a persistent factor in religious freedom cases. In this case, the Court attempted to balance two competing interests:

(1) that "teachers ... do not shed their constitutional rights to freedom of speech or expression at the schoolhouse gate" (*Tinker v. Des Moines*), and (2) that public employees, per *Garcetti*, are limited in their free speech when acting in the capacity of their job duties. In short, the Court attempted to balance restrictions on employee religious expression with the religious freedom of teachers on campus. The Court ruled to protect the football coach who was fired for praying at the 50-yard line after games. It ruled that the football coach was not engaging in government religious speech because he was not engaged in the immediate duties of coaching a football game. Specifically, his religious expression occurred "during the postgame period when coaches were free to attend briefly to personal matters and students were engaged in other activities"[95] and he "was not instructing players, discussing strategy, encouraging better on-field performance, or engaged in any other speech the District paid him to produce."[96]

The fears related to this case manifested in at least three ways: the fear that students would be coerced into prayer for fear of losing benefits that come from positive relationships with coaches and peers, the fear of being shot due to media attention, and the fear of being fired for praying in public. Those who were opposed to Coach Kennedy's prayer expressed the fear of coerced prayer rooted in the fear of losing favor with the coach and peers. Justice Sotomayor noted in her dissenting opinion that Kennedy's prayer practice "implicated the coercion concerns at the center of the Court's Establishment Clause jurisprudence" (i.e., that students would be coerced into prayer). She wrote, "The reasons for *fearing* this pressure are self-evident. This Court has recognized that students face immense social pressure."[97] She then names pressures that would lead a student to seek their coach's approval, including to get extra playing time, get a stronger letter of recommendation, and gain help in the college recruiting process. She substantiated her claim by citing the district court record that "some students reported joining Kennedy's prayer because they felt social pressure to follow their coach and teammates."[98]

After the head coach recommended that Kennedy not be rehired as a coach, the head coach himself resigned after eleven years in the position. In his resignation, he expressed "*fears* that he or his staff would be shot from the crowd or otherwise attacked because of the turmoil created by

Kennedy's media appearances. Three of five other assistant coaches did not reapply."[99] The school district responded to the fears of student coercion and the expressed fears of other coaches for their safety by firing Coach Kennedy.

As for Coach Kennedy, he and his supporters expressed a fear of God and/or a fear of being fired for engaging in prayer in public places. For example, Coach Kennedy expressed that, as a child, he *"feared* [God]" at a moment where he felt like nobody cared for him while he was alone in a church.[100] The televangelist page for *The Jim Bakker Show* showed a picture of Coach Kennedy, and under the photo's caption there was a quote from the Bible (Exodus 18:21) instructing people to "look for able men from all people, men who *fear* God, who are trustworthy and hate a bribe."[101] The fear of God is coupled with the fear of getting fired. For example, Kelly Shackelford, president, CEO, and chief counsel for First Liberty noted that the Supreme Court decision was "a victory for Coach Kennedy and religious liberty for all Americans. . . . Our Constitution protects the right of every American to engage in private religious expression, including praying in public, without *fear* of getting fired."[102] Like in *CLS v. Martinez* and *Burwell v. Hobby Lobby*, there was no shortage of fears and fear appeals in the controversial *Kennedy v. Bremerton School District* case.

SUMMARY

This chapter demonstrates that the establishment clause is central to many fears in American life. These fears range in intensity according to time and place. The fears of the founding era stemming from the European tradition have continued into the era of the Roberts Court. One fundamental difference between the founding era and the Roberts era is the collision in the Roberts era of equal protection and religious freedom. The fallout of this collision has reexposed persistent fears in American life. Many religious Americans have a very visceral fear of being targeted. Whether it be Islamophobia, Christians who fear government and secular groups, Jews who fear hate crimes, atheists who fear religious groups, or any other groups organized around (non)religious identification, many fears accompany religious belief. Add these fears to the plethora of fears felt by those working to ensure equal protection under the law,

CHAPTER 4

and controversy unsurprisingly ensues. Fear has been a central feature in the history of church and state relations, and until those fears are addressed in a meaningful (and rhetorically sensitive) manner, fear will continue to define First Amendment battles over the establishment clause.

5

Fear at the Burial of a Soldier

Snyder v. Phelps

THE FIRST AMENDMENT'S RIGHT to "assemble peaceably" invokes at least two fears. The most visceral is the fear of mob rule. As we saw on January 6, 2020, such rule can do damage. It can even overthrow a government, as the world saw with the French and Russian Revolutions. The second fear is that without the right to assemble, people will have their voices suppressed and injustices will be tolerated. The right to assemble has a rich tradition in America. In 1770, Boston was alive with dissent. The trouble began in 1765, when the British Parliament imposed an internal tax on its American colonies by insisting that all transactions carry a stamp of approval that had to be paid for. Once tax collectors began to be tarred and feathered and Patrick Henry gave an impassioned speech against the tax, it was repealed within twelve months. Henry's speech was reprinted in Boston newspapers; in reaction, the Sons of Liberty formed in the city. Acceding to Benjamin Franklin's argument that no *internal* taxes should be applied to the colonies, the Parliament in 1767 imposed the Townshend Duties, a tariff that had to be paid at points of entry on incoming products from England. The colonists responded with boycotts of certain goods. The Boston merchants imported tea from the Netherlands and smuggled other goods into the

CHAPTER 5

colonies. The British sent troops to the city to keep it calm and enforce the tariff. However, by 1769, the importation of British goods had fallen by 40 percent.

On March 5, 1770, a hostile mob in Boston surrounded British troops under the command of Captain Preston. The mob threatened violence, and Preston ordered his men to shoot to protect themselves. The Boston Massacre was a major impetus for the revolution that followed, even though John Adams successfully defended Captain Preston of the charges brought against him. Importantly for our purposes, this tragedy was one of the reasons the word "peaceably" was inserted into the First Amendment where it grants the right to assemble.

Two fears frame the tension that has occurred in mob action. The mobs feared a loss of their freedoms; the forces of law and order feared for their lives and the lives of others. Whether it be the union members rioting in Haymarket Square in Chicago, or suffragists chaining themselves to the White House fence during World War I, or students being shot at Kent State University, demonstrators have been an integral part of American history. And this has led to a number of important Supreme Court rulings on the subject. The case studied in this chapter, *Snyder v. Phelps*, focuses on a particular kind of protest: the protest of the obnoxious.

This chapter explores *Snyder v. Phelps* in three stages. First, it examines the case law leading up to the ruling, then it examines the arguments of the justices, and, finally, it looks at the implications of the ruling. In the end, we observe a continuing and persistent role for the rhetoric of fear in First Amendment disputes that appear in the Roberts Court and in the history of American conflicts over the nature and scope of First Amendment rights.

PRECEDENTS FOR PROTECTING PRIVACY

At the intersection of freedom of expression and the right to privacy are several fears that have motivated different laws and rulings by the courts. For centuries, Anglo-Saxon rulers have been forbidden to cross the doorsteps of their subjects without a proper warrant. That tradition can be traced back to the Charter of Liberties of 1100 and the Magna Carta of 1215, the latter being drawn up by nobles and forced on King John. It was codified into British common law in 1628 by Sir Edward Coke in

THE BURIAL OF A SOLDIER

The Institutes of the Lawes of England, which specified that "a man's home is his castle." John Locke incorporated the rule into the English Bill of Rights of 1689 following the "Glorious Revolution." Prime Minister William Pitt, the great commoner, enhanced the tradition when he claimed in 1763 that "the poorest man may in his cottage bid defiance to all forces of the crown. It may be frail—its roof may shake—the wind may blow through it—the storm may enter—the rain may enter—but the King of England may not enter."

We fear invasions of privacy and unauthorized invasions of our space with good reason. Privacy is essential to quality of life; it is essential to intimacy and security. However, the government often fears that private citizens in their homes are protecting criminals or are engaged in criminal activity. With the attacks of 9/11, national security trumped privacy concerns as the war on terror began. Library records are now open to government inspection, as are telephone records if you make one or more calls to a foreign nation. At airport security stations, even your body can be scanned and/or touched in uncomfortable ways. These invasive procedures have certainly chilled some freedom of expression.

The relevant case law that applies to *Snyder v. Phelps* concerns how much privacy citizens have outside of their homes. To put it another way, does our privacy travel with us? Does it protect us from demonstrators at the funeral of our child? The right to privacy has been deduced from the Fourth Amendment and reinterpreted in Louis Brandeis and Samuel Warren's "The Right to Privacy" as the right to be left alone.[1] One of the most important cases in this regard is *Frisby v. Schultz,* involving the picketing of a home.[2] In Brookfield, Wisconsin, Sandra Schultz and Robert Braun, who strongly opposed abortion, picketed the house of a doctor who facilitated the procedure. The city passed an ordinance prohibiting the picketing of residential houses for the "protection and preservation of homes." Schultz and Braun brought suit, claiming the ordinance violated their First Amendment rights. Their suit set up a classic confrontation between two amendments to the Constitution, the First and the Fourth.

The Supreme Court overturned lower court rulings and upheld the law. Justice Sandra Day O'Connor penned the 6–3 majority opinion. Since the ban was "content neutral," that is, it applied to all picketing on any topic; since there were alternate means of communication available to speakers; and since the law advanced a compelling government interest,

115

CHAPTER 5

namely, keeping peace in neighborhoods, it was allowed to stand.[3] Thus, in this case, the right to privacy trumped First Amendment rights, and the doctor's home and its environs became his castle.

But what if we are not in our homes? Do we carry our right to privacy into the streets? In 1972, Jacqueline Kennedy Onassis obtained an injunction against paparazzi photographer Ron Galella because she claimed he was harassing her and her children, often yelling at them to look at his camera. In *Galella v. Onassis*, a district judge ruled that Mrs. Onassis and her children had the "right to be left alone, and to define one's circle of intimacy; to shield intimate and personal characteristics and activities from public gaze; to have moments of freedom from the unremitted assault of the world and unfettered will of others in order to achieve some measure of tranquility for contemplation and other purposes, without which life loses its sweetness."[4]

He imposed a 150-foot bubble of protection around Mrs. Onassis and a 225-foot bubble around her children. Though the general ruling was upheld by the Second Circuit Court of Appeals, it reduced the distances to 25 feet for Mrs. Onassis and 30 feet for her children, effectively eviscerating the lower court ruling.[5] This small bubble of protection has been extended to women entering abortion clinics. In *Hill v. Colorado*, the Supreme Court ruled that we cannot be compelled to listen to speech, particularly if we are in a captive audience.[6] Women entering an abortion clinic were deemed to be a captive audience. How else were they to get into the clinic without going through the entrance? The Court upheld a narrow law preventing people from coming within eight feet of those entering or leaving an abortion clinic, thus preventing in-your-face demonstrations. Eight feet was a minimal distance and did little to relieve the epithets women entering an abortion clinic would endure.

The Supreme Court has been more stringent in applying the "captive audience" standard to prevent the imposition of an ideology on the unwilling. In *Lee v. Weisman*, the Supreme Court ruled that "at a minimum, the Constitution guarantees that government may not coerce anyone to support or participate in religion or its exercise."[7] In this case, the Court protected the captive audiences at graduation ceremonies from having to endure religious invocations. In 1996, in *Moore v. Ingebretsen*, the Supreme Court disallowed prayers at school functions and reinforced that decision in *Santa Fe Independent School District v. Doe*.[8]

THE BURIAL OF A SOLDIER

Thus, in terms of privacy, precedent holds that you do take some measure of privacy with you when you leave your home, especially when you are faced with unwanted speech and/or you are part of a captive audience. As we shall see, these rights were important in the case of *Snyder v. Phelps*.

PRECEDENTS FOR PROTECTING OBNOXIOUS SPEECH AND ASSEMBLY

At least three important rulings and their progeny are also relevant to the ruling in *Snyder v. Phelps*. The first is *Cantwell v. Connecticut*, which struck down a prohibition on door-to-door religious solicitation. The second is *Tinker v. Des Moines*, which extended First Amendment protection to symbolic speech, as reviewed in chapter 2 of this book. The third is *Chaplinsky v. New Hampshire*, which attempted to define fighting words contextually.

Just before the start of World War II, Connecticut passed a law banning door-to-door religious solicitation. The case arose from Newton and addressed Jesse and Russell Cantwell's door-to-door solicitation of people to join the Jehovah's Witnesses, read its literature, or listen to a recording about the literature. The Cantwells had failed to register with the secretary of the Public Welfare Council, as required by Connecticut law. Many citizens of Connecticut had complained about the aggressive solicitations by the Witnesses and had requested the council to stop their activities.

In *Cantwell v. Connecticut*, Justice Owen Roberts, writing for the unanimous Supreme Court, ruled that states can impose content neutral time, place, and manner restrictions on door-to-door solicitations, but they may not ban them completely.[9] Furthermore, and particularly in Connecticut's case, the empowering of a government official, in this case a council secretary, to decide who may solicit and who may not constituted an arbitrary licensing system that implicated religious freedom as well as free speech.

Almost three decades later, a group of students enrolled in a school in the Des Moines Independent School District wore black armbands to school to protest the war in Vietnam. They were suspended for disruptive behavior. School officials argued that even if their protest was not

117

CHAPTER 5

disruptive, it endangered the students, who may face retaliation from classmates with relatives serving in Vietnam. Furthermore, they argued that since the students were not engaged in speech, per se, their symbols should not be afforded First Amendment protection. And finally, students should not enjoy First Amendment rights when in school because they were underage and not in a public forum.

The Supreme Court disagreed on all counts in *Tinker v. Des Moines*.[10] Justice Hugo Black, a strict constructionist, failed to persuade his colleagues that symbolic speech should not be protected by the First Amendment. He argued that the Founders meant words when they wrote about "speech" and "press." However, the majority extended protection to symbolic speech, believing it was "expression" that the Founders sought to protect. Furthermore, the landmark ruling held that students do not "shed their constitutional rights to freedom of speech or expression at the schoolhouse gate." The Supreme Court rolled back some of this freedom in subsequent cases, culminating in *Morse v. Frederick*, the subject of study in chapter 2 of this book.

However, the Supreme Court has consistently protected symbolic speech ever since the *Tinker* decision. Particularly relevant to our study of *Snyder v. Phelps* is the Court's ruling in *Texas v. Johnson*, in 1989.[11] Five years prior to the final disposition of the case, Gregory Johnson had burned a flag on the steps of the Dallas convention center hosting the Republican National Convention. He was arrested under a Texas law that prohibited desecration of the US flag. In prosecuting Johnson, Texas sought to protect the flag as a sacred symbol of the sacrifice made by many Americans and to reverse the *Tinker* standard on symbolic speech. Among other arguments, Texas argued that flag burning was conduct, not speech, and therefore not protected under the First Amendment. In a narrow 5–4 decision, the Court overturned the Texas law, as it would a subsequent US law, the Flag Protection Act. Writing for the majority, Justice William J. Brennan argued that Johnson presented no threat to the peace and that forbidding his symbolic action advanced no compelling interest of the state. The majority also argued that determining what was desecration could prove difficult. Would wearing an American flag bikini constitute desecration? Since the term "desecration" was vague, it could be enforced in an arbitrary and capricious way, which violated the Fifth Amendment. The dissenters argued that preserving the sanctity of the flag was a compelling government interest and that burning the flag clearly could be interpreted in no way other than desecration.

This line of cases clearly establishes that symbolic speech is protected even if it is as offensive as burning a symbol of the nation. We now turn to a set of cases that define what constitutes "fighting words," that is, speech that might cause emotional distress, because one of the issues in the *Snyder* case was the emotional distress the demonstrators' placards caused.

Chaplinsky and Its Progeny

Chaplinsky v. New Hampshire made it unlawful to "address any offensive, derisive or annoying word to any other person who is lawfully in any street or other public place."[12] While America was at war with the Nazis, Chaplinsky referred to a local marshal as a "damned fascist." The Supreme Court ruled that in the context of the time, Chaplinsky had in fact thrown the first punch, because fighting words are "those by which their very utterance inflict injury or tend to incite an immediate breach of peace."[13] There are two items of note here. First, the Court feared that if it did not stop it, violent speech would be mistakenly protected by the First Amendment. Second, the Court *used the context of the times to determine the meaning of the speech.*

The fighting words doctrine is fraught with peril for freedom of expression. Under this standard, legitimate speech advancing an idea might not be protected if in its context someone is so offended that retaliatory violence occurs. The Supreme Court has revisited the issue several times, and dialed it back in each case. First came *Terminiello v. The City of Chicago* in 1948. The case has precedential heft, since it is often cited by the courts and advocates before the courts. Essentially, the Supreme Court overturned a conviction because the sitting judge had instructed the jury that all the prosecution needed to show was that the speech in question "stirs the public to anger, invites disputes, brings about a condition of unrest, or creates a disturbance."[14] Writing for the majority, Justice William O. Douglas claimed that protected speech might invite dispute: "It may indeed best serve its high purpose when it induces a condition of unrest, creates dissatisfaction with conditions . . . or even stirs people to anger. Speech is often provocative and challenging. It may strike at prejudices and preconceptions and have profound unsettling effects as it

CHAPTER 5

presses for acceptance of an idea."[15] For some, this opinion was a repudiation of *Chaplinsky*. But it was certainly not the last time the Supreme Court visited the issue. In two cases during the Vietnam War, it again protected provocative, offensive speech. Those fearing that offensive language could hurt others seek laws that remove First Amendment protection from such language. However, those fearing a contraction of the free marketplace of ideas seek to protect all speech, often arguing that sticks and stones will break your bones but words will never hurt you.

First, in 1969, as mentioned in the opening of this book, the Supreme Court protected the offensive speech of Ku Klux Klan member Brandenburg, who advocated violence against Black people and Jews. It is worth repeating that in dealing with this difficult case, the Supreme Court specifically defined the burden of proof that had to be met by those who would restrict offensive speech: a "state [may not] forbid or proscribe advocacy of the use of force or of law violation except where such advocacy is directed to inciting or producing *imminent* lawless action, and is likely to produce such action."[16] Prosecutors have to prove not only that the advocate was calling for immediate action but that such action was plausible. The Court also ruled that the rhetoric must be aimed at a specific individual or individuals if it is to be restricted or punishable.

Second, in 1971, the Supreme Court protected the speech of a young man named Paul Cohen, who wore a jacket into the Los Angeles County Courthouse with the words "Fuck the Draft" written on the back. Thus, this case goes right to the question of what can be put on banners, placards, T-shirts, and the like. Prosecutors argued that the slogan was obscene and harmful and/or offensive to people, including children, who happened to be in the courthouse. Cohen was sentenced to thirty days in jail for disturbing the peace by offensive conduct. Cohen's conviction was reversed by the Supreme Court. Justice John Marshall Harlan II wrote in the majority decision, "This case cannot be said to fall within those relatively few categories of instances where prior decisions have established the power of government to deal more comprehensively with certain forms of individual expression simply upon showing that such a form was employed. This is not, for example, an obscenity case."[17]

Perhaps the most notable case in regard to protecting offensive speech occurred in Skokie, Illinois, in the late 1970s. Frank Collin, the head of the National Socialist Party of America (Nazi Party), planned

THE BURIAL OF A SOLDIER

to march to the city's village green area, even though (or probably because) half of the population of over sixty-two thousand people was Jewish and one in six members of the population was a Holocaust survivor. Fearing violence, the city of Skokie filed to enjoin the march scheduled for May 1, 1977. The Cook County Circuit Court issued an injunction on April 28, 1977, stopping the march. The village of Skokie then passed three ordinances that effectively banned Nazi marches. For example, one of the ordinances required the Nazis to post a very-high-cost insurance bond to cover liability. Another said that wearing Nazi paraphernalia was illegal because that wearing such appeal would invite physical attacks.

On June 14, 1977, in *National Socialist Party of America v. Village of Skokie*, the United States Supreme Court ordered the courts of the state of Illinois to deal with the injunction expeditiously.[18] At this point, the ACLU had entered the case on Collin's side. The Anti-Defamation League entered on the opposing side and appealed for a separate injunction on June 27.

On July 13, the state appellate court upheld the original injunction on the grounds that the march might lead to violence. This ruling raised the issue of the heckler's veto: can't any demonstration be stopped if someone claims it will result in violence? Isn't it the responsibility of the forces of law and order to prevent violence so that free speech will be protected? That was the position of the ACLU when it formally challenged Skokie ordinances in August 1977. It wasn't until January 1978 that the Illinois State Supreme Court lifted the injunction against the American Nazi Party, and the banning of wearing swastikas, arguing that the swastikas were protected symbolic speech under the *Tinker* precedent and did not constitute fighting words under the *Chaplinsky* precedent. The court also dismissed the case brought by the Anti-Defamation League.

On February 23, the US District Court for the Northern District of Illinois struck down the Skokie ordinances, a ruling that was affirmed by the Seventh Circuit US Court of Appeals in May 1978. Frank Collin then proposed to drop plans to march in Skokie if he could hold a demonstration in Marquette Park in Chicago. On June 12, the US Supreme Court refused to intervene regarding a march in Skokie that was planned for June 25. On June 20, the district court ordered the city of Chicago's Parks District to provide Collin with a permit to march or demonstrate. On July

CHAPTER 5

9, Collin called off the Skokie march and led the demonstration in Marquette Park despite attempts by the ADL to stop it.

Here was a classic dialectic between the fear of stifling freedom of expression and the fear of inciting violence. The resolution was that offensive speech, even if it is symbolic and/or might provoke retaliation, is protected especially if it is in a public space. Here, then, we have a classic case of the right to peace and privacy confronting the right to demonstrate.

Snyder v. Phelps

On March 2, 2011, the Supreme Court handed down its decision in the highly controversial *Snyder v. Phelps* case.[19] The case involved the Reverend Fred Phelps, who headed the Westboro Baptist Church of Topeka, Kansas, and for two decades had led protests at various sites, among them more than six hundred military funerals. His demonstrations condemned the practice of allowing gay men to serve in the military, argued that America was becoming "Sodom," and accused the Catholic Church of scandals involving its clergy. The case at bar involved Phelps and five others who participated in demonstrations in Annapolis at the US Naval Academy, the Maryland Statehouse, and the funeral of Marine Lance Corporal Matthew Snyder, who had been killed in Iraq. Unlike forty-three other states and the federal government, Maryland at that time did not have a law prohibiting demonstrations proximate to cemeteries. The Westboro group notified authorities of their planned demonstrations and was in compliance with state and local ordinances when they assembled thirty minutes before the funeral on a public street across from the cemetery. Their signs included such phrases as "Semper Fag," "Thank God for Dead Soldiers," "Fags Doom Nations," "Priests Rape Boys," and "You're Going to Hell." In an attempt to block the signs, the motorcycle group Patriot Guard Riders (PGR) lined the road to the cemetery. Albert Snyder, Matthew's father, saw only the tops of the signs on his way into the cemetery; he did not learn what they said entirely until he watched the evening news later in the day.

Albert Snyder filed a diversity action against Phelps, those who traveled with him, and the Westboro Baptist Church. Snyder won his tort for emotional distress at the jury trial and was awarded $10 million. Phelps challenged the verdict on the grounds that his group's speech was protected by the First Amendment no matter how much stress it caused. The district court upheld the verdict against Phelps but reduced the damages by half. On appeal by Phelps, the decision was overturned by the US Court of Appeals for the Fourth Circuit. Citing *Hustler Magazine, Inc. v. Falwell*, the court of appeals ruled that the Westboro Church's speech was protected from tort action by the First Amendment's protection of public discourse on public issues of concern.[20] The Supreme Court granted certiorari and ruled 8–1 in favor of Phelps and his church, with only Justice Samuel Alito dissenting.[21]

One could argue that if the Supreme Court had properly contextualized the communication of the Westboro group, it would have seen that enough of the speech at the funeral site was private and aimed at particular persons to warrant upholding the tort awarding damages for the imposition of "emotional distress" on Matthew Snyder's parents.[22] In *Chaplinsky*, the Supreme Court ruled that context creates meaning; a close reading of the words of the protestors at the cemetery in context constituted a personal attack, which should not have been afforded First Amendment protection. One of the results of our subsequent analysis is that Chief Justice John Roberts's case citations and arguments can be used to reach a very different conclusion than he did. In other words, we explore the possibility that the majority opinion may fall under its own weight.

CONTEXT HELPS DETERMINE MEANING

We have already reviewed *Chaplinsky*, in which the Supreme Court used a contextual reading of a situation to show how the immediate context converted words (speech) to a "first punch" (action). Another important example of the importance of context lies in the pervasive use of the originalist method of interpreting the Constitution introduced by Justice Hugo Black, a staunch defender of the First Amendment. In his opinions, Black often argued that if passages in the Constitution were vague, they should be read within the context of the original meaning of the authors of those passages.[23] He used this method to advance his liberal agenda against the notion of "judicial restraint" embraced by Justice Felix Frankfurter and others on the Supreme Court. As we know, this method is sometimes appropriated by current conservatives on the Supreme Court to support their opinions.

However, a fulsome reconstruction of the context of Phelps's protest

CHAPTER 5

was not established by the majority in *Snyder v. Phelps*. They could have found the speech near the grave site to be personal in its context, but they did not. They could have used a compelling government interest to prevent emotional distress to uphold the lower court ruling, but they did not. They could have used a compelling government interest to prevent an invasion of privacy to uphold the lower court ruling, but they did not. A closer look reveals why the decision may be as seriously flawed as Justice Alito asserted in his dissent.

In his majority opinion, Chief Justice Roberts rightly points out that "whether the First Amendment prohibits holding Westboro liable for its speech in this case turns largely on whether that speech is of public or private concern as determined by all the circumstances of the case."[24] However, later in his opinion, he admits that "even protected speech is not equally permissible in all places and at all times."[25] Picketing of particular residences has been prohibited even when performed on public streets, as Roberts points out citing the *Frisby* ruling we reviewed at the beginning of this chapter.[26] Thus, shouldn't it be possible to hold people actionable for picketing a funeral? This issue becomes even more telling when Roberts admits that "the boundaries of the public concern test are not well defined."[27] At best we are on shaky ground here, and that is crucial when it comes to overturning a jury's verdict that was upheld by a district court, which had in fact happened in the *Snyder* ruling. Thus, and rightly, Roberts invites a hermeneutic approach when he writes, "Deciding whether speech is of public or private concern requires us to examine the 'content, form, and context' of that speech."[28] So let's examine those circumstances to see if Justice Roberts's ruling stands by his own standard or whether Phelps's speech was private and, therefore, not eligible for First Amendment protection.

First, Roberts argues that the demonstrators were engaged in public speech on a public street and, therefore, deserve First Amendment protection. He rejects the argument that the protest was conduct as opposed to speech. In most cases, that is true. However, one wouldn't condone treason simply because it was committed in a public space. And couldn't a speaker make a personal attack and then embed it in public discourse to obtain First Amendment protection under Roberts's rule? In fact, Snyder made just a such claim against Phelps, and Roberts summarizes Snyder's argument this way: "The church members in fact mounted

THE BURIAL OF A SOLDIER

a personal attack on Snyder and his family, and then attempted to 'immunize their conduct by claiming that they were actually protesting the United States' tolerance of homosexuality or the supposed evils of the Catholic Church."[29] However, Roberts rejects the claim: "We are not concerned in this case that Westboro's speech on public matters was in any way contrived to insulate speech on a private matter from liability."[30] A hermeneuticist would ask, why not? Shouldn't the Court parse public versus private rhetoric given the damages and privacy interests at stake? Why can't one break the discourse apart and treat each part separately for what that discourse says and what damage it does? Wouldn't an examination of the discourse in terms of its context, including location and *other communication* from the offending group, support exactly the analysis Roberts seeks to avoid? As Justice Alito points out in his dissent, "A physical assault may occur without trespassing; it is no defense that the perpetrator had 'the right to be where [he was].' . . . Neither classic 'fighting words' nor defamatory statements are immunized when they occur in a public place."[31] For that reason, Alito accepts the premise that if, in context, Phelps's protest was conduct, not speech, then he was not protected just because he uttered the words in a public venue. For Alito, the First Amendment does not give protestors the right to "engage in such conduct."[32] The protestors, according to Alito, had "brutalize[d]" Snyder with a "vicious verbal assault."[33]

Second, Roberts points out that the demonstrators used the same rhetoric at the Maryland Statehouse and the United States Naval Academy as they did at the Snyder funeral; therefore, the rhetoric was general discourse on public issues and not a personal, private attack. This contention is enormously problematic. Location determines context in this situation. While demonstrations at a statehouse or a military academy can be seen as general public speech, those same signs become a personal attack when moved to the street outside a cemetery where a marine is being buried and the signs in context become a personal attack on him, his father, and his mother. At the time of the demonstration, only Matthew Snyder's funeral was being conducted; therefore, those driving into the cemetery could reach no other conclusion than that a marine was being defamed at his funeral.

The contention that this rhetoric is personal and not public is reinforced by the fact that it was an invasion of privacy. Does anyone believe

CHAPTER 5

that Phelps would have been on that street corner if Matthew Snyder was not being buried at that time? The fact is Phelps put out a press release stating that his group was going "to picket the funeral of . . . Snyder," whom he claimed was killed by God. The release goes on to state that Snyder "died in shame, not honor—for a fag nation cursed by God. . . . [He is n]ow in Hell." The intent here can be seen as nothing but a personal attack. Chief Justice Roberts himself admits, "The speech was indeed planned to coincide with Matthew Snyder's funeral."[34] Once in proximity to the grave site, once they have named Snyder's parents in their press release, and once they have named them on the church website, Phelps's group is no longer engaging in a broad public appeal; it is attacking the parents of a dead soldier.

The importance of the press release and website to the determination of public versus private speech is evident in the 1983 ruling in *Connick v. Myers*. The ruling makes clear that such determinations should rely on the "content, form, and context of a given statement, as revealed by the whole record."[35] The Court in *Snyder* is well aware of this ruling and even admits that it "provides some guidance." Roberts then cites the very language quoted previously. Thus, the decision to exclude the press release and website from scrutiny is a horrible mistake.[36]

Roberts's next move is also highly problematic. He establishes the burden of proof for the privacy concern when he quotes from *Cohen v. California* that restriction of speech is "dependent upon showing that substantial privacy interests are being invaded in an essentially intolerable manner."[37] It would be difficult to think of any event better able to justify privacy than the burial of a soldier by his family. We can think of few invasions that would be more intolerable and obnoxious than associating the soldier and his family with Satan and the sins of the Catholic clergy, not to mention using bigoted language to address the sexual preferences of the soldier. This kind of personal attack, especially on a *captive audience in a private moment*, is not protected speech. As we saw earlier in this chapter, the Supreme Court has regularly held that captive audiences can seek relief from imposed ideological or religious beliefs; surely, they can seek relief from defamation and emotional stress at a grave site.[38]

Third, using Roberts's logic, one could easily conceal a vicious personal attack on another person by uttering it at different places and times and claiming it was not aimed at that person but his or her class in

THE BURIAL OF A SOLDIER

general. The lie is given to Phelps's claim in this regard when one examines the quoted press release and his church's website. There, one finds an attack directed at Matthew Snyder's parents, which reads:

> God blessed you, Mr. and Mrs. Snyder, with a resource and his name was Matthew. He was an arrow in your quiver! In thanks to God for the comfort the child could bring you, you had a DUTY to prepare that child to serve the Lord his God—PERIOD! You did JUST THE OPPOSITE—you raised him for the devil. Albert and Julie RIPPED that body apart and taught Matthew to defy his Creator, to divorce, and to commit adultery. They taught him how to support the largest pedophile machine in the history of the entire world, the Roman Catholic monstrosity. Every dime they gave the Roman Catholic monster they condemned their own souls. They also, in supporting satanic Catholicism, taught Matthew to be an idolater. . . . Then after all that, they sent him to fight for the United States of Sodom, a filthy country that is in lock step with his evil, wicked and sinful manner of life, putting him in the cross hairs of a God that is so mad, He has smoke coming from his nostrils and fire from his mouth! How dumb was that?

This posting demonstrates what Justice Alito fears, that the discourse goes beyond "commentary on matters of public concern" and makes a personal attack on "private figures."[39] It names the parents; it defames their child and causes emotional distress. Furthermore, Alito makes clear that these remarks and the signs at the cemetery are tantamount to fighting words, which are not protected by the First Amendment under the *Chaplinsky* standard.[40] To be clear, the comments in the press release and on the website contextualize the demonstration at the cemetery and convert that part of the day's demonstrations into a personal attack and fighting words, which fall outside of protection under the First Amendment and therefore are rightly open to a tort for libel and emotional distress.

That fact leads us to a final point: In the trial that Snyder won, the burden of proof he met was enormous. Very few emotional distress cases have been won in Maryland. Furthermore, the law of torts, as Justice Alito points out, is very narrow, with requirements that "are rigorous and difficult to satisfy."[41] The jury in Snyder's case was so instructed by the

127

CHAPTER 5

presiding judge, and yet Snyder prevailed. And in fact, in their appeals, Phelps's lawyers never contest the sufficiency of the evidence that Snyder provided to establish emotional distress. One would think that reversing the jury's decision that was upheld by district court using "rigorous" standards would require much better grounding than Roberts provides. The district court upheld the findings of infliction of emotional distress, invasion of privacy, and civil conspiracy. The burden of proof rests with those who would overturn such a ruling. The presumption lies with Snyder, not with Phelps. As we pointed out, Roberts acknowledges that the boundaries of the "public concern test are not well defined." Giving Phelps the benefit of the doubt on the basis of concerns about ambiguous public speech undermines a jury that met rigorous and clear standards.

Roberts rightfully points out, "To succeed on a claim for intentional inflictions of emotional distress in Maryland, a plaintiff must demonstrate that the defendant intentionally or recklessly engaged in extreme and outrageous conduct that caused the plaintiff to suffer severe emotional distress."[42] The fact is that Snyder's situation met Roberts's standard; the jury and the district court to which the case was appealed believed he had suffered emotional distress. Remarkably, Roberts admits as much at various places in his opinion. He writes, "The record makes clear that the applicable legal term—'emotional distress'—fails to capture fully the anguish Westboro's choice added to Mr. Snyder's already incalculable grief."[43] Near the end of his opinion, Roberts writes, "Westboro's funeral picketing is certainly harmful and its contribution to public discourse may be negligible. . . . Speech is powerful. It can stir people to action, move them to tears of both joy and sorrow, and—as it did here— inflict great pain."[44] Perhaps that is why Roberts writes that "our holding today is narrow."

IMPLICATIONS FOR THE FUTURE

It is remarkable that the fear of suppressing viewpoint protected speech motivated eight justices to protect obnoxious speech that inflicted severe emotional distress. Only one justice in this case feared the danger of providing a blueprint for circumventing legitimate laws protecting individuals from harmful speech. This precedent's damage is trickling down through the lower courts.[45]

THE BURIAL OF A SOLDIER

Correctives have been put in place, but they have yet to be tested. Some states, such as Maryland, have passed laws prohibiting demonstrations proximate to cemeteries. On September 18, 2012, California's Governor Jerry Brown signed a law keeping demonstrators at least three hundred feet from a funeral or making them subject to a $1,000 fine and six months in jail, the same rules used for federal cemeteries. The author of the legislation, State Senator Ted Lieu, commented, "We've all been disgusted by hateful protests at military funerals, and that should now be reduced or stopped."[46] However, three hundred feet is not a great distance. The demonstrators at Snyder's funeral were farther away than that. The emotional stress suffered was because of what the signs said, not because of where they were placed.

One hopes that the Supreme Court will, as it has in the past, see the error of its ways and issue a corrective.[47] That process will start when a majority on the Court realize that Roberts's opinion is not only narrow but flawed. The demonstrators may have had a right to occupy a street corner, but what they said and wrote was not protected from tort action, because it constituted a personal attack when read in its context, including Westboro's web page and press release. Furthermore, once at the cemetery, the Snyder family constituted a captive audience because they had nowhere else to bury their son, and the Court has often found that captive audience situations provide exceptions to First Amendment protection.[48] Surely this was also a matter of protecting the right to be left alone with one's dead son. The least the Supreme Court could have done on behalf of Snyder was to remand the case for rehearing with instructions.

129

6

Fear and Protecting Depictions
of Violence in Video Games

Brown v. Entertainment Merchants Association

SHAKESPEARE'S *HAMLET*, LIKE MANY classic stories, uses violence to make a point. Ophelia commits suicide to underline her unrequited love for Hamlet. Hamlet then orders the death of Rosencrantz and Guildenstern, who had been hired to assassinate him. We are forced to watch the play within the play that depicts the murder of Hamlet's father; poison is poured into his ear while he sleeps. Hamlet browbeats his mother, claiming he is "cruel only to be kind," and then runs poor Polonius through, who is hiding behind a curtain in her chamber. Eventually, the queen accidentally drinks poison; Laertes is killed in a duel with Hamlet; the king is forced to drink poison; and Hamlet dies from a wound inflicted by a poisoned rapier. This play would make a great video game and may have been made into one if video game technology existed at the time. If the video game were made today, would it be subject to censorship?

Many fear that violence in the media, particularly in vicious video games, can spur aggressive and harmful behavior. Is there, they ask, a way to treat violence, particularly gratuitous violence, in the same way as we regulate indecency or obscenity? This chapter examines a case in which just such a law was tested.

ATTEMPTS AT CENSORSHIP

A host of national policy makers has brought pressure on producers of violent programming to curtail "gratuitous violence." In 1954, Senator Estes Kefauver (D-TN) investigated the relationship between juvenile delinquency and television programs. This issue was revived in the early 1960s by Senator Thomas Dodd (D-CT), who in 1968 got President Johnson to establish the Eisenhower Commission on the Causes and Prevention of Violence. Since its conclusions were not in accord with his impressions, in 1969, Senator John Pastore (D-RI) requested that the surgeon general issue another report on the problem. Three years later, under the watchful eye of Congress, a report was published that hinted at a weak correlation between the viewing of violence and violent activity: "The effect is small compared with many other possible causes, such as parental attitudes or knowledge of and experience with the real violence in society. [The evidence does not] warrant the conclusion that televised violence has a uniformly adverse effect . . . [or] an adverse effect on the majority of children."[1] Nonetheless, the surgeon general appeared before Pastore's committee and claimed a causal link had been documented, though "carefully phrased and qualified in language acceptable to social scientists."[2]

By the fall of 1974, the chairman of the Federal Communications Commission, Richard Wiley, was urging the three networks to voluntarily curtail "sex and violence" on television. Unfortunately, this call of conscience intertwined the issue of indecency with the issue of violence. The commission made clear that "industry self -regulation" was preferable to governmental regulation and that such standards were highly subjective and raised "serious constitutional questions."[3] In reaction, the networks and the National Association of Broadcasters Television Review Board adopted the "family viewing" policy, which moved violent and sexual programming into the 9:00 to 11:00 p.m. time slot. In November 1976, the courts found the "family viewing" hour unenforceable and unconstitutional.[4]

The issue was revived in 1994, when Congressman Edward Markey

CHAPTER 6

(D-MA) told the television networks to figure out a way to label violence in programming or he would do it for them. In 1995, he attached legislation to the communications bill that would require the installation of a V-chip in all new television sets. The chip, while not yet developed at that point, would, Markey speculated, detect ratings of programs that would be applied by producers.

But the issue was confused in the same year when Senator Paul Simon (D-IL) told the National Association of Broadcasters that while cartoons such as *Tom and Jerry* were too violent for television, he wouldn't mind seeing the film *Schindler's List* on television.[5] Reed Hundt, chairman of the Federal Communications Commission, warned that networks may be legally responsible for the effects of their programs and that the Federal Communications Commission has the power to regulate the content of programs. Speaking before the Executive Committee of the National Association of Broadcasters in February 1994, Hundt called for "new family programming" to "educate and instruct" children. Appearing before Markey's committee later that year, Surgeon General Joycelyn Elders attacked the networks for not doing enough to reduce violence on television. When Elders was fired for seeming to endorse including the subject of masturbation in children's sex ed classes as a method of avoiding AIDS, Attorney General Janet Reno emerged as the point person on this issue for the Clinton administration. In a frightening statement, she told Congress that regulating the content of programming does not damage the rights of broadcasters, because they are second-class citizens under the First Amendment.[6] And she would extend content regulation to computers.

She found many friends in Congress. In February 1995, Senator Kent Conrad (D-ND) introduced a bill to ban "gratuitous violence" from television between 8:00 a.m. and 10:00 p.m.[7] Senator Bob Graham (D-FL) coerced the Defense Department, the postal service, and Amtrak to agree not to place advertisements in "excessively violent" broadcast programming. Senator Fritz Hollings (D-SC) introduced legislation to ban violent television programs when children are "reasonably likely" to compose a "substantial part of the audience." The bipartisan nature of the proposed censorship was evident when Senators Joseph Lieberman (D-CT) and John McCain (R-AZ) held hearings and warned producers that regulation was just a bill away.

Finally, Clinton's last surgeon general, Dr. David Satcher, issued a report in his final week linking violence with the media. It came under immediate attack by numerous scholars. Karen Sternheimer, a sociologist at the University of Southern California and a researcher at the Center for Media Literacy, wrote, "One of the studies the surgeon general cites equates programs as diverse as cartoon and police dramas with video games and action movies."[8] Such comparisons are misleading and dangerous because they ignore the more likely causes of violence such as "alcohol abuse, the deterioration of public education and the lack of economic opportunity in impoverished areas."[9] As we shall see, censorship is feared to this day, as is the threat of violence stemming from various media.

THE SUPREME COURT ON REGULATING INDECENCY

The problem with trying to censor violence became clear in 1948 in *Winters v. New York*. The state of New York had arrested Winters under a statute that prohibited the sale of stories of bloodshed. After three arguments before the Supreme Court, the law was deemed unconstitutional on the ground that it was too vague. The Supreme Court ruled that the "line between . . . informing and . . . entertaining is too elusive. . . . Everyone is familiar with instances of propaganda as fiction. What is one man's amusement, teaches another's doctrine."[10] That was an important finding, because *Winters* is one of the few Supreme Court cases that deals with the question of the effect of violence in media.

The vagueness of the term "violence" is one of the most persistent problems for those who seek to regulate it, because it encourages arbitrary regulation that violates free, let alone creative, speech. Television programs, from *The Three Stooges* to *Will & Grace*, achieve comic effects using what some have called violent activity. However, one could argue that violence in such programming is not taken seriously because of the humorous context. Though, as we will demonstrate, studies have not shown it to be true, some argue that a dramatic context for violence makes it more dangerous. However, defenders of serious drama argue that violence is not gratuitous if it is used to reinforce in the mind of audience members what is moral and what is immoral. Other studies show that violence in programming, even if gratuitous, is cathartic and might actually prevent further violence.[11]

CHAPTER 6

Given this history, this chapter addresses a key question: Does the guarantee of freedom of expression extend to media in such a way as to preclude states and/or Congress from making laws affecting portrayals of violence? There are several important sub-questions that situate this debate inside the context of the struggle over the past decade to give broadcasters parity with newspapers when it comes to content controls. They include the following: (1) Can "violence" and related terms like "gratuitous" be defined in such a way as to preclude their arbitrary and capricious use? We fear the arbitrary and capricious use of terms because they can be applied in unfair ways, usually to punish minorities. Thus, the Supreme Court has regularly overturned regulations that contain terms that can be applied in arbitrary and capricious ways to censor minority views. (2) Does violence in media, particularly video games, constitute a clear and present danger, and does regulation of it by the government advance a significant and legitimate government interest? We fear clear and present dangers, such as converting our children into aggressively violent actors who could hurt themselves or others. This chapter proceeds by answering these sub-questions and then addressing the major question in the Court's analysis of *Brown v. Entertainment Merchants Association* of whether violent games cause violence.

Content Controls over Broadcasting

Those who believe that video games present a clear and present danger because of their impact on the human psyche often justify the regulation of video games by comparing it to the regulation of broadcast media. The analogy is flawed for several reasons. First, broadcasters are licensed by the federal government and subject to certain "public interest" standards established as far back as 1924. Video game producers face no such regulatory scheme. Second, in recent years, the broadcast standards, while maintained by the Supreme Court, have become irrelevant because they do not apply to cable broadcasting, which is the way most Americans receive broadcast programming. Third, a strong case can be made that broadcasters should be afforded the same freedom as newspapers; in other words, they should be de-regulated from all content restrictions and subject only to defamation laws. Steps were taken in that direction with the suspension of the so-called fairness doctrine in 1987 and its progeny in 2000. These "content controls" were removed by the lower courts and Congress.

134

It is important to note that these reforms were encouraged by the Supreme Court in 1984 when they invited a review of the fairness doctrine in *FCC v. League of Women Voters* : "In light of the substantial increase in the number and types of information sources, we believe that the artificial mechanism of interjecting the government into the affirmative role of overseeing the content of speech is unnecessary to vindicate the interest of the public in obtaining access to the marketplace of ideas."[12] After its own hearing in 1985, the FCC also concluded that the doctrine was counterproductive and constitutionally suspect.[13]

Additional clarification came with *Turner Broadcasting System, Inc. v. FCC*, a further injunction against content-based controls.[14] The Supreme Court ordered that the terms of the regulation be examined to see whether, on its face, regulation confers benefits or imposes burdens based on the content of the speech regulated. Second, it must be determined, even if the regulation's plain language does not mandate a finding of content discrimination, whether there are indications that the rule's manifest purpose is to regulate speech based on the message it conveys.[15] Clearly, the fairness doctrine, or a regulation concerning violence, would not meet this standard and would therefore be declared unconstitutional.

This conclusion is supported by a number of constitutional scholars, the most prominent of whom wrote in 1995 that it "is not necessary to retain a separate First Amendment jurisprudence for broadcasters. . . . We believe that the growing telecommunications convergence should lead the Court to embrace these principles explicitly while discarding the false notion that 'broadcasting' (whatever that is) requires or deserves a separate First Amendment jurisprudence. . . . The general principles of law and regulation underlying all non-broadcast mass media would be just as workable, and should be fully applied, to broadcast media."[16] Thus, even if violence in video games were parallel to broadcasting, it is doubtful that it should be regulated.

Arbitrary and Capricious Use of Terms

It is a long-standing matter of constitutional law and administrative review that the arbitrary and capricious use of laws or regulations is prohibited. In *Cox v. New Hampshire* (1941), the Supreme Court struck down a law giving a licensing board arbitrary power and unfettered discretion over parades, due to the fear that law could be used to censor unpopular

CHAPTER 6

or minority views.[17] A whole line of cases has held that for literary works, including film, to be considered obscene and therefore censurable, they must meet very specific standards, not some vague arbitrary formula such as "I know obscenity when I see it."[18] Thus, even if violence were allowed to be regulated as obscenity and indecency are, regulators would face a very heavy burden of proof.

The problem of defining violence has been compounded by disagreements in the social sciences. If we cannot specifically define violence, then we cannot to any degree of certainty know what is causing the fear that motivates the regulation of violence. Sometimes violence is described as aggressive behavior; sometimes it is described as verbal abuse, bullying, hate speech, or even teasing. Constitutional scholars Thomas Krattenmaker and Scott Powe put the problem this way in their landmark, two-hundred-page review of social scientific research: "Finally, and most damaging to proponents of the violence hypothesis, no one yet has been able to suggest an acceptable operational definition of the very kind of behavior sought to be measured: 'violence.' To be useful as a basis for policy making, studies of the causes of violence must rest upon a definition incorporating normative, social connotations. To illustrate, if violence is defined simply as a willingness to stand one's ground when physically attacked, it is extremely unlikely that violence caused by television would produce an outcry for increased regulation. What then can the researcher take as an objective observable conception of violence capable of measuring behavior that produces social concern?"[19] In the wrong hands, and perhaps in any hands, using a phrase like "gratuitous violence" to write policy creates a broad sweep that would include many instances of creativity or even innocuous speech and/or programming. It is, therefore, unconstitutional and dangerous to allow the government to censor "gratuitous violence" and/or other such undefinable phrases.

CLEAR AND PRESENT DANGER; COMPELLING GOVERNMENT INTEREST

This leads us to ask, under what circumstances is the government allowed to infringe on the First Amendment? The Supreme Court stated that a "government regulation is sufficiently justified if it is within the constitutional power of the Government; if it furthers an important or substantial government interest; if the government interest is unrelated to the suppression of free expression; and if the incidental restriction on alleged First Amendment freedoms is no greater than is essential to the furtherance of that issue."[20] In *Edenfield v. Fane* (1992), the Supreme Court ruled that proof of a real harm must be demonstrated before speech can be restricted. In other words, policy makers must be able to define violence in operational policy terms and then prove that there is a causal link between portrayed violence on media and serious crime on the streets, or some other significant harm, in order to restrict content.

That leads us to the O'Brien test: Does the proposed law advance a "compelling interest"?[21] In the case we are examining, the question becomes whether there is a problem that can only be solved by banning violence in video games. In the case of violence, those seeking to ban it must show that the portrayal induces significant harm and that the banning of specific portrayals of acts of violence in video games will alleviate that harm. To pass the lesser levels of scrutiny applicable to content-neutral regulations, such regulation must also be "narrowly tailored to serve a significant governmental interest, and . . . leave open ample alternative channels for communication of information" because it was influenced by a bias against video games.[22]

There is much literature on the effect broadcast violence has on its audience. As Marjorie Heins of the ACLU has made clear, much of this literature is a summary of other studies.[23] Most of those studies are seriously flawed or based on responses from hormonally challenged first- and second-year students subjected to who knows what kinds of video violence.[24] The laboratory tests are not scientific, are not representative of the population, and do not use an operational definition of violence. No wonder the Department of Education concluded that "a disturbing amount of scholarship has been slipshod."[25] Other studies have carefully reviewed the social scientific data in favor of censorship and found it seriously deficient in making its case.[26] And still others have found no correlation between watching violent video games and engaging in actual violence when studies were conducted properly.[27] To put it another way, the social scientific community has failed to produce evidence that there is something in video games to fear.

For example, Wiegman et al. (1992) conducted a cross-cultural longitudinal study investigating the extent to which the viewing of violent

CHAPTER 6

content caused aggressive behavior in children. The study examined subjects in The Netherlands, Australia, Finland, Israel, Poland, and the United States over a period of three years. The researchers reported, "On the basis of the data of all countries participating in this study, we may conclude that there is almost no evidence for the hypothesis that television violence viewing leads to aggressive behaviour."[28] The statistical relationship between aggression and television that some social scientists have found disappears, according to Wiegman et al., when the data are corrected to reflect such factors as a child's intelligence and preexisting level of aggression. In another study, Feshbach tried to establish a correlation between viewing violence and being aggressive. Others were unable to replicate the study. Feshbach's coauthor later said that their work actually supported the null hypothesis and "shows no support for the theory that viewing of aggressive television increases real life aggression."[29] Richard Rhodes, a Pulitzer Prize–winning scientist, told ABC News, "There is no good evidence that watching mock violence in the media either causes or even influences people to become violent."[30] Major field studies support this latter view. The most significant was by Milgram and Shotland in 1973 and Lynn, Hampson and Agahi in 1989.[31] These studies were recently updated by Przybylski and Mishkin with regard to violent video games and hence are particularly relevant to this chapter. After observing 110 teenage boys and 107 teenage girls in 2014, the researchers from Oxford University found that moderate access to violent games, an hour a day or less, actually *led to less aggressive behavior* than those who engaged in no access to a game at all.[32]

Because there are so many other factors that contribute to violent behavior, and because the best studies on the subject are inconclusive at best, it is irresponsible to claim that watching violent behavior causes violence in society. It has yet to be demonstrated that banning such programming advances a substantial government interest. As we shall see, more research is needed on two fronts: (1) to determine whether games have a cathartic effect; and (2) to determine whether graphic representations of violence or sex trigger painful psychological effects.

What the Courts Believe

No court has granted monetary compensation for harm allegedly caused by a video program, because the courts doubt the existence of a provable

VIOLENCE IN VIDEO GAMES

link between television and violence.[33] In *Zamora v. Columbia Broadcasting System, Olivia N. v. NBC, Walt Disney Prod. v. Shannon*, and *DeFilippo v. NBC*, the plaintiffs were denied damages when they alleged that they were victims of violence incited by copycat video viewers.[34] Instead, the courts sided with the defendants' claim to a First Amendment right to freedom of expression. Only advocacy of "imminent lawless action" that is capable of being produced has been ruled restrictable, and the Supreme Court has specifically ruled that video violence does not fall into that category, especially if it is entertainment.[35] Other courts have held that holding media companies responsible for actions committed by others "stretches the concept of foreseeability" beyond reason.[36]

This line of thought was reinforced in the Supreme Court's unanimous protection of the Internet in June 1997 in *Reno v. ACLU*. The Court would not subordinate the freedom of adults to the purported interest of protecting children. Instead, the Court struck down the provision of the law that prohibited the "display" of indecent materials online, and, importantly to the case under review in this chapter, voted 7–2 to void the provision that banned the transmission of indecent information to a minor. In the process of striking down the Communication Decency Act of 1996, the Court warned about the "vagueness" of the term "indecency." One of the strongest points made in the unanimous decision was that the government's interest in protecting children from what might be harmful "does not justify an unnecessarily broad suppression of speech addressed to adults." Writing for the Court, Justice John Paul Stevens argued that the government may not, in an effort to protect children, "justify an unnecessarily broad suppression of speech addressed to adults."[37] Thus, even if violence could be conflated with indecency, it could not be banned in video games.

GOING AFTER VIDEO GAMES

In reaction, those seeking to censor violence in media moved on to compare it to obscenity, which is censurable, even though, again, the evidence of harmful effects of obscenity is hard to find. For example, the Indianapolis City Council wrote an ordinance that bracketed "graphic violence" with obscenity, arguing that graphic violence caters to a "morbid interest," is "patently offensive to prevailing standards in the adult community as

CHAPTER 6

a whole," and "lacks serious literary, artistic, political or scientific value." Second, the ordinance defined "graphic violence" as "amputation, decapitation, dismemberment, bloodshed, mutilation, maiming, or disfigurement." The local judge approved implementation of the ordinance, and it became a model for others who sought to restrict video games, including the legislature of the state of California.

However, when the Indianapolis ordinance was brought before to the US Court of Appeals for the Seventh Circuit in 2001, Judge Richard Posner issued the unanimous ruling of the court in *American Amusement Machine Association v. Kendrick* in which he argued that "no showing has been made that games of the sort found in the record of this case" induce violence. "The grounds" for such an ordinance "must be compelling" and not merely plausible, because "children have First Amendment rights." Posner compared the video games to literature containing graphic violence and concluded that video games, despite their interactive nature, were still stories that taught lessons. His opinion influenced the case that is the subject of this chapter; in fact, he is quoted in the majority decision, as we shall see.[38]

At the Supreme Court level, Posner's position was consistent with two other important rulings: *Ashcroft v. Free Speech Coalition* and *Ashcroft v. American Civil Liberties Union*, which followed four weeks later.[39] The first case, with a 5–4 majority, struck down provisions of the Child Pornography Prevention Act of 1996 as overly broad. Justice Anthony Kennedy argued that the provisions could be used to censor such films as *Lolita* and *Traffic*, because in each of them an actress portrayed an underage woman involved in sexual activity. The second *Ashcroft* case assessed the Child Online Protection Act (COPA), which, in his majority opinion, Justice Clarence Thomas found to violate the First Amendment. He argued that there were less restrictive means to solve the problem of depictions of child pornography, that the law restricted adult access to material they had a right to view, and that the problem was better controlled by parents than by Congress. It is hard to imagine that if the Supreme Court extended First Amendment protection to these kinds of materials, they would not extend it to violent video games.

Despite these rulings, the staff at the Federal Communications Commission issued a report that argued that it would not violate the Constitution to equate violence with indecency. All it would take is an act of

140

VIOLENCE IN VIDEO GAMES

Congress giving the FCC the power to regulate indecency on the Internet or computers, as it does with broadcast media. Senator Jay Rockefeller (D-WV) then formed a bipartisan coalition that pushed for the legislation in 2005. It went nowhere.

The real issue here is whether these games induce violence. If they do, that might constitute a harm significant enough to trump First Amendment rights. However, as we have seen, the most recent evidence does not support those who would censor video game violence. In 2000, Jonathan Freedman, of the University of Toronto, who has studied violence and the media for many years, concluded that none of the two hundred or so recent violence studies support a causal relationship between violence in programming and violence in society. In 2001, President George W. Bush's surgeon general concluded that there was "insufficient evidence to suggest that video games cause long-term aggressive behavior." In April 2004, the *Journal of the American Medical Association* summarized available research and agreed with the surgeon general. They also noted that while video game participation has increased, "youth violence has been decreasing." Dmitri Williams published a study in *Communication Monographs* that examined 213 video game players after they had played games for a month. He found no increase in aggressiveness among the participants.[40]

More important, the portrayal of violence is often essential if one wishes to convey a moral message. Dr. Rhoda Baruch, president of the Institute for Mental Health Initiatives (IMHI), reminds us that violence is a natural part of life and may offer some prosocial benefits. Violence is an "element of our folk tales and our best literature—from *Hansel and Gretel* to *Hamlet*.... Storytellers have traditionally used violence to teach youth about danger, safety, courage, injustice and honor."[41] She cautions that removing violence from media will not expel violence from society but may eliminate important values from the same media. "To put it succinctly, in mainstream programs, good triumphs over evil, honesty is the best policy, the righteous inherit the Earth."[42]

BROWN V. ENTERTAINMENT MERCHANTS ASSOCIATION

Fearing that violent games could trigger violent acts among teenagers, the state of California attempted the same end run that had been used

CHAPTER 6

in the aforementioned Indianapolis case. The California law prohibited the sale of "violent video games" to minors and required the games to be labeled as intended for people over the age of seventeen.[43] The law defined violence to "include killings, maiming, dismembering, or sexually assaulting an image of a human being" if depicted in a way that a "reasonable person, considering the game as a whole, would find appeals to deviant or morbid interest of minors," if "patently offensive to prevailing standards in the community as to what is suitable for minors," and if the game, "as a whole . . . lacks serious literary, artistic, political, or scientific values for minors."[44] The penalty for violating the act was set at $1,000.

Fearing censorship and the loss of revenue, representatives of the video game and software industries brought suit to enjoin the law. The US District Court for the Northern District of California ruled in their favor on First Amendment grounds.[45] The US Court of Appeals for the Ninth Circuit affirmed this ruling, and it was granted certiorari by the Supreme Court in 2010. The merchants argued that the games were creative expression that should be protected just as films and plays are. Among other arguments, California responded that because of their interactive nature, playing the games constituted conduct not speech. In his majority opinion of 2011, Justice Antonin Scalia relied heavily on the Court's precedent set in *United States v. Stevens*, a case that focused on a federal law prohibiting the sale and distribution of so-called crush videos of animal cruelty.[46] In *Brown*, Justice Scalia specifically rejected California's argument; instead, he claimed that all literature was interactive and communicative. Government, therefore, cannot regulate the ideas being conveyed in games without advancing a substantial government interest, a burden California failed to meet. He was joined by Justices Kennedy, Ginsburg, Sotomayor, Kagan, Alito, and Roberts, the latter two filing a joint concurring opinion. Justice Thomas and Breyer filed dissenting opinions on two very different grounds, as we shall see.

Ignoring the outlined history of media censorship, Justice Scalia advanced the position that "'the basic principles of freedom of speech and the press . . . do not vary' when new and different medium for communication appears."[47] Then he refuted parts of Justice Alito's concurrence by stating that just because video games are a new form of media does not afford them the same protection as the examples Scalia cites. Furthermore,

142

he argued that video games communicate ideas and therefore qualify for First Amendment protection, unless they are obscene, induce imminent incitement to crime, or are significantly harmful in some other provable way. In the *Stevens* case, the law was carefully crafted around the *Miller v. California* obscenity standards, which exempted depictions with "serious religious, political, scientific, educational, journalistic, historical or artistic value."[48] But even that law, which is very like the California law, was struck down as an unwarranted content-based restriction. Fearing censorship of redeemable literature, Justice Scalia extended the *Stevens* precedent to *Brown*.[49]

Like Posner, Scalia feared conflating obscenity with violence. He chastised California for trying to make "violent-speech regulation look like obscenity regulation."[50] He was adamant that violence is not like obscenity and, therefore, cannot claim protection under *Ginsberg v. New York*.[51] He condemned California for trying to create a new category of unprotected speech directed at children, which he claimed was unprecedented and mistaken. Relying on *Erznoznik v. City of Jacksonville*, he argued that children have First Amendment rights, a position perfectly consistent with *Tinker* but not, as we shall see, with the dissent of Justice Thomas in this case, which Justice Scalia specifically attacked in footnote 3 of his opinion.[52] Justice Scalia argued that parents are not free to infringe on the speech and religious rights of their children unless some compelling interest can be shown.

In fact, Scalia pointed out that historically and traditionally children have had access to violent depictions in literature; he specifically cites the Brothers Grimm version of the Cinderella story, in which her wicked sisters have their eyes pecked out by birds, and Hansel and Gretel, who baked their nemesis in an oven. He gave many more examples to make his point, ranging from the *Odyssey* to *Lord of the Flies*. He continued his refutation of Alito by acknowledging his extensive research into video game material but ultimately concluded that even "disgust is not a valid basis for restricting expression."[53] He concluded this section of his opinion by stating that he feared that Alito's position opens the door to using disgust as a way to censor, and that is what Scalia believed California was up to with this law. In short, Justice Scalia feared that the California law would open the door to a massive amount censorship of material that has not been proven to be harmful.

143

CHAPTER 6

He next considered whether the restrictions on content in the California law pass the strict scrutiny test of whether there is a compelling government interest to justify the restrictions. Because California failed to show a direct causal link between violence in video games and harm to minors, it did not meet the test. That is to say, California's fears were unsupported. As we did ourselves, Justice Scalia cited psychological studies that rely on correlational findings, not causal findings, and that are often in conflict with one another or invalid. In fact, he pointed out that the very studies that California relies on have been rejected "by every court to consider them."[54] He ridiculed the studies for alleging only minor harms that correlate with viewing violence. Worse yet, claimed Scalia, the law does not include the very items that were used to produce the tested results.

He also showed that the law put the control of the games in the hands of parents, further watering down its effectiveness: "By requiring that the purchase of violent video games can be made only by adults, the Act ensures that parents can decide what games are appropriate."[55] He argued that California was using a third party to carry out its regulation and thus violated the rights of minors established in the *Erznoznik* ruling. He believed the voluntary rating system set in place by the video game industry was a better model for guiding parents and protecting minors. It is at this juncture that Scalia also rebutted Justice Breyer's argument that those minors without parental supervision provide a compelling government interest that justifies the law. This argument occurred inside Breyer's attempt to shift the framing of the decision from freedom of speech to protection of children, relying on the *Ginsberg* precedent. Justice Scalia answered that *Ginsberg* concerned obscene material, not violent material, and that the percentage of children who fall into Breyer's category of neglect does not justify imposing the same kind of ban that applies to alcoholic beverages or obscenity.

Justice Scalia concluded that the California law did not stand up to strict scrutiny because it failed to define a narrow class of speech, failed to show that the regulation would solve a problem, and offended the rights of minors. The law was also condemned for being underinclusive in terms of the games it covers and overly inclusive in terms of the children it covers.

Justice Alito was joined by Chief Justice Roberts in a concurring opinion. They agreed with Scalia that the California law was not "framed

VIOLENCE IN VIDEO GAMES

with precision."[56] For example, the law should have had a narrower list to depict graphics that meet the *Miller* standard. Instead of imposing its own standards, the California legislature relied on vague societal or community standards. The law dumped all young people into one category instead of separating the impact on various groups of minors, such as grade school children versus high school students. Furthermore, terms such as "deviant" and "morbid" were not defined in the statute, and they feared that would lead to arbitrary and capricious enforcement.

However, Justice Alito did not believe the California law to fall under the *Stevens* standard. While the crush video law applied to all persons, the California law applied only to minors. Therefore, the law did not restrict the creation of games or their sale to adults. Parents could buy the games for their children if they so wished. Worse yet, the Supreme Court created a situation in which states could restrict the sale of "girly magazines" to minors but couldn't restrict the sale of graphically violent video games.

Justice Alito was less reluctant to regulate new forms of media, which, he feared, so mirror reality that they can cause harm. He was particularly concerned with the fact that video games require active participation, which novels and plays do not. Current video games are much more realistic than novels, plays, or even films. In his most telling argument, Justice Alito pointed out, "By wearing a special vest or other device, a player will be able to experience physical sensations supposedly felt by a character on the screen."[57] He went on to point out that the amount of violence in some of the games is way beyond that which one finds in *Grimms' Fairy Tales* or *Hamlet*. Many of these games purposely debase societal values in a very cynical way. Players can even take on the identity of the killers at Columbine High School or Virginia Tech. Fearing that the simulations are so real they can deform the psyche of the player, Alito wrote, "The objective of one game is to rape a mother and her daughters; in another, the goal is to rape Native American women."[58] For him, the interactive quality and the excessive, debasing violence voided the argument that video game violence falls into the same category as written or passively viewed violence and further voided the use of psychological data from the latter category. Only psychological studies testing the effects of interactive video games should be included in making a decision about how to regulate them, and the Supreme Court should not be so quick to

CHAPTER 6

include interactive video games in the free speech/print category for First Amendment protection. However, Justice Alito might have wanted to note that the Pew Internet & American Life Project of 2008 found that 81 percent of Americans between the ages of nineteen and twenty-nine play video games, but nowhere near that number of people engage in acts of violence after they have played them. As of yet, despite Alito's fear, no correlation between participation in such games and actions that follow has been established.

In his dissent, Justice Clarence Thomas came at the problem in a unique way. He argued that minors do not have First Amendment rights; the Founders intended such rights only for adults. Not surprisingly, Thomas justified his dissent using the precept of original meaning. Relying on his understanding of the Founders, Thomas would exclude from First Amendment protection "speech to minor children bypassing their parents."[59] He clearly feared that granting such rights to minors would undercut parental control and family values. He argued that the Founders placed full authority for supervision of children in the hands of their parents. Therefore, it is nonsense to believe they would have granted freedom of speech to children, thereby preempting parental control. Thus, his fear was not only that children will be damaged by video games but that parental control will be attenuated by this ruling, thereby destabilizing the family unit.

After reviewing colonial practices, Thomas turned to such Enlightenment thinkers as John Locke and Jean-Jacques Rousseau to buttress his argument. These philosophers, who influenced America Founders, saw children as "blank slates" that were highly "malleable." They lacked decision-making abilities and so required parental supervision. Thomas cited the common law commentaries of William Blackstone to prove his point. This position was reflected in Thomas Jefferson's thoughts on the education of children. Justice Thomas cited the letters of Jefferson to his daughters for further evidence for his argument. Marriage and military service required parental consent of a child who was not of age. Obviously, children can't vote or serve on juries, so why should they be granted First Amendment rights?

The doctrine of in loco parentis passed this duty along to teachers, to whom the responsibility of guiding and supervising children was further extended in society. For further support on this point, Thomas cited

146

VIOLENCE IN VIDEO GAMES

Morse v. Frederick (see chapter 2 of this book) from 2007 in which he concurred. He also pointed out that parents and teachers were expected to decide what books children could read, including the condemnation of certain literary works. For Thomas, it is only a small step to allow legislatures to reinforce this parental function, particularly in the case of harmfully violent video games that do not qualify as speech in his use of the term.

Justice Breyer's dissent was quite different. Since he bought the social science claims about the inherent damage video games can do to the psyche of children, he feared these games and wanted them regulated. At some length, he cited studies that he claimed provided "causal" evidence of heightened aggression in children after interactive violent video games have been played.[60] Furthermore, Breyer deferred to the opinions of medical experts with regard to these findings, being no expert himself. He then cited a number of medical reviews upholding the findings. Because they demonstrate the potential harm to minors that violent video games may cause, the state may take on a parental role to protect its minors and guide their parents.

Breyer believed the California law to be constitutional on its face and therefore required those seeking its suspension to meet a very high burden of proof. For example, since the law provided fair notice of its intent, it is not unconstitutionally vague. He drew a comparison with the *Ginsberg* ruling, which upheld a New York statute regarding the sale of obscene material and of course, with *Miller*, which the California statute imitates.[61] He argued that the definition of "deviant" behavior in the California law was no vaguer than the definition of "prurient" appeals in the *Miller* case. Since, like *Miller*, the California law protected any video game that has serious literary, artistic, political, or scientific values, it was facially sound, and the fears of those who believe the law could be used to censor legitimate discourse were without merit.

Another part of his rationale lies in the fact that the law regulates action as well as speech, and Breyer believed action is not protected by the First Amendment. He would sort out the action elements from the expressive speech elements and then determine if the California law was narrowly tailored to restrict the action elements. The "modest restriction" that the California law did impose was justified by a compelling interest to protect minors from engaging in gratuitous violence.[62] And, like Alito,

147

CHAPTER 6

Breyer believed engaging in the simulated violence makes it a different form of activity from protected speech. He also believed that such engagements are damaging to minors based on the social scientific evidence he would accept.[63]

Breyer went on to argue that there is no other less restrictive alternative to the California statute, because the statute itself was not very restrictive. Adults could still buy these video games and give them to their children if they so choose. Thus, the state has the right to regulate the sale of such a product to minors.

CONCLUSION

This chapter explains why those fearing infringement on First Amendment protections prevailed over those like Justice Breyer, who fear that those playing video games will visit harm on society. One of the oddities of this case is that it opens us to the contrary fears among those who find sexual material indecent or obscene but have no objection to graphically portrayed violence. Justice Alito in his concurring opinion and Justice Breyer in his dissent explore just how graphic, that is, realistic, portrayals of violence have become. And Breyer provides evidence that portrayals of graphic violence probably cause more psychological damage than does obscene material. But neither examined what might be seen as a hypocritical stance by the majority with regard to condemning obscenity but protecting depictions of violence.

Fearing the censorship of material with literary merit, the Supreme Court's majority relied on several contentions that strongly mitigate against the labeling of video games. It ruled that the content of programming should be no more restricted than that of newspapers and that the Constitution prohibits the imposition of restrictions on programming based on its contents: "Selective exclusions from a public forum may not be based on content alone, and may not be justified by reference to content alone."[64] Furthermore, the majority contended that courts in general believe that studies that have tried to link violence in society with violence in video games are severely flawed and that other studies show that causation cannot be established, despite Justice Breyer's claims to the contrary.

The dialectic of fears in this case is rather unique and complicated. Justice Breyer would allow censorship of games that contained graphic

148

depictions of violence, because he feared a contagion of violence among impressionable minors. If the California law had been crafted more carefully, Justice Thomas would have allowed regulation of video games, because he fears that giving children First Amendment rights undercuts parental control and hence family values. If the proper law could be written and harkening back to the regulation of new media, Justice Alito would have allowed censorship because this new media is virtual and untested. He was afraid that since its consequences were unknown, it could result in tragedy. On the other side of the dialectic, Justice Scalia and the majority feared that conflating violence with obscenity was a ruse that would lead to censorship of material having literary merit. They also feared that laws containing vague descriptions could lead to arbitrary and capricious applications.

None of us like all of the things that are contained in video games; many are horrendously violent or offensive. However, few of us want the government arbitrating matters of taste or taking on a parental role. The Supreme Court's ruling in *Brown* provides a rare instance of prohibiting the government from regulating a new form of communication. Historically, the United States has acted like an old-world principality, imposing controls over new forms of content, whether it be radio, television, or film. It has taken time for each new medium to free itself of these shackles. Beginning with the Creel Committee, movies were severely censored in this country from 1915 to 1952, first because they were thought to be subversive to the war effort in 1917 and then because they were thought to be indecent. Created in 1949 to relieve the prohibition of editorials by broadcasters, the well-meaning but abused fairness doctrine was not suspended until 1987. The government feared the power of broadcasters to promote one ideology over another, a fear that has resurfaced with the explosion of media, social and otherwise. Fake news and the big lie have led to calls for new restrictions and censorship.

The First Amendment was not established to protect the easy cases. It was created to protect the "romantics," as Steve Shiffrin calls them, "those who would break out of classical forms: the dissenters, the unorthodox, the outcasts."[65] We need to remember that there were those in this country who arrested citizens who defended the French Revolution and made fun of President John Adams. President Andrew Jackson forbade the distribution of abolitionist tracts in the South. President Lincoln

CHAPTER 6

incarcerated editors who criticized his administration. Union leaders were regularly jailed by federal judges at the end of the nineteenth century. And if you don't think it can happen in modern times, just revisit the McCarthy era, which so cruelly punished screenwriters, producers, and actors.

A first, virginal viewing of Shakespeare's *Hamlet* should shock the system. You should fear what is happening to the characters. If you don't, the play won't provide catharsis, which most psychologists believe is good for the psyche. If violent entertainment is the cause of our ills, and if that cause is to be exterminated, then a great many works of art will be destroyed in the process. Perhaps that is why Franklyn Haiman warned: "If our problem is that we do not respect each other enough, that we exploit each other's gullibilities, that we resort to violence too easily, that we lust too much and love too little, I do not understand how improvement will be achieved by the censorship of communication, which is itself a coercive tool that treats us as objects to be manipulated by the censors rather than as human beings with the capacity to learn and choose for ourselves what is better and what is worse."[66] Censorship is often the first step to mind control and the imposition of an ideology.

7

Fear and Indecent, Obscene, and Graphic Speech

FCC v. Fox Television Stations, Ashcroft v. American Civil Liberties Union, and *United States v. Stevens*

THERE IS NO SHORTAGE of people in America who are offended by sexual, excretory, or otherwise graphic material that is shared in public spaces. In the twenty-first century, we have already witnessed several incidents make their way through the legal system because of claims regarding the offensiveness of language and images. *FCC v. Fox Television Stations* I and II (2009 and 2012) involved four separate incidents that were aired and that viewers found objectionable. In December 2002, Cher used the word "fuck" in her Billboard Music Award acceptance speech: "I've had my critics for the last 40 years saying I was on my way out every year. Right. So fuck 'em. I still have a job and they don't." In January 2003, U2's Bono used the word "fucking" in his Golden Globe Award acceptance speech: "This is really fucking brilliant." In February 2003, a portion of an episode of *NYPD Blue* showed the side of a woman's breast and a full view of her back before panning down to a shot of her buttocks for a few seconds. In December 2003, Nicole Richie used the words "shit" and "fucking" in her speech at the Billboard Music

CHAPTER 7

Awards: "Have you ever tried to get cow shit out of a Prada purse? It's not so fucking simple."

In 2004, while approximately ninety million people were tuned in to the Super Bowl halftime show, many Americans were disturbed when Janet Jackson's "wardrobe malfunction" exposed her breast. The FCC fined CBS a record $550,000, CBS fought the fine in the Supreme Court, and the case was remanded to the US Court of Appeals for the Third Circuit, which ruled against the fine. In 2010, the Supreme Court heard the case of *United States v. Stevens* involving three videos of pit bulls engaging in attacks against other animals, one of which depicted "a 'gruesome' scene of a pit bull attacking a domestic farm pig."[1] And, in 2015, the FCC fined Virginia television station WDBJ $325,000 when viewers complained about an image of "a naked, erect penis and sexual manipulation"[2] that was aired for three seconds in a small box on the side of a web page image during a news broadcast report on Tracy Rolan (also known by her porn star name, Harmony Rose), who became an EMT.

As these examples suggest, there has been no shortage of controversy concerning the types of "graphic" materials that confront Americans in daily life. The purpose of this chapter is to focus on the rhetoric of fears that are persistent in American life and have made their way into recent cases in the Roberts Court. Many of these fears have a long history in Western civilization. To investigate some of these fears, we have structured this chapter in five sections. In the first section, we highlight some of the significant fears throughout history regarding the regulation of indecent and graphic material. As in the last chapter, we include the contradictory fears of those who find sexual material indecent or obscene but have no objection to graphic violence. We then analyze three significant cases pertaining to indecent and graphic material that have made their way to the Roberts Court: *FCC v. Fox Television Stations*, the Child Online Protection Act cases, and *United States v. Stevens*. Finally, we offer a summary and concluding remarks.

FEAR IN THE HISTORY OF REGULATING
INDECENT AND GRAPHIC MATERIAL

There are many fears undergirding the concerns about graphic, indecent, and/or obscene material, though one of the most persistent fears is the "decline of civilization." This fear harkens back to early American history. For example, American laws pertaining to the regulation of indecency and obscenity have their roots in English law where "obscene speech tended to be prosecuted as a disturbance of the peace or 'public lewdness.' Written and pictorial materials thought to be obscene were prosecuted because of the belief, by legislatures and judges, that exposure to such materials tended to corrupt and debase the reader."[3] Obscenity, indecency, and profanity are legally distinct categories in American jurisprudence even as they are bound together by a "common sense of decency" concerning sexual and/or excremental "appropriateness." Generally speaking, obscenity refers to expression via *images* that refers to sexual and/or excretory functions, whereas indecency refers to expression via *words* that refer to sexual and/or excretory functions. Profanity more generally is associated with expression that is a "nuisance." In her comprehensive book on the history of swearing, Melissa Mohr noted that these types of expressive material are rooted in a "*fear* that civilization is a thin veneer, barely covering a state of chaos. We worry that this fragile membrane can be ripped apart by swearing, which violates so many dictates of polite, rational discourse and gives voice to so many unruly impulses."[4] This fear is coupled with other fears in significant cases on obscenity, indecency, and profanity.

Legally, indecency and obscenity have come to mean different though related things, "A thing may be 'indecent,' but not *obscene*. However, the reverse proposition is not true: all things obscene *are* indecent."[5] The first case to take up the question of whether obscenity was to be protected by the First Amendment was *Roth v. United States*. At issue in the case was the constitutionality of 18 U.S.C. § 1461, a provision that "makes punishable the mailing of material that is 'obscene, lewd, lascivious, or filthy . . . or other publication of an indecent character."[6] The Court upheld the obscenity laws, holding that "obscenity is not within the area of constitutionally protected freedom of speech or press either (1) under the First Amendment, as the Federal Government, or (2) under the Due Process Clause of the Fourteenth Amendment, as to the States."[7]

Fear was embedded in the rhetoric of both the opinion of the Court and Justice Harlan's dissent. Justice Brennan wrote the majority opinion in *Roth* and shared the fear that sex and obscenity may be treated synonymously to the detriment of speech and press about sex. Thus, he sought

CHAPTER 7

to clarify this distinction to work through the fear that obscenity statutes may inhibit the freedom of speech and press. He wrote, for example, "sex and obscenity are not synonymous. Obscene material is material which deals with sex in a manner appealing to prurient interest. The portrayal of sex, e.g., in art literature and scientific works, is not itself sufficient reason to deny material the constitutional protection of freedom of speech and press."[8] According to Justice Brennan, sex has "indisputably been a subject of absorbing interest to mankind through the ages; it is one of the vital problems of human interest and public concern."[9] Justice Brennan then explicitly referred to the fear of regulating speech and press about sex by citing *Thornhill v. Alabama*: "The freedom of speech and of the press guaranteed by the Constitution embraces at least the liberty to discuss publicly and truthfully *all matters of public concern* without previous restraint or *fear* of subsequent punishment."[10] In short, Justice Brennan reasoned that people ought not fear speaking about sex even though obscenity may be regulated as a distinct type of speech (that targets the prurient interest).

Justice Harlan did not agree with the opinion of the Court in *Roth*. His fear was that the ruling would essentially make it more difficult for the courts to effectively regulate the enforcement of obscenity. Justice Harlan expressed his concern as a fear: "The opinion paints with such a broad brush that I *fear* it may result in a loosening of the tight reins which the state and federal courts should hold upon the enforcement of obscenity statutes."[11] Justice Harlan's fear is directed toward what he believed to be decisions determined by a jury's judgment without consideration of constitutional reasoning. He explained, "Many juries might find that Joyce's 'Ulysses' or Bocaccio's 'Decameron' was obscene, and yet the conviction of a defendant for selling either book would raise, for me, the gravest constitutional problems, for no such verdict could convince me, without more, that these books are 'utterly without redeeming social importance.'"[12] Justice Harlan expressed being "very much afraid that the broad manner in which the Court has decided these cases will tend to obscure the peculiar responsibilities resting on state and federal courts," encouraging "them to rely on easy labeling and jury verdicts as a substitute for facing up to the tough individual problems of constitutional judgment involved in every obscenity case."[13] Thus, Justice Harlan did not believe that indecency regulation's First Amendment considerations

GRAPHIC SPEECH

would be meaningfully resolved in *Roth*. His belief would become manifest in the landmark case of *Miller v. California*.

In *Miller v. California*, Chief Justice Burger began the majority opinion with Justice Harlan's writing on obscenity, noting that *Miller* is "one of a group of 'obscenity-pornography' cases being reviewed by the Court in a reexamination of standards enunciated in earlier cases involving what Mr. Justice Harlan called 'the intractable obscenity problem.'"[14] The case pertained to Marvin Miller's mass mailing campaign to advertise the sale of "adult" illustrated books. When the manager of a restaurant and his mother opened an envelope containing brochures for four books titled "Intercourse," "Man-Woman," "Sex Orgies Illustrated," and "An Illustrated History of Pornography" and a film titled "Marital Intercourse," the recipients complained to the police. Miller was charged with a misdemeanor for violating California law, which prohibited knowingly distributing obscene matter. Miller challenged the misdemeanor charge, arguing that he had the First Amendment right to speech in the form of his mailers. The Supreme Court vacated and remanded the case while holding that obscene material is not protected by the First Amendment and establishing a three-prong test to guide the evaluation of what constitutes obscene speech: "(a) whether 'the average person, applying contemporary community standards' would find that the work, taken as a whole, appeals to the prurient interest, (b) whether the work depicts or describes, in a patently offensive way, sexual conduct specifically defined by the applicable state law, and (c) whether the work, taken as a whole, lacks serious literary, artistic, political, or scientific value."[15]

The most prevalent fear resulting from *Roth* and *Miller* is perhaps of chilling speech in light of the "contemporary community standards" clause of the test. This is especially the fear expressed by many concerning the regulation of obscenity on the Internet. For example, Ernest J. Walker explained that the standard "poses a unique difficulty when applied to the Internet. The problem stems from a question as to what the applicable community should be. In a conventional transaction, the speaker is aware of those communities into which the speech is distributed. However, when speech is distributed over the Internet, that speech potentially reaches all communities." He continued by explaining the fear of a chilling effect in applying *Miller's* community standard to the Internet, because on the Internet "the speaker would have to conform to the

155

CHAPTER 7

standards of the most restrictive community. This was not the intent of the 'contemporary community standard.' Such a result would likely cause a chilling effect because speakers on the Internet would be unwilling to speak for *fear* of prosecution."[16]

Prior to the Internet, however, the fear of chilling speech emerged in the regulation of indecent and profane speech in the context of national broadcasting. Most notably, the fear was manifest in the case of *Pacifica Radio Foundation v. Federal Communications Commission* (hereafter *Pacifica*). *Pacifica* involved the question of whether Pacifica Radio Foundation had a First Amendment right to broadcast George Carlin's satiric monologue titled "Filthy Words." A father complained to the FCC after hearing the broadcast while driving with his young son. The FCC issued a declaratory order granting the complaint (without formal sanctions) and included in the station's license file that if subsequent complaints were received, the FCC would decide whether it would utilize available sanctions. The station argued that the FCC's declaratory order violated its First Amendment right, and therefore, the note should not be attached to the station's license file. The Supreme Court ruled in favor of the FCC's ability to regulate indecent material in the broadcast medium. The Court reasoned that given the unique pervasiveness of public broadcasting in American homes, viewers may be subject to unwanted speech acts.[17] Scholars refer to this rationale as the "intrusion upon seclusion," "passive act of consumption," and "the surprise rationale."[18] Moreover, the Court ruled that because children may reasonably be in the audience during certain hours, the government has an interest in protecting children from indecent material, defined as "language that describes, in terms patently offensive as measured by contemporary community standards for the broadcast medium, sexual or excretory activities and organs, at times of the day when there is a reasonable risk that children may be in the audience."[19]

Pacifica argued in the case that *Miller* should not guide the FCC's regulatory power because broadcasts were not akin to mailed materials in mailboxes. The Court disagreed: "Pacifica's position would, of course, deprive the Commission of any power to regulate erotic telecasts unless they were obscene under *Miller v. California*. Anything that could be sold at a newsstand for private examination could be publicly displayed on television."[20] Thus, the Court reasoned that, although different

GRAPHIC SPEECH

in important ways, *Miller* was relevant to the regulation of speech in the broadcast realm.

Pacifica brought to the forefront a host of fears surrounding both indecent material and the overreach of governmental regulation of free speech. At the outset, fear of defeat became a factor for the FCC to consider in whether it would even challenge the lower court ruling to the Supreme Court: "Commission attorneys recommended against seeking Supreme Court review for *fear* of a further defeat."[21] However, the commissioners decided not to fear making an appeal—they "insisted on testing the extent of their authority to deal with indecent programming."[22] Historically, there was a guiding expressed fear that airwaves would be "used as 'a purveyor of smut and patent vulgarity' without controls."[23] At the same time, with the regulation of indecent material came the fear of the FCC's sanction and ill will and, by extension, a chilling of constitutionally protected speech. Even within the FCC itself, commissioners expressed the fear-provoking nature of the FCC's indecency policy: "Opposing a penalty issued by the FCC in *In re Application of Jack Straw Memorial Foundation,* Commissioner Cox found the indecency standard to be 'so indefinite [that it] is probably unconstitutionally vague.' . . . When the Commission bases its penalties upon such a vague indecency standard, 'licensees may avoid the use of many, many more words out of *fear* that they may be on the Commission's secret list.'"[24]

FCC V. FOX TELEVISION STATIONS

Pacifica would provide the foundation, many years later, for the cases of *FCC v. Fox Television Stations* I (2009) and II (2012). These cases concerned the issue of "fleeting expletives"—whether the FCC had the authority to regulate expletives that refer to sexual or excretory functions if they were *merely* broadcasted in a manner where speakers did not dwell on them. The distinction at issue was the perceived difference between George Carlin's monologue in *Pacific* and, for example, Bono's award acceptance speech that used the phrase "really fucking brilliant." In the former, Carlin's monologue used expletives in a sustained manner as the subject of the speech. In the latter, Bono said one expletive in passing while expressing excitement for winning an award. The Court's decision in both of these cases was, at the risk of oversimplification, to uphold the

CHAPTER 7

authority of the FCC to regulate indecent speech so long as it provides fair warning and presents a clear standard for regulating such content. At the same time, the Court largely agreed with the fact that the issue may be moot going forward since public broadcasting is mostly of limited significance in the contemporary landscape compared to private broadcasting with Internet streaming and private cable networks.[25]

Justice Breyer, in his dissent in *Fox I*, explained the impact of fear on smaller networks when it comes to the new FCC policy of regulating fleeting expletives. He noted that fear of substantial fines on smaller networks may cut back live broadcasting by those networks, "The result is that smaller stations, *fearing* 'fleeting expletive' fines of up to $325,000, may simply cut back on their coverage."[26] Justice Breyer shared the fear of possible elimination of live TV as a fundamental service that the smaller networks provide to localities: "'Afraid of taking chances' of getting fined under the FCC's new policy, 'local broadcasters are responding by altering—or halting altogether—the one asset that makes local stations so valuable to their communities: live TV.'"[27] Justice Breyer continued by sharing the words of one local station manager who chose to minimize risk based on the fear of crippling fines: "To lessen the risk posed by the new legal framework . . . I have directed [the station's] news staff that [our station] may no longer provide live, direct-to-air coverage' of 'live events where crowds are present. . . . Thus, news coverage by [my station] of live events . . . will be limited to civil emergencies.'"[28] Justice Breyer reasoned that the fear of censoring live events was justified because the FCC said nothing about these kinds of consequences: "What did the FCC say in response to this claim? What did it say about the likely impact of the new policy on the coverage that its new policy is most likely to affect, coverage of *local* live events—city council meetings, local sports events, community arts productions, and the like? It said nothing at all."[29] Thus, for Justice Breyer, the fear of broadcaster censorship in the wake of the FCC regulation of fleeting expletives was reason enough to dissent in this case.

The fear of penalty is not limited to local broadcasters and to fines but extends also to monetary liability. Even larger networks feared a "Forfeiture Penalty," which could mean losing their broadcasting license. Courtney Livingston Quale explained, "Today, broadcasting networks such as the American Broadcasting Company ('ABC'), the network formerly

158

GRAPHIC SPEECH

known as Columbia Broadcasting System ('CBS'), the National Broadcasting Company ('NBC'), the Fox Broadcasting Company ('FOX'), and the Public Broadcasting Service ('PBS'), live in constant *fear* that they will be assessed a Forfeiture Penalty, a monetary fine imposed by the FCC for failing to meet the Commission's broadcasting standards."[30] Quale continued, "These broadcasters' *fears* are real because recently the Commission has been overturning FCC precedent and more aggressively assessing Forfeiture Penalties and issuing Notices of Apparent Liability ('NAL') against broadcasters."[31]

These fears are manifest in tangible forms of prior restraint where networks have chosen to stay away from even newsworthy programming (chilled speech) because of their fear of fines. For example, CBS affiliates refused to rebroadcast *9/11—A Documentary* because of this fear: "The chill in the airwaves is unmistakable, and the viewing public is the big loser. The most recent example involves dozens of CBS affiliates who refused to rebroadcast the documentary '9/11' for *fear* they would be fined for the coarse words uttered by rescuers."[32] Jim Dyke, executive director of TV Watch, wrote a letter to the FCC, documenting in his "Exhibit A" at least sixteen other actual instances where broadcasts were chilled, including even shows like PBS's *Antiques Roadshow* that featured famous lithographs of Marilyn Monroe and illustrations of the female form in artwork from World War II bombers.[33]

The chilling of speech is rooted in more than the fear of penalties and liabilities. The chilling of speech is also rooted in the fear of paying legal fees associated with even the possibility of facing accusations and charges. The ACLU argued in its amici curiae supporting respondents brief that when faced with the choice between possibly being put out of business as a result of legal fees and proactively censoring questionable indecent programming, stations will choose the latter.[34] As Sarah Herman noted, "Self censorship is further induced by the related fear of having to pay for any consequential legal fees needed to respond to FCC investigations."[35] Thus, taken together, the fear of penalties, liabilities, legal fees, and going out of business based on those costs function collectively to chill the speech of the broadcasters.

The impetus for the FCC to become involved in the first place in terms of regulating content like Janet Jackson's "wardrobe malfunction" during the halftime show is rooted in "moral panics" that cultivate fears.

159

CHAPTER 7

Clay Calvert reviewed much of the literature on moral panics as it relates to FCC regulations. Drawing on the work of Stanley Cohen, Erich Goode and Nachman Ben-Yehuda, Shahira Fahmy and Thomas Johnson, and Tom Morton and Eurydice Aroney, Calvert explained, "Moral panics are 'over-heated periods of intense concern.' They arise when many people harbor 'intense feelings of concern about a given threat which a sober assessment of the evidence suggests is either nonexistent or considerably less than would be expected from the concrete harm posed by the threat.'"[36] According to Calvert, there are three factors that may coalesce to produce a response from the legal system: (1) "the media generally play a role in fanning the flames of fright, be it intentionally or otherwise," (2) key players, such as the moral crusades of interest groups (e.g., professional associations, the police, parent organizations), draw public attention to, and curtail, a specific set of actions, and (3) these responses often emanate from a key event.[37] Moral panics are closely related to the fear of concrete harms, like moral crusades against indecent speech for fear of cultivating a rise in teenage pregnancies, sexually transmitted diseases, or sinful behavior. This idea is perhaps why, "more than any variety of media content, it is sexual expression that launches moral panics in the United States."[38]

Importantly, the fears leading to the regulation of the public media landscape have resulted in a significant shift away from the dominance of a publicly owned media infrastructure to a mostly privately owned communication infrastructure, such as cable television or streaming. Rather than hassle with public regulations, entertainers merely shift their attention to the private sphere, where they often experience even more commercial success than they would on public channels of communication. As Justice Alito noted in oral arguments, "Well, broadcast TV is living on borrowed time. It is not going to be long before it goes the way of vinyl records and 8 track tapes."[39] Howard Stern may agree, since he has found a much more lucrative career on private broadcasting airwaves than he ever did on public broadcasting. His last contract for public broadcasting was a five-year, $10 million deal. He became the FCC's number one target for fines, $2.5 million in total. He then signed a private contract with SiriusXM worth $500 million and now has an estimated net economic worth of $650 million. Perhaps this is a case wherein the fears of those concerned with regulating indecency contribute to economic demand in the private market.

GRAPHIC SPEECH

ASHCROFT V. AMERICAN CIVIL LIBERTIES UNION

In *Fox I*, Justice Thomas noted the transformation from the dominance of public broadcasting to that of cable and the Internet: "Traditional broadcast television and radio are no longer the 'uniquely pervasive' media forms they once were. For most consumers, traditional broadcast media programming is now bundled with cable or satellite services. . . . Broadcast and other video programming is also widely available over the Internet."[40] With the rise of broadcasting on the Internet, Congress passed the Child Online Protection Act (COPA) of 1998 to protect children from exposure to obscene material. COPA, however, drew on the language of *Miller v. California*'s obscenity standard, and the Court ruled in 2002 that when it comes to the Internet, COPA was unconstitutional because it was not narrowly tailored to advance the government interest on at least three grounds: (1) obscene speech is already unprotected and the interest may be met with existing obscenity standards; (2) there were no technological means for senders to prevent minors from accessing materials while making protected material available for adults (including international web companies that evade US regulation); and (3) there were other means available on the recipient's (i.e., parent's) end to block children from accessing obscene material on the Internet. The Court affirmed the injunction, remanded the case to the Third Circuit, and then granted certiorari again in 2004 and reaffirmed the original preliminary injunction remanded to the lower courts, which held again that COPA was unconstitutional. The case was appealed a third time, but the Court denied certiorari and terminated COPA without it ever having gone into effect.

From COPA's inception to its end, debates about COPA highlighted many fears. The fear giving rise to the legislative adoption of COPA was rooted in what the pornographic material would do to minors and in parents' inability to prevent children from accessing obscene material while searching the Internet. For example, Laith Paul Alsarraf, testifying before the House Subcommittee on Telecommunications, Trade, and Consumer Protection leading up to COPA's adoption, explained, "This bill will provide to parents a degree of assurance that their children can surf the net without *fear* that they will be exposed to harmful or indecent materials."[41] Peter Nickerson testified about the need for filtering Internet material on the receiver's end based on the fear of exposing kids to

161

CHAPTER 7

inappropriate material in schools. His objective was to "provide schools with a suite of Internet services that allow [school administrators] to fully utilize the educational opportunity of the Internet, without *fear* of exposing students to inappropriate material."[42] Taken together, many proponents of COPA expressed parents' fears that no matter what they did, without governmental regulation, children would be exposed to obscene material while surfing the web.

Another fear expressed in the preliminary hearings was that if website providers were liable under COPA, then they may be incentivized to require credit card information as a safeguard, which would increase the likelihood of credit card information falling into the wrong hands. Aside from the fact that many kids can simply gain access to their parent's credit cards, participants in the COPA hearings expressed the fear that such requirements would lead to illicit activity and even more credit card fraud. Lawrence Lessig stated, "There are many people who are obsessed with their *fear* of putting credit cards on the Internet. I think they are exaggerating things. But, Mr. Chairman, I think the last people in the world that we should require individuals to turn their credit card numbers over to before they get access to speech that is protected are online pornographers."[43] Thus, opponents of COPA expressed the fear that credit cards would become the normalized means of regulating material that may be inappropriate for children and that such a norm would proliferate fraud and criminal activity.

Moreover, there was the fear of chilled speech, resulting from those who generate web content erring on the side of self-censoring their constitutionally protected speech rather than risking different interpretations under COPA. For example, Judge Reed of the US District Court of Eastern Pennsylvania wrote in his ruling against COPA, "The plaintiffs have persuaded me that at least with respect to some plaintiffs, their *fears* of prosecution under COPA will result in self-censorship of their online materials in an effort to avoid prosecution. This chilling effect will result in the censoring of constitutionally protected speech, which constitutes an irreparable harm to plaintiffs."[44] Thus, we find the same theme here as we found in *Fox I and II*—the conflict between the fear of chilling valuable speech for adult citizens and the more intense fear that protecting that speech will expose children to material that crosses the line into the obscene.

162

GRAPHIC SPEECH

Judge Reed had been persuaded by the chilling argument based on the fear of liability for several reasons. Johanna Roodenburg explains that the plaintiffs "asserted six reasons for *fearing* liability under COPA."[45] She breaks these reasons down as follows: (1) "information present on their Web sites may violate the 'harmful to minors' standard in some communities"; (2) "the plaintiffs *feared* civil liability under the COPA because a federal prosecutor anywhere in the country could seek civil penalties simply by filing a complaint" and the civil standard is lower than the criminal standard; (3) "the plaintiffs *feared* liability for materials created by others but available on the plaintiffs' Web sites" as the language of "knowingly solicits . . . materials" does not require authorship; (4) COPA contains unclear language, leading to confusion over "the relevant 'community' for what is 'harmful to minors' on the global Internet"; (5) "the affirmative defenses provided in the COPA are technologically and economically unavailable to them"; and (6) "because the currently available age verification methods are technologically and economically unattainable by the plaintiffs, the plaintiffs have no way to take advantage of the affirmative defenses supplied by COPA."[46] Thus, "because of these reasons, there were two alternatives for the plaintiffs: risk prosecution or civil penalties under the COPA or engage in self-censorship and thereby deny adults and minors access to constitutionally protected material."[47]

Related to the fear of liability is the fear that the least tolerant community will end up being the judge of whether material is obscene or valuable; this is reminiscent of giving book burners in one community the authority to burn another community's books of choice. In other words, according to this fear, the danger of leaving COPA in the hands of a community standard is that while the Internet exists as a global and national network, restricting content at the source would privilege the most restrictive community over the least restrictive community. Kristin Ringeisen highlights part of Justice Stevens's rationale when she argues, "because the web publisher cannot control where his materials reach it is excessively restrictive to confine him to the community standards that any particular community holds. . . . The Justice *fears* that standards will be determined by the least tolerant community and, therefore, what is available for viewing will be that which is suitable to that community."[48] For example, whereas Justice Breyer reasons that the Kenneth Starr report online would not be liable under COPA, Justice Stevens fears that

163

CHAPTER 7

leaving it up to the least tolerant group may result in a community standard that views the material as not suitable for children, obscene, and the poster of the material as liable.

Taken together, the fears surrounding COPA and the *Ashcroft v. American Civil Liberties Union* case extend many of the concerns expressed in *Fox I* and *II*. Namely, there is a tension between the fear of exposing children to obscene or indecent material and the fear that limiting this exposure will also limit the political speech and exposure to questionable content that is often required for the populace to participate fully informed in democratic shared governance. Moreover, the tension exists between whether the responsibility should lie with the sender of messages or with the receiver of those messages, who may or may not have access to technology that works to filter material they may or may not want to receive.

UNITED STATES V. STEVENS

The tension between chilled speech and exposure to obscene material (and criminal acts that may result from such exposure) is also relevant to the case of *United States v. Stevens*. Robert Stevens ran Dogs of Velvet and Steel, a business with a website that sold videos of pit bulls engaging in dogfights and attacking other animals. He was convicted under a federal statute that criminalized "the commercial creation, sale, or possession of certain depictions of animal cruelty. The statute does not address underlying acts harmful to animals, but only portrayals of such conduct."[49] The statute defines "animal cruelty" as occurring when "a living animal is intentionally maimed, mutilated, tortured, wounded, or killed," if the "conduct violates federal or state law where 'the creation, sale, or possession takes places.'"[50] The code exempts depictions of animal cruelty that have "serious religious, political, scientific, educational, journalistic, historical, or artistic value."[51]

The Court reversed Stevens's conviction on the basis that the criminal statute was overly broad in terms of its potential application to protected First Amendment speech. At the risk of oversimplification, we focus on two central arguments: (1) the "depiction" of animal cruelty did not require that cruelty to animals actually took place (and if the cruelty was criminal, then the cruelty itself could be prosecuted; hence, there already

164

GRAPHIC SPEECH

existed a mechanism for convicting people for actual crimes against animals) and (2) defining depictions of cruelty based on local standards in federal law means that owners could commit a crime by creating material that is legal in one area of the country but is then distributed in areas of the country where it is not legal (because the "creation" of the material, regardless of where that creation occurred, is criminal under the code). For example, a hunter may create a video and sell it in Montana where hunting is legal, but if it appears in the District of Columbia where hunting is illegal, the hunter may be found guilty even though she or he created it legally in the first place. There were other reasons the Court gave for ruling in favor of Stevens, but the important point for our purposes is that there were also many fears surrounding this controversial case.

One of the fears that gives rise to the popularity of dogfight videos, including the ones Robert Stevens sold, is the fear of prosecution for attending a dogfight in person. Justice Alito explained in his dissent that many dogfights are held specifically to create the videos due to the dangers of live dogfights. He explained, "some dogfighting videos are made 'solely for the purpose of selling the video (and not for a live audience.)' In addition, those who stage dogfights profit not just from the sale of the videos themselves, but from the gambling revenue they take in from the fights; the videos 'encourage [such] gambling activity because they allow those reluctant to attend actual fights for *fear* of prosecution to still bet on the outcome.'"[52] In other words, according to Justice Alito, fear of prosecution for attending dogfights bolstered the dogfight video market, and thus the need to regulate the video market was essential to curbing dogfighting itself (which is illegal in all fifty states and the District of Columbia). Restricting the dogfight video market was critical to restricting dogfights.

The criminal law under which Stevens was convicted occurred in the context of a legislative history that intended to punish animal crush videos. Chief Justice Roberts noted, "The legislative background of §48 focused primarily on the interstate market for 'crush videos.'"[53] He continued, "such videos feature the intentional torture and killing of helpless animals, including cats, dogs, monkeys, mice, and hamsters. Crush videos often depict women slowly crushing animals to death 'with their bare feet or while wearing high heeled shoes,' sometimes while 'talking to the animals in a kind of dominatrix patter' over the 'cries and squeals of

165

CHAPTER 7

the animals, obviously in great pain.'"[54] In his testimony before the Senate Judiciary Committee hearing on "Prohibiting Obscene Animal Crush Videos in the Wake of United States v. Stevens," Kevin Volkan explained, "Paraphilias and fetishes (which are often not well-differentiated in the psychological literature) have been described as far back as the turn of the century as the association of something pleasurable (usually sexual) with some object other than a whole human.... Freud associated fetishes with the *fear* produced by the castration anxiety of the Oedipal complex. In this conception using the fetish object for sexual gratification was safe."[55] Thus, the idea of animal crush videos as rooted in fear made its way into the Senate testimony over the decision in *United States v. Stevens*.

In response to the *Stevens* decision, the legislature expressed an array of fears while advocating for a more narrowly tailored version of the unconstitutional law. For example, because of the rapid growth in the number of users of the Internet between the original legislation in 1998 and the Supreme Court overturning it in 2010, there was a fear that animal cruelty videos would be more widespread than ever before. For example, after explaining that the Court overturned §48, Senator Gary Peters (D-MI) argued, "Over a decade after §48's enactment, with far more internet users than there were during the 1990s, I fear that these unconscionable videos could become even more widespread than before if new legislation is not passed to stop the creation and distribution of depictions of these heinous acts."[56] Without regulation, and with increased users, the senator and others feared the widespread presence of the animal cruelty videos.

One of the more nuanced fears expressed in the attempt to regulate depictions of animal cruelty involves the human identification and empathy with the fear of animals. In other words, the presumed fear that animals experience is shared by the humans who seek to protect them. This fear, for example, was expressed in the account shared by Officer Paul LeBaron of the Long Beach Police Department, who described to Congress the content of a video in which a small guinea pig's "paws are being bound down by wires, that are pulling tightly in four opposite directions. The animal occasionally squeals, and squeaks, possibly from *fear*, possibly from pain."[57] The fear that attends identifying with both the fear and the pain that an animal suffers during the acts of cruelty featured in the video involves a transference of the emotional energy. As sentient beings,

166

GRAPHIC SPEECH

humans fear for the animals' lives because, in part, they imagine what it would be like to be subject to the same kind of treatment.

Perhaps a tangential fear informing the arguments that favor banning animal cruelty videos is that if such videos were to become commonplace, they could threaten the animal agricultural industry. In short, the agricultural industry fears backlash should the public view audio and video of slaughterhouses. As Gabriela Wolfe explained, industrial animal agriculture is a "system that revolves around high-speed, systematic killing of living beings," and "if the public were given audio and visual access to slaughterhouse activities, it may, as the industry *fears*, prompt demands for a radical shift in the way the industry operates."[58] Thus, there is a host of legislation adopted, and advocated by the agriculture industry, to target food libel.

Much of this legislation became popularized by an *Oprah Winfrey Show* episode that showed the dangers of mad cow disease. The Texas Beef Group sued Oprah Winfrey and former cattle rancher turned critic Howard Lyman, alleging the show violated Texas's False Disparagement of Perishable Food Products Act of 1995. The jury found that Winfrey and Lyman did not engage in libelous speech, even though fear may potentially play a role in fending off critics—Winfrey no longer speaks about mad cow disease in public and declines to make the original interview available to journalists.[59] The food disparagement laws "grew out of a 1989 CBS-TV '60 Minutes' report on Alar and its use on apples, which gave rise to the Alar litigation."[60] Thirteen states have passed food disparagement legislation to quell the agriculture industry's fears about false reports from the media that may kill their economic market.

Of course, when it comes to *United States v. Stevens*, critics of the decision note that exceptions built into §48 could have allowed for some material to be published and distributed if it met the act's requirement to protect "any depiction that has serious religious, political, scientific, educational, journalistic, historical, or artistic value." In other words, such critics contend the Court could have punished material like crush videos that §48 intended to target while also continuing to protect videos like Oprah Winfrey's coverage of mad cow disease and hunting videos. In reviewing the Court's interpretations of §48, Harold Anthony Lloyd notes that the legislative history easily provided the interpretive power to make it "indisputable at this point that §48 addresses cruelty and not,

167

CHAPTER 7

for example, the humane slaughter of a cow"; however, the Court was reluctant to leave it up to a jury to decide whether a "slaughter" could be "humane," even though the constitutionality of legislative history could trump any jury decision. He continued by noting that hunting videos could easily have been defined by the Court as distinct from dogfighting and crush fetish videos because, "remembering that meaning includes both intended and perceived meaning, hunting videos can easily be intended to fall in every exception category. Those who believe in gun and hunting rights could see hunting videos as valuable political statements. Those who study hunting methods or enjoy hunting could see videos as having scientific and educational value. Those who report on hunting or hunting videos could find them to have journalistic value."[61]

The Court's fears on this front, however, are that §48 does not allow for a mechanism to discriminate between the depicted acts of cruelty and that juries (and lower courts) may not have a mechanism to prevent §48 from being either completely ineffective (because dogfighting videos and crush videos may use a similar defense) or used to restrict the hunting videos. The Court can imagine, for example, dogfighting video producers making similar arguments. For example, they could argue that their intent is to make a political statement based on their belief in dogfighting rights. Those who study dogfighting methods or enjoy dogfighting could see the videos as having scientific and educational value. Those who report on dogfighting videos could find them to have journalistic value, and so on. In other words, hunting involves killing animals. Dogfighting involves killing animals. At base, the videos seek to define the act of killing, and such definition is a rhetorical act, contingently defined by humans who struggle to define killing as kind/cruel. Thus, the Court ruled to keep the power of interpretation out of the hands of juries unless Congress could more narrowly tailor the law to protect First Amendment rights.

CONCLUSION

As the preceding cases and controversies suggest, Americans continue to struggle through a variety of fears based on sexual, excretory, or otherwise graphic material that is shared in public spaces. These fears have existed throughout history. The fears range from the influence of such material on children's psyche and behaviors, the fear of the "decline of

GRAPHIC SPEECH

civilization," the fear of chilling valuable speech as a cost of regulating graphic speech, and the fear of economic consequences of a given legislative restriction and/or lawsuits to the fear at heart in the creation of moral panics, the fear of parental failure, the fear of crimes such as credit card fraud and identity theft, the fears that may give rise to particular fetishes, and the fear of animal cruelty. Taken together, these fears are manifest in the rhetorical process whereby humans attempt to create laws that are general enough to apply to a number of specific cases while also not being so specific that crimes are allowed be committed in the service of protecting speech.

We have made a number of important observations in undertaking our research for this chapter. In studying fears surrounding obscene, indecent, and/or graphic speech, we found several iterations of the relationship between threatening communication and the First Amendment. For example, the Roberts Court has cited *Virginia v. Black* on a number of occasions. In *Virginia v. Black*, a case involving whether a cross-burning ordinance was constitutionally protected, Justice Thomas (who said almost nothing during oral arguments between 1995 and 2002) spoke out to note, "Now, it's my understanding that we had almost 100 years of lynching and activity in the South by the Knights of Camellia [*sic*] and the Ku Klux Klan, and this was a reign of terror, and the cross was a symbol of that reign of terror."[62] He continued, "My fear is . . . that you're actually understating the symbolism" and "there was no other purpose to the cross. There was no communication of a particular message. It was intended to cause fear and to terrorize a population."[63] As grounded in the history of violence by the Ku Klux Klan and other groups that have committed acts of racist violence, this type of speech exploits the reality, according to John C. Knechtle, "that minority groups may have more legitimate fears of violence being perpetrated upon them than the majority does, particularly if there is a history of injuries being inflicted by the dominant racial, religious or ethnic group."[64] As Justice Thomas noted, there is a symbolic quality to such speech that is meant to instill fear in a population.

Sometimes the speech intended to cause fear becomes directed at particular people, as is the case with threats against people in domestic disputes. This was precisely the issue in *Elonis v. United States*. After his wife left him, Anthony Douglas Elonis "under the pseudonym 'Tone

169

CHAPTER 7

Dougie,' used the social networking website Facebook to post self-styled rap lyrics containing graphically violent language and imagery concerning his wife, co-workers, a kindergarten class, and state and federal law enforcement."[65] Although Elonis claimed he was expressing himself artistically, "many who knew him saw his posts as threatening" including "his boss, who fired him for threatening co-workers, and his wife, who sought and was granted a state protection-from-abuse order against him."[66] Elonis was convicted on four of five counts of a federal crime for transmitting in interstate commerce a threat to injure another person, violating 18 U.S.C. Sec. 875 (c), which prohibits transmitting in interstate commerce "any communication containing any threat . . . to injure the person of another." At the trial, Elonis's lawyer requested that the jury be instructed that the prosecution had the burden of proving that Elonis's communication constituted a "true threat." However, the court instead instructed the jury that all that was required was that the threat be *perceived* as true. While the Court ruled in favor of Elonis on a jury instruction question, the remand of the case resulted in his conviction. Thus, the law continues to be in force regarding threatening speech in interstate commerce.

What may be common ground on this front is that it is a moral wrong to direct speech at people with the intention to invoke fear as a consequence of that symbolic speech act. The extent to which people express emotions such as fear, anger, and rage, and the extent to which that speech crosses the line into invoking fear in others, is simultaneously clear and unclear. It is clearer when the Ku Klux Klan burns a cross in a person of color's front yard and less clear when a rapper in an artistic setting produces a song lyric about "wanting to" commit a violent act against a person. Specifically, in *Elonis*, the Court laid out the dialectic, namely, "whether, consistent with First Amendment and *Virginia v. Black*, 538 U.S. 343 (2003), conviction of threatening another person requires proof of the defendant's subjective intent to threaten, as required by the Ninth Circuit and the supreme courts of Massachusetts, Rhode Island, and Vermont; or whether it is enough to show that a 'reasonable person' would regard the statement as threatening, as held by other federal courts of appeals and state courts of last resort."[67]

Justice Alito reasoned in Elonis's case that he could not claim to be a rapper on social media because, "Statements on social media that are pointedly directed at their victims, by contrast, are much more likely to

GRAPHIC SPEECH

be taken seriously," whereas "'taken in context,' lyrics in songs that are performed for an audience or sold in recorded form are unlikely to be interpreted as a real threat to a real person."[68] So, according to Justice Alito's reasoning, Elonis was more likely to be threatening than the rapper Eminem because of the medium of communication and the marketability.

The fears in play here run between the possibility of restricting satiric or humorous expression and the possibility of a true threat to do violence to a specific person. Thus, *Elonis* fits into a line of cases ranging back to *Brandenburg v. Ohio*, which held that only threats that were aimed at a specific person at an imminent specific time and were capable of being carried out were prohibitable.[69] The Supreme Court updated that ruling in *Virginia v. Black*, a cross-burning case that examined the issue of perception.[70] Virginia law prohibited the burning of crosses as a symbolic true threat to African Americans. However, the Supreme Court ruled that the law blurred the distinction between the right to express an opinion and the presentation of a true threat. Since the cross was burned on private property owned by the cross burner, his right to expression was paramount. The Court ruled that true threats include "statements where the speaker means to communicate a serious expression of an intent to commit an act of unlawful violence to a particular individual or group of individuals."[71]

As we have shown, the majority did show restraint in *Snyder* and *Fox Television Stations* but did not in *Brown* or *Citizens United*. Roberts concluded that Elonis's conviction was premised solely on how his posts would be viewed by a reasonable person, a standard feature of civil liability in tort law that is inconsistent with the conventional criminal conduct requirement of "awareness of some wrongdoing."[72] Thus, the Court avoided clarifying the difference between objective and subjective intent, and whether the media in question, cyberspace and rap, were to be included in the calculus of the case. In his dissent, Justice Alito claimed that this dodge was "certain to cause confusion and serious problems."[73]

At the same time that it ruled on *Elonis*, the Supreme Court issued *Walker v. Texas Division, Sons of Confederate Veterans*, concerning vanity license plates that would have contained a Confederate battle flag.[74] Justice Alito's dissent set out the grounds for the decision on both sides of the aisle. Quoting from *Pleasant Grove City v. Summum*, Alito argued that "the Free Speech clause restricts government regulation of private

CHAPTER 7

speech; it does not regulate government speech."[75] Alito then argued that the license plates were private speech and, therefore, protected by the First Amendment. However, Justice Thomas crossed over to form a majority with the four liberal justices who ruled that the license plates were instances of government speech and, therefore, not protected. Texas could control the content of what appeared on specialty license plates. This was a clear constriction of First Amendment rights, quite consistent with the Supreme Court's past reliance on judicial restraint, this time in favor of a state's right to control the content of speech.

In each of these cases, the First Amendment problem, of course, is how to best create rules to prevent governments from fining and/or imprisoning people for reasons opposite of the intended effect. This is the crux of many of the difficulties in labeling some speech as "hate speech" and regulating speech on that basis. For example, advocates of regulating hate speech in France were traditionally aligned with their ideologically left-wing parties. The law in France prescribes imprisonment or a fine of up to $50,000 for parties that "provoke discrimination, hatred or violence toward a person or group of people on the grounds of their origin, their belonging or their not belonging to an ethnic group, a nation, a race or a certain religion."[76] Even though perhaps well intentioned, the law must be interpreted by people, and thus, the law that was advocated by France's left was used to convict leftist activists who arrived at a supermarket wearing shirts with the words "Long live Palestine, boycott Israel" and handing out fliers saying that "buying Israeli products means legitimizing crimes in Gaza."[77] Thus far, therefore, the First Amendment errs on the side of protecting much speech that may be considered *by some* to be hateful, obscene, indecent, graphic, or otherwise offensive. Erring on that side is an attempt to prevent juries from prosecuting people based on their subjective interpretations of "community standards," and other standards, so that activists in American of all ideologies may not fear political persecution by consequence of laws like those passed in France (that may be well intentioned).

There are at least two other findings that emerged from our research on fear and the Roberts Court when it comes to obscene, indecent, and graphic speech. First, we found that invective rhetoric has a long history in the United States as a political type of rhetoric. Invective rhetoric is defined as "a railing speech or expression" that "proceeds from an

172

GRAPHIC SPEECH

enemy, and is intended to give pain or to injure."[78] For example, on the campaign trail in Colorado, vice presidential nominee Sarah Palin told crowds that Obama was "palling around with terrorists," to which the crowd responded by yelling, "Kill him," "Traitor," "Terrorist," "Treason," "Liar," and "Off with his head."[79] According to Jeremy Engels, this kind of rhetoric could very well be "constitutive of community itself—that an imagined community is made real, if only for a moment, by the collective act of denunciation."[80] The problem is that such rhetoric may function either to further democratic leveling or, conversely, in the service of authority. Engels notes, on the one hand, that invective "can take the shine off our heroes, bringing them down to the level of the people."[81] In this manner, "invective was central to the formative years of American democracy because it was potentially open to anyone and everyone."[82] On the other hand, Engels advises, "we should not miss the chance to understand how invective acted as an instrument of authority. In democratic culture, persuasion is power."[83] When a leader draws on invective as a rhetorical strategy, they may further their interests in maintaining their authority (e.g., Palin, a multimillionaire, becomes "one of the people").

Thus, whether invective rhetoric comes with expletives, threats, or graphic communication, it has played a historical role in American politics from at least 1826 (as Engels observes) into the twenty-first century. Drawing on the lessons of invective as constitutive of community, we might conclude that indecency functions in a similar manner. In any case, if cursing and invective can be constitutive of community, then it can always already function politically, and thus indecency regulation itself is called into question. In other words, when Bono says the Golden Globe Award is "really fucking brilliant," he not only uses an expletive but also communicates his part in a community of rock 'n' roll stars who engage in that kind of communication, and hence it signifies his being part of the community that engages in, for example, the politics of rock 'n' roll.

Finally, through our research into the Roberts Court cases in this chapter, we also found research about catharsis and other positive effects that have the potential to disrupt censorship rationales that are rooted in fear. A host of research indicates a possible cathartic effect of participating in the consumption or deployment of indecent, obscene, and graphic speech. That is, communicating in indecent, obscene, or graphic ways may prevent people from acting out the content in real life. For example,

173

CHAPTER 7

a study of traffic situations indicated that "swearing is a type of verbal aggression and possible way to cope with anger."[84] Furthermore, recent evidence suggests that "social and physical pain are functionally similar and that swearing attenuates social pain."[85] And, of course, there is evidence that such material may function as both a stimulation to action and catharsis depending on the content *and* the person.[86] In the end, these complications make it difficult to discern where to draw lines when it comes to the First Amendment. Two things, however, are relatively clear—such lines will continue to involve a rhetorical contest over the interpretive aspects of what constitutes indecent, obscene, and graphic communication that is worthy of censorship. And fears surrounding indecent, obscene, and graphic speech are likely to endure.

8

Themes and Implications of Fear and the First Amendment

Plato tell us that when the gods created humans, they inculcated their souls with "fear" among other emotions.[1] Plato's most famous pupil, Aristotle, presented a much more pragmatic analysis of the emotions in his book *On Rhetoric*. He established various polarities in each emotional state. For example, he claims that anger and calm are on opposite ends of the same continuum and therefore one cannot be angry and calm at the same time. He pairs fear with confidence, arguing that one can't be fearful and confident at the same time. He then explores the causes of fear to help speakers build appeals to that emotion and move their audiences by channeling the fear of something into a call for action to relieve their fear. Causes of fear include such things as pain, death, loss, the unknown, or being overpowered. These causes then need to be brought closer to the audience in terms of space and time if the appeal is to be effective. An audience member is much more fearful of a bear at the door than a bear in the woods.

Frans de Waal built on Aristotle's analysis to argue that emotions such as fear serve as building blocks for our moral structures.[2] These emotions are also organized into systems to alert us to various things. The fear system alerts us to approaching danger. Many recent studies have taken this analysis a step further, which may help with our analysis

CHAPTER 8

of patterns of the appearance of fears in the Supreme Court's decision-making. These new studies argue that liberals and conservatives have genetic differences, "most of them related to neurotransmitter functioning, particularly glutamate and serotonin, both of which are involved in the brain's response to threat and fear."[3] Thus, it is entirely possible that conservative and liberal justices reach different conclusions because they react differently to fear on a genetic level.

In the various cases we have examined in this study, fears of various intensities often motivated the justices, and the justices often invoked fear of various intensities to persuade their audiences to their point of view. They also used proxemics to bring their fears closer to their audiences in an attempt to persuade them. For example, in the case we examined on prohibiting the sale of video games to minors, Justice Alito feared that new forms of the video games may be more violence-inducing than prior forms. To bring this fear close to his audience, he cited examples of interactive video games that provide physical sensations to match the action on the computer screen, including the wearing of a vest that feels like it is being hit with bullets. Justice Breyer used the same fear in his dissent and brought it close to his audience by arguing that "extremely violent games can harm children by rewarding them for being violently aggressive in play."[4] He also accepted a good deal more of the social scientific and medical data presented by the state of California to intensify the fear of creating violent children.

One caveat to the use of appeals to fear should be considered. Sometimes justices, like any other persuaders, use appeals to fear to buttress their opinions when in fact they do not themselves suffer from that fear. Does a justice really believe that censoring video games for teenagers will have a chilling effect on his or her own speech? Or is the invocation of this fear a way of appealing to a broader audience? Does a justice really believe that allowing students to hold up a nonsensical sign will enhance students' free speech rights? Or is this argument a way of making his or her ruling more appealing? Because we can't get into the mind of a justice, we have chosen in this study to take them at their word. However, it would be unrealistic to think that in every case the reaction to fear appeals or the invocation of fear appeals are consistent with deeply held motives. We leave it to the free marketplace of ideas and the dialogues among Supreme Court justices to produce as authentic an opinion as

IMPLICATIONS OF FEAR

possible. That is why their speech along with ours is protected. Other scholars have supported this view.

In 1963, Thomas Emerson provided a rationale for protecting speech. If free speech facilitated the discovery of the truth, educated the public so that our democracy could function properly, and/or allowed for self-discovery and creativity, then that speech should be given full protection under the Constitution.[5] From political leaders such as James Madison and Thomas Jefferson to jurists such as Emerson and Oliver Wendell Holmes, there has always been a fear that the government will encroach on speech in such a way as to prevent these goals. Many governments before and after our founding have hampered the search for truth, fearing it would undermine their credibility. They fear an educated public because it might seek reforms that take power from the leadership. They fear self-discovery because it leads to empowerment, and empowerment can lead to revolution. They fear creativity because it inspires spirituality, which can also lead to revolutions against powerful material interests.

Thus, a dialectic operates between the fear of loss of freedoms and the fear of what those freedoms might to do those in power, those holding majority opinions, or those with dogmatic beliefs. In a way, this provokes a fear of democracy, because a majority may overcome a minority or democracy may breed demagogues. Jeremy Engels addresses with this problem when he writes:

> The fear of democracy, Benjamin Barber observes, is "as old as political thought itself," and it was deeply engrained in the United States. While radical pamphleteers including Thomas Paine argued for a more democratic government in the 1770s, democracy was unthinkable for much of the early republic and thus the Founders did what they could to tame, discipline, and transform the democratic urges of the Revolutionary War into something more stable and hierarchical. The French Revolution taught many Americans that democracy was synonymous with guillotines and blood running through the streets. In 1814, [John] Adams, who was profoundly skeptical about the possibilities of popular government, mused, "Democracy never lasts long. It soon wastes, exhausts, and murders itself. There never was a democracy yet that did not commit suicide."[6]

CHAPTER 8

Luckily, we do not live in a brutal democracy, though at certain moments in our history it may appear that we do; however, the dialectic of fears emerges in many of our contestations, including the attack on the Capitol in 2021. As we have seen in the cases examined here, national security often trumps freedom of expression in times of crisis. Laws that restrict the distribution of obscene or indecent materials trump creativity. The need to maintain a learning environment trumps the right of students to speak out, even while they are off school property. On the other side of the dialectic, we have also seen the Court take the protection of freedom of expression to excess, as in the case of the Westboro Baptist Church. The majority's fear of chilling free speech protected an invasion of privacy and speech that caused emotional distress. It is clear that fear provides a liminal space for discursive disputation that can motivate an audience to act and to accept or reject an opinion.

Before we begin a summary of the cases examined in this book, we note the obvious. If you are arguing before the Supreme Court, you are going to have to deal with appeals to fear. Whether the fears are real or imagined, or whether some fears are thought to be more significant or realistic than others, or whether the fears are ephemeral or enduring, fear is endemic as a factor in the rhetoric of First Amendment cases. There are several ways to accomplish the task of thinking about the significance of fear in a given case. First, advocates can surface and label appeals to fear. Many people believe appeals are sophistic and/or irrational. Merely labeling them in some environments is enough to refute them. Second, advocates can refute them by revealing that the fears have no basis in evidentiary fact. The fear that vaccinations for COVID-19 causes impotence is factually untrue. In this case, the credibility of the source of information is also subject to question. Third, advocates can present a counter appeal to a stronger or more intensely felt fear. It can be enhanced by bringing the cause of the fear closer to the intended audience in terms of time and space. Death is scarier than illness. And if the cause of death can be bought closer in time and space than the cause of illness, it will be the more persuasive appeal. Finally, one can attempt to work through the fears in order to develop solutions with an invented constitutional interpretation that may work best to minimize the fears of competing parties (though perhaps it is impossible to make everyone happy) in a given case. In any case, because fears are realistically manifest in the rhetoric of

IMPLICATIONS OF FEAR

First Amendment cases, fear must be considered as a significant factor. We have evidenced a range of fears throughout this book in a number of Roberts Court cases.

MORSE V. FREDERICK

As we have seen, the censorship of expression results from that expression's controversial nature. This dialectic raised two important questions for the Supreme Court. Did students retain First Amendment rights after entering a school? Or is it time to once again trim those rights as in the *Fraser* and *Hazelwood* cases? Furthermore, if students retain First Amendment rights, do they extend to off-campus activities under the supervision of the school? The case was further complicated by the fact that the sign the student brandished, "Bong Hits 4 Jesus," was unclear in what it intended to convey.

Many of the fears that surfaced in this case are deeply rooted in the American educational system. The fear that children would not receive a proper education at home was relieved by sending them to public schools. The more intense fear that children could be indoctrinated in these schools was overcome by resting the control of content in school boards. Furthermore, concerned parents could, with proper certification, educate their children at home or place them in private schools. The Founders believed that children needed to be educated not only to obtain vocational skills but to become good citizens. Thomas Jefferson did not believe that democracy could function properly unless the citizenry was properly educated. Thus, if this educational process is disrupted, students will not only fail to gain important skills, but they will also not become proper citizens and democracy will fail.

Public education in America is caught between two sometimes contrary motivations. On the one hand is the freedom to learn, generally enhanced by academic freedom, an open process seeking to investigate all legitimate pathways to the truth. On the other hand is the need to control the classroom to make sure that the proper learning environment is assured. In other words, academic freedom cannot be allowed to fall into chaos, or all is lost. The question in this case revolved around Frederick's free speech rights in the name of academic freedom and the school's rights to maintain an orderly learning environment.

CHAPTER 8

Frederick's case might have been clearer had he held up a sign that read "The Olympics are a capitalistic money-grubbing operation." Such a message would not only have been clearer than the one he held up, but it could not have been linked to urging students to commit an illegal act. For some, the sign he held up was disruptive, not protected political speech. His disruption, if not contained, could have led to a contagion of prankish activities by the students on the sidewalk and back at school the next day. For others who conceived of his speech as harmless, restricting what Frederick held up raised the fear of increasing censorship of students, a trend evident in *Fraser*, which involved disruptive innuendos, or *Hazelwood*, which involved abuse of school sponsorship of discourse.

The *Morse* ruling also has to be seen in the context of violence on campuses and drug use among students. The most intense fear in this case was that loosening control of the learning environment makes it easier for students to bully, use drugs, or even shoot one another. Thus, among some justices there may have been a desire to return authority to school officials so they could control the learning environment and prevent criminal activity. Justices Alito, Kennedy, and Roberts specifically cited drug use as a threat to students and the learning environment.

At the same time, the fact that Justices Alito and Kennedy fell back on judicial restraint indicates that the ruling was narrow and should not be used to regulate protected speech of the kind singled out in the *Tinker* decision. The fear of overregulation led these justices to endorse the heart of the *Tinker* ruling, which protected peaceful political protest, such as the wearing of a black armband to protest the Vietnam War.

Justice Thomas was more adamant about siding with forces of control against the forces of chaos. He worried that undisciplined students and students uneducated about drug abuse would overrun the learning environment if *Tinker* were taken to its logical conclusion. As we shall see in the next case under review in this conclusion, Justice Thomas would strip students of their First Amendment rights altogether in the name of original meaning. However, it should be noted that in this case, Justice Breyer showed some sympathy for Justice Thomas's side of the dialectic in that Breyer believed it was important to enhance the credibility of school administrators in the name of an orderly educational process. Morse did not want the public to believe that the school endorsed marijuana use. That would certainly undercut her credibility and her ability to provide a proper learning environment for her students.

Undoubtedly, Morse feared bad publicity for her school and perhaps for public officials in Juneau in general. However, a more salient fear was legal in nature. Schools also live in our litigious environment and are rightly fearful of lawsuits, particularly those stemming from past in loco parentis rulings. In this case, not only was the school district named in the lawsuit, but Morse was personally named and, thus, subject to civil damages. As a result of such legal maneuvering, administrators may be overly cautious about the kinds of speech activities they allow. Certainly, that was the position of the dissenters who saw Frederick's sign as at worst a prank and at best political speech. Justice Stevens, for example, saw the taking of the sign as an infringement on Frederick's right to express himself on an important issue. And since Frederick was not on school property at the time, many feared that the ruling would leak into other off-campus activities such as those conducted on the Internet.

And that leads to a final fear: if the school is authorized to overregulate student speech, then it sets an example for the future students who may follow that authority. In short, a school that chills free speech may create students who believe chilling speech is permissible in other circumstances. Both sides in this case were asking a very important question based on their own fears: what kind of example are we setting for our children? The dialectic is clear: Are we endorsing drug use by leaving the sign in place? Are we endorsing censorship by taking the sign down? In this case, there was no battle over evidence but only over which fears were felt more intensely. In an America rife with school shootings, the fear of death undoubtedly trumps all others.

The questions raised by this case have yet to be resolved by the courts. And they are unlikely to be resolved as the schoolhouse gate becomes virtual and these questions enter cyberspace. The fear of bullying on school grounds has already moved to cyberbullying. Many of the other things we fear and try to restrict on the playground and in the hallway are also moving onto the Internet. Name calling, racial slurs, and hate speech are not uncommon on students' social media. The balance between control and chaos will be important for a long time to come.

CHAPTER 8

CITIZENS UNITED

In the mid-1970s, based on the precept that consumers had the right to receive certain information, the Supreme Court reversed government suppression of commercial speech and extended to corporate advertisers the right to sell such products as drugs and such services as abortions to their clientele. However, because of the fear of the appearance of corruption, the amount of money that corporations could contribute to federal candidates and the ways they could spend on behalf of them was severely curtailed in the wake of the Watergate scandal. While commercial advertising continued to expand in terms of freedoms granted into the twenty-first century, corporate involvement in federal political campaigns was restricted.

All that changed with the *Citizens United* ruling. Those favoring granting First Amendment rights to corporations overcame those who favored restricting corporations and unions in the political realm. *Citizens United* reified not only corporate and union freedom of expression but also extended the public's right to receive information via corporate and union advertising for federal candidates. While consistent and arguably constitutional, the wisdom of extending these rights with regard to public policy has been contested for the last five years.

The dissenters in *Citizens United* appealed to several fears. First and foremost was the undue influence of corporations and unions on political campaigns. If corporations and unions can spend unlimited amounts of money in federal campaigns, they could overwhelm the contributions of average citizens seeking to voice their support. The dissenters accepted evidence of corporate and union spending as a form of pollution of the marketplace of ideas, but the majority did not. Lying behind the dissenters' fear was another fear that went unspoken but was loudly voiced by editorialists: by unleashing corporations, the Supreme Court tipped the balance of spending power toward the Republican Party, which most corporations support.

To refute the arguments of those who oppose negative advertising, its defenders often point out that the two most common kinds of such advertising—attacks on the opponent's legislative record and attacks on their character—tend to level the playing field among candidates. Challengers would be put at a disadvantage if they were not allowed to attack

182

incumbents' records, given incumbents' advantage in terms of name recognition. Finally, relying on one of the tenets of judicial restraint, dissenters feared that *Citizens United* would overturn precedents going back to 1906 and as recent as *Austin* and *McConnell*. Justice Kennedy answered that rules prohibiting corporate and union political speech flew in the face of the intent of the Founders. Citing historical evidence, Kennedy argued that during of the time of the ratification of the Bill of Rights, political campaigns were vigorous and often rough and tumble, and newspapers were filled with corporate speech and attack editorials. If there was any speech the Founders sought to protect, it was political speech. Furthermore, since the 1970s, corporate speech has been protected, particularly in its commercial form.

The majority in *Citizens United* voiced fears of their own, the most compelling of which was Justice Kennedy's position that limiting corporate and union spending would deprive political consumers of information in the marketplace of ideas. Voters have a right to hear all arguments that are not libelous or slanderous. In fact, the marketplace is protected against such corruption by defamation laws and by corrupt practices committees. Thus, the government had no compelling interest in closing down the free marketplace of political ideas.

Any way you look at it, *Citizens United* is a landmark ruling that reveals a dialectic of fears that, in this case, became synthesized into the conservatives' majority. Our elections are still sorting out the expected and unexpected consequences in terms of public policy and constitutional law.

CHRISTIAN LEGAL SOCIETY AND HOBBY LOBBY

Our analysis of cases revolving around religious freedom in the last decade uncovered several primal fears. The first was fear of religious persecution mandated by government regulation. This fear is intensified by regulations that dictate how children are to be educated, medicated, and/or housed. By preventing certain practices such as homeschooling, the government may allow children to be weaned away from their religious roots by exposing children to peer pressure in public schools.

On one side of the dialectic, the fear of the government is intensified by the fear that religious ceremonies and traditions can be trumped by

CHAPTER 8

the government's interest in preventing some harm or crime, such as drug use, or discrimination. Congress tried to protect such interests when it passed the Religious Freedom Restoration Act, but that act was quickly limited by the Supreme Court, as we have seen. Limitations to religious freedom were reinforced in the *CLS* ruling, for example, which upheld Hastings Law School's right to deny association status to student groups that discriminated against LGBTQIA+ membership, even though CLS core beliefs oppose gay marriage and sex out of wedlock. Justice Alito expressed this fear best when in his dissent he pointed out that the majority's endorsement of a "content neutral" standard quashed the free speech rights of CLS. If a religious campus group has to accept "all comers," as Hastings required, then it ceases to be a religious group with core standards. Alito pointed out that CLS was the only campus group ever denied association status, which certainly censored CLS's freedom of expression and free exercise of religion. This fear can be traced back to the Founders' fear of the government promoting one religion over another and all the way to the present time, when some practices, such as state governments providing vouchers for children to attend Catholic schools, seem to disproportionately favor one religious organization over another.

On the other side of the dialectic, rulings such as *Hobby Lobby* lead to the fear that expanding the freedom of exercise of religion may provide a cover for avoiding the law. It is one thing to say that an individual is free to not use a condom. It is quite another to say that a corporation has the same free exercise rights as that individual and therefore does not have fund condoms for the health of its employees. The *Hobby Lobby* ruling is certainly at odds with the *CLS* ruling, which should come as no surprise, because the only judge each ruling has in common is Justice Kennedy, who is known for his swing votes. In *Hobby Lobby*, he joined his conservative colleagues in concurring with Justice Alito's majority opinion. Like *Citizens United*, the ruling extended First Amendment rights to corporations, in this case, not to have their religious beliefs overburdened by government regulations in the Affordable Care Act. The mandate to supply or fund condoms was envisioned as religious persecution.

Legal scholars now fear that the ruling opening the door to one religious exemption could open the door to many more, such as providing blood transfusions or inoculations to children. Alito's majority opinion tried to deal with this objection by arguing that if a mandate is "the least

184

restrictive means" to obtain the government's goal, then it would be allowable assuming that the government's goal achieved a significant interest or prevented a significant harm.

There is also the fear that the *Hobby Lobby* ruling could rationalize discriminatory hiring practices, particularly against LGBT people, if those practices were couched in religious terms. What if a corporation argues that forcing it to hire LGBT persons overburdens its religious freedom because its personnel believe in traditional marriage and/or that LGBT sexual practices are immoral based on the teachings of the Bible? Legislation that could be used for this purpose has been passed in several states, including Texas and Indiana, based on the federal RFRA. Here again, *Hobby Lobby* and *CLS* are at odds, and the Court will need to work this contradiction out in the future.

SNYDER V. PHELPS

Perhaps the most unique case studied in this book concerns the demonstrations by the Westboro Baptist Church at the funerals of soldiers who, in fact, gave their lives for the church's right to demonstrate. This case touches on issues of privacy, religious freedom, and freedom of expression. Its raises visceral fears about the cost we pay to have freedom of expression. And yet, this case mustered the most lopsided majority, 8–1, of any of the cases we reviewed.

The chief justice, writing for the majority, acknowledged the difficulty of the situation and the grief the family felt. However, he believed that the right to protest overrode the right to privacy and compensation for emotional distress. Roberts concluded that the protestors were involved in a public protest because they had carried the same signs with the same messages to the state capital in Annapolis nearby. But to reach that conclusion, Roberts had to ignore very real evidence provided by Snyder: the press release and the website post that specifically targeted the Snyder family and their dead son. Justice Alito used this evidence to argue that the expressions of Phelps in public protest amounted to a private attack launched during a private moment to a captive audience and thus should lead to actionable emotional distress. He raised the fear that despite Roberts's attempt to narrow the ruling to the case at hand, the ruling would trickle down through the court system, undercutting tort

CHAPTER 8

law in other states. Alito feared that the Supreme Court's decision provided a blueprint for avoiding torts related to emotion distress. The ruling undercut state legislation that imposed a huge burden of proof on the plaintiff. If I want to inflict emotional pain and get around the law pertaining to it, in this case, Maryland's law regarding emotional distress, all I have to do is connect my discourse to a public campaign of humiliation and repeat it on the steps of the state capitol. Remarkably, Alito's fears appealed to no other justice.

The majority also chose to ignore the fighting words doctrine established in the *Chaplinsky* ruling during World War II that claimed words could be tantamount to actions. In fact, the majority provided one of many steps back from the *Chaplinsky* ruling, such as the ones we have reviewed including *Terminiello, Obrien, Tinker,* and *Texas v. Johnson.*

BROWN V. ENTERTAINMENT MERCHANTS ASSOCIATION

In this case, the majority struck down the California law prohibiting the sale of video games to minors. It did so for a variety of reasons. The law was vague. It conflated violence with obscenity, which the majority rejected. The law was so porous that it was unlikely to achieve its ends. Finally, the California legislature relied on social scientific data, which the majority rejected either because of contrary social scientific data or owing to the position that no social scientific data is reliable. Thus, more than any other case we have studied, this one became a battle of refutation based on the limits of evidence. Even Justice Alito in his concurring opinion argued that the most recent video games are so realistic that they should be tested anew to determine if their highly interactive qualities make them more likely to induce violently aggressive behavior. While he believed the California law was misguided, he did not rule out the possibility that the government could establish a compelling interest for restrictions if they could document such findings.

In his dissent, Justice Breyer supported this contention by accepting the social scientific and medical evidence of violence inducement presented by California, breaking with the majority and most jurists across the land. He also believed that California had the right to accept the evidence provided to its legislature in creating the law and that the Supreme

Court was overreaching by making a different determination regarding the validity of that evidence.

Justice Breyer provided another rationale by borrowing from obscenity rulings. He would apply the "reasonable person" test to determine if the video games had any serious literary, artistic, political, or scientific value for minors. If a game does not, then it would fall under the California statute. Thus, Breyer not only broke with the majority over the question of acceptable evidence, but he also took a step toward censorship by allowing violent video games to come under the standards that in the past had been applied only to obscenity. Part of his rationale for this unorthodox move is that he sought to *protect children*, which makes this a very different case than those that would apply it to adult entertainment.[7] Since the *Ginsberg* ruling protects children from depictions of obscene material, Breyer would simply carry the mandate over to violence in the name of protecting children from depictions of violence that have no redeeming merit. In short, he claimed the California law meets the *Ginsberg* and *Miller* standards of being narrowly enough crafted to ameliorate the majority's concerns. It must meet these standards because, in the end, Breyer believed there are enough "literary elements" to overcome the opinion that the video games can be seen as action instead of speech.[8]

Justice Thomas made the most radical claim of all in this ruling: minors do not have First Amendment rights. Thomas would reverse *Tinker* and its progeny by stripping children of First Amendment and many other constitutional rights altogether. His argument is well documented in terms of original meaning. He cited a raft of evidence from colonial times to the passage of the Bill of Rights of 1791 to show that children were not meant to be included among citizens with rights. Thomas would turn responsibility over to parents for the most part but allow the government to invoke protections of children, since they are incapable of making correct judgments for themselves. He claimed that the Founders believed that children were "not fit to govern themselves."[9] He also pointed out that minors are restricted in many ways by many states with many laws including when they can drive, drink, vote, marry, and/or smoke. Thomas was frank in admitting that his opinion may be "inconsistent with precedent,"[10] thus providing an example of "original meaning" overturning judicial restraint.

CHAPTER 8

FCC V. FOX TELEVISION STATIONS, ASHCROFT V. AMERICAN CIVIL LIBERTIES UNION, AND UNITED STATES V. STEVENS

Three cases dealt directly with the fear of obscene or indecent material and its impact. As we have seen in other cases, for speech to be proscribed, it must present a true threat. However, in the case of obscene or indecent material, that is not the case. To lose its First Amendment protection, the material must appeal to prurient (sexual) interests; when taken as a whole, it must have no serious literary, artistic, political, or scientific value; and it must offend contemporary community standards. That's a heavy burden of proof for prosecutors and lawmakers, but it is a burden that is laden with problems. To start with, the last part of the burden, the "community standards," will be used to generate evidence. But how does one define "community?" Is it the local city, the county, or the state? These standards are based on local morality, which can vary greatly from one location to another. The standards in West Hollywood, California, are far different than the standards in Topeka, Kansas, and for that matter the standards in West Hollywood are different than the standards of nearby Beverly Hills. Thus, what is obscene in Topeka or Beverly Hills may not be deemed obscene in West Hollywood. And what does it mean to have no socially redeeming value? Almost any work can send some sort of message. And what about appealing to sexual interest? Showing people kissing can be sexually arousing.

These questions made it difficult for lawmakers and justices to deal with the cases examined in the preceding chapter of this book because they rely on the "reasonable person" test. That person must sit in judgment of items as diverse as the genre of videos in which animals are deliberately crushed for a viewers' amusement or arousal, or a simple fleeting expletive, such as when golfer Justin Thomas referred to himself as a "faggot" on national television after missing a putt.[11] Furthermore, there is a big difference between a slip of the tongue and intentionally using offensive words in a monologue or scripted presentation.

Those attempting to tame these moments of indecency are motivated by the fear of decadence, a decline in civilization, and an erosion of moral values, especially among minors. In their worldview, teenage pregnancies, sexually transmitted diseases, and sinful behavior are real problems for society. However, the guardians of virtue are constantly challenged by emerging technology that vastly complicates the communication environment. The shift to cable and streaming, which have been invited into the home, removed a good deal of discourse from the FCC's purview. To correct this perceived defect, Congress passed the Child Online Protection Act in 1998. This led to a legal challenge that eventually succeeded because the law was porous and too broad and deprived adults of programming in the name of protecting children.

Often, the penalties imposed, such as the indecency standard for broadcasters, manifest themselves in fines and confiscations that lead to more expenditures to fund a legal defense. The chilling effect has been real since radio became popular in the 1920s and broadcasters were required to operate in the "public interest." In the current era, section 230 of the Communication Act was passed to stimulate the growth of the Internet, designating it a common carrier that could not be sued for libel or slander. With the emergence of rich and immensely popular platforms such as Twitter and Facebook, legislators are considering rewriting section 230, to force online platforms to monitor what they publish.

Rhetorical Framing: Original Meaning and Judicial Restraint

Throughout this study, we have seen justices appeal to the original meaning of the Founders to buttress their opinions. These justices fear that abandoning the precept of "original meaning" would make the Constitution into a malleable instrument that could be shaped to fit almost any cause. The use of "original meaning" is common to both the liberal and the conservative sides of the Supreme Court. In the infamous gun control ruling in *District of Columbia v. Heller*, Justice Scalia relied heavily on originalism for his majority opinion, as does Justice Stevens for his dissent. In the cases reviewed in this study, originalism has surfaced many times. Based on his reading of the Founders, Justice Black would not extend First Amendment protection to symbolic speech. Justice Stevens would not protect flag burning. Justice Thomas would not extend First Amendment rights to minors. Justice Kennedy would extend First Amendment rights to corporations.

Originalism is often misrepresented as a current invention of such literalist justices as Antonin Scalia. But that is not the case. And since original meaning is used so often and now dominates the court, this

CHAPTER 8

might be a good place to review its evolution and proper use. Originalism is a hermeneutic precept that can be traced back to Thomas Jefferson and James Madison. For example, on December 27, 1821, fearing distortion of the Constitution, Madison wrote that the document must be interpreted according to "its true meaning as understood by the nation at *the time of its ratification*" (emphasis ours).[12] In June 1823, Jefferson wrote that we ought to return "to *the time when the constitution was adopted*, recollect the spirit manifest in the debates, and instead of trying what meaning may be squeezed out of the text, or invented against it, conform to the probable one in which it was passed" (emphasis ours).[13]

More recently, original meaning was revived not by conservatives but by a progressive seeking to move the Supreme Court away from "judicial restraint" to a more aggressive stance on habeas corpus rights. In 1947, Justice Hugo Black issued a full-scale defense of original meaning in his lengthy dissenting opinion in *Adamson v. People of the State of California*. He sought to apply the Bill of Rights to the states using the original meaning of the Fourteenth Amendment:

> Past history provided strong reasons for the apprehensions which brought these procedural amendments into being and attest to the wisdom of their adoption. For the fears of arbitrary court action sprang largely from the past use of courts in the imposition of criminal punishments to suppress speech, press, and religion. Hence, the constitutional limitations of courts' powers were, in the view of the Founders, essential supplements to the First Amendment, which was itself designed to protect the widest scope for all people to believe and to express the most divergent political, religious, and other views. But these limitations were not expressly imposed upon state court action. . . . In deciding the particular point raised, the Court there said that it could not hold that the first eight amendments applied to the states. This was the controlling constitutional rule when the Fourteenth Amendment was proposed in 1866.[14]

Black went on to read the Fourteenth Amendment according to the context of its passage, thereby resuscitating Jefferson's and Madison's calls for relying on original meaning. He then argued that the Fourteenth Amendment could be used to incorporate the Bill of Rights under its "due process" and "equal protection" provisions and apply those rights to the states. In the 1960s, Black's theory was embraced by the *liberal* Warren Court to incorporate basic rights guaranteed in the Bill of Rights against states' infringements. To name but three landmark cases, *Mapp v. Ohio* prevented unwarranted searches by state authorities. *Gideon v. Wainwright* guaranteed the right to counsel in state criminal trials. *Pointer v. Texas* guaranteed the right to confront witnesses in state criminal trials.

When reading the Constitution, particularly its more ambiguous or vague passages, various justices argue that it is important to re-create the contexts of these passages to better understand their meaning. This method has been refined into the precept of "original meaning" articulated more recently by legal scholars at the University of Chicago such as Robert Bork, who inspired the creation of the Federalist Society. "Original meaning" was then embraced by President Reagan's attorney general Edwin Meese in a speech before the American Bar Association in July 1985. From that point on, the Federalist Society recommended potential nominees to Republican presidents, many of whom embraced "originalism" and were appointed to the Supreme Court.[15]

Those who question "originalism," such as Catherine Langford, Joseph Ellis, and others, admit that while the method is valid, its historiography is often flawed.[16] Historical facts are cherry-picked to create a context that will produce or reinforce the desired result.[17] The solution to this problem is not to abandon a legitimate hermeneutic method but to refine it by relying on accurate and robust historiography.

As we move further into the twenty-first century, we will see more cases wherein fear provides a hermeneutic frame that enlightens our understanding of what motivated the opinions of the justices of the Supreme Court. These fears run from a fear of an uneducated public electorate to the definition of a "true threat" of violence. However, these rulings revealed another fear of the Supreme Court: the fear of overstepping its own bounds. Should the Supreme Court follow precedent? Should it show judicial restraint?

From the beginning of the nation, the role of the Supreme Court as the interpreter of the law of the land has been vague. A giant step forward for the Court came in the *Marbury v. Madison* ruling of 1803, which established almost by fiat the Supreme Court's right to review congressional legislation in terms of its constitutionality. However, to maintain its

CHAPTER 8

credibility and avoid accusations of legislating from the bench, the Supreme Court, with noted exceptions such as the Warren Court, has exercised judicial restraint. It manifests itself in several ways that are apparent in the cases we reviewed earlier. First, the Supreme Court often rules as narrowly as possible. For example, in *Snyder v. Phelps*, Justice Roberts took great pains to say that the ruling applied only to the case at hand. Second, the Supreme Court usually shows great respect for precedent and is often cited by both majority and minority commentary. Third, as in *Masterpiece Cakeshop*, the Court will rule on other grounds to avoid a constitutional judgment. President Franklin Roosevelt became so frustrated with the Court's judicial restraint that he tried to add members to it in 1937. As we have seen, Justice Black became so frustrated that he retrieved the notion of original meaning from Jefferson and Madison to get the Court to move on civil liberties.[18]

As we have mentioned, at least two fears ground the rhetoric of judicial restraint. One is the fear of being accused of legislating from the bench and the other is the fear of violating precedent, that is, causing chaos by overturning previous rulings. A prime recent example of judicial restraint came in *Masterpiece Cakeshop v. Colorado*. The Supreme Court had the opportunity to address two major concerns: (1) Does a commercial business have the right to deny sales to minorities? (2) Does the Colorado statute requiring sales to minorities overburden certain religious beliefs, thereby violating the free exercise and/or establishment clauses of the First Amendment? Instead, Justice Kennedy, writing for the majority, recognized but sidestepped these issues because a member of the Colorado Commission that heard the case made derogatory remarks about the baker's religion.

The *Elonis* ruling provides another example of judicial restraint. In 2015, Anthony Elonis was granted certiorari by the Supreme Court, which then overturned the ruling of the US Court of Appeals for the Third Circuit that had convicted him of issuing a threat via cyberspace. However, the ruling did not clarify what kind of discourse is protected in cyberspace nor nettlesome issues surrounding what constitutes a "truth threat" in First Amendment law. In *Elonis*, Chief Justice Roberts claimed it was "not necessary to consider any First Amendment issues."[19] Roberts held that the Third Circuit's instruction, which required only negligence with respect to the communication of a threat, was not sufficient to support a conviction. Thus, after calling for a consideration of a "true threat" interpretation, the Supreme Court dodged the issue, thereby conforming to its penchant for judicial restraint.

We conclude that fear provides a way into the thinking of the justices of the Supreme Court and the advocates that appear before them. It can function as a powerful framing device for decisions, and competing fears certainly motivate many rulings. Anyone arguing before the Supreme Court who ignores these practices does so at their peril.

Notes

CHAPTER I

1. As of this writing, Ornato and Engel were negotiating the terms of testifying before the House committee.

2. The federal statute regarding "incitement to riot" can be found at 18 U.S. Code Section 2102. The more relevant statute regarding "incitement to rebellion or insurrection" can be found at 18 U.S. Code Section 2383: "Whoever incites, sets on foot, assists, or engages in any rebellion or insurrection against the authority of the United States or the laws thereof, or gives aid or comfort thereto, shall be fined under this title or imprisoned not more than ten years, or both; and shall be incapable of holding any office under the United States."

3. *Abrams v. United States*, 250 U.S. 616, 627, 630 (1919).

4. 250 U.S. 616, 627, 630 (1919).

5. *Schenck v. United States*, 249 U.S. 41, 52 (1919).

6. *Chaplinsky v. New Hampshire*, 315 U.S. 568 (1942).

7. 337 U.S. 1, 20 (1949).

8. 337 U.S. 1, 3 (1949).

9. 337 U.S. 1, 4 (1949).

10. 395 U.S. 446, 447. Using authorial discretion, we have chosen to bowdlerize the word in this quotation although it is not bowdlerized in the original quotation.

11. 395 U.S. 446–47 (1969).

12. The "viewpoint" standard was reinforced in 1973 in *Hess v. Indiana* when the Supreme Court ruled that Gregory Hess's call to "take the fucking street" was protected speech. 414 U.S. 105 (1973).

13. Craig R. Smith and David M. Hunsaker, *The Four Freedoms of the First Amendment* (Long Grove, IL: Waveland Press, 2004), 22.

14. Smith and Hunsaker, *The Four Freedoms of the First Amendment*, 30.

15. Craig R. Smith, "The Alien and Sedition Crisis," in *Silencing the Opposition: How the U.S. Government Suppressed Freedom of Expression During Major Crises*, ed. Craig R. Smith, 2nd ed. (Albany: State University of New York Press, 2011), 10.

16. For more on Lincoln's suspension of the writ of habeas corpus, see Craig

NOTES

R. Smith and Stephanie J. Hurst, "Lincoln and Habeas Corpus," *Silencing the Opposition*, 27–56.

17. Andrew Sachs, "Silencing the Union Movement," *Silencing the Opposition*, 146.

18. Sachs, "Silencing the Union Movement," 146.

19. For an analysis and account of many of these incidents, see Katie L. Gibson and Amy L. Heyse, "Suppression of the Suffrage Movement," *Silencing the Opposition*, 151–74.

20. Craig R. Smith, "The Red Scares," *Silencing the Opposition*, 176.

21. Justice Marshall is citing from the Supreme Court decisions in *Baggett v. Bullitt* and *Cramp v. Board of Public Instruction*.

22. For more details about these cases, see John Charles Kunich, "Natural Born Copycat Killers and the Law of Shock Torts," *Washington University Law Quarterly* 78 (Winter 2000): 1157–270; John D. Zelezny, *Communications Law: Liberties, Restraints, and the Modern Media*, 5th ed. (Belmont, CA: Thomson Higher Education, 2007), chapter 3.

23. Michael J. Mannheimer, "The Fighting Words Doctrine," *Columbia Law Review* 93 (1993): 1527–71.

24. *Chaplinsky v. New Hampshire*, 315 U.S. 568 (1942).

25. Eric B. Easton, "The Colonel's Finest Campaign: Robert R. McCormick and *Near v. Minnesota*," *Federal Communications Law Journal* 60 (2008): 183–228.

26. A similar fear manifests itself in *New York Times Co. v. Sullivan*. In 1960, the *New York Times* published a full-page advertisement to solicit funds to defend Martin Luther King Jr. against an Alabama perjury indictment. The advertisement reported King had been arrested seven times instead of four by the Montgomery, Alabama, police commissioner L. B. Sullivan. Sullivan feared that the inflated number of arrests negatively tarnished his reputation, and so he sued and lost in the Supreme Court.

27. See, for example, Glenn McNatt, "Larry Flynt Isn't Worthy, but Freedom of Speech Is," *Baltimore Sun*, January 12, 1997.

28. For further reading on this analysis of fear, see Alicia J. Bentley, "*Hustler Magazine v. Falwell*: The Application of the Actual Malice Standard to Intentional Infliction of Emotional Distress Claims," *Ohio State Law Journal* 49 (1988): 825–40.

29. For an analysis of First Amendment issues involved in student dress codes, see Kevin A. Johnson, "The First Amendment and Rhetorical Style: The Politics of School Dress Codes," in *The Politics of Style and the Style of Politics*, ed. Barry Brummett (Lanham, MD: Lexington Books, 2011), 173–90.

30. Patent offensiveness is determined by the contemporary community standards.

31. We are referring here to the Jeffersonian "wall of separation" as affirmed in the Supreme Court case of *Everson v. Board of Education*. For an account of

NOTES

the wide variety of fears in the establishment clause of the First Amendment, see Philip Hamburger, *Separation of Church and State* (Cambridge, MA: Harvard University Press, 2004).

32. Brian Calabrese, "Fear-Based Standing: Cognizing an Injury-in-Fact," *Washington and Lee Law Review* 68 (Fall 2011): 1445–1503. Calabrese is influenced by the work of Corey Robin. See Corey Robin, *Fear: The History of a Political Idea* (New York: Oxford University Press, 2004).

33. For example, Joanna Bourke noted how fear can move into anxiety and vice versa: "The uncertainty of anxiety can be whisked away by processes of naming an enemy (it may be a plausible or implausible enemy), converting anxiety into fear. The 'work' of fear is commercial work: converting anxieties into fears is the function of a range of new professionals and, in pharmaceutical terms, is big business. It also has a political function: scapegoating, for instance, enables a group to convert an anxiety into a fear, thus influencing (for instance) voting preferences against an 'outsider' group.... If anxiety can be turned into fear, and thus provide an enemy to engage with, fear can, similarly, be converted into anxiety." See Joanna Bourke, *Fear: A Cultural History* (Emeryville, CA: Shoemaker and Hoard, 2006), 190.

34. Craig R. Smith, *Rhetoric and Human Consciousness: A History*, 2nd ed. (Long Grove, IL: Waveland Press, 2003), 83.

35. Smith, *Rhetoric and Human Consciousness*, 83. We would be remiss if we did not also quote Yoda: "Fear is the path to the dark side. Fear leads to anger. Anger leads to hate. Hate leads to suffering." George Lucas, *Star Wars: Episode I—The Phantom Menace* (Los Angeles: Twentieth Century Fox, 1999).

36. Kierkegaard would couple fear with trembling as a paradoxical Christian base. He wrote, "According to *Fear and Trembling*, all Christianity is rooted in the paradoxical, whether one accepts it as a believer, or rejects it precisely because it is paradoxical. Aye, it lies in fear and trembling, which are the desperate categories of Christianity, and of the leap." See Søren Kierkegaard, *Concluding Unscientific Postscript*, trans. David F. Swenson and Walter Lowrie (Princeton, NJ: Princeton University Press, 1968), 96.

37. Friedrich Wilhelm Nietzsche, *Beyond Good and Evil*, trans. Helen Zimmern (New York: MacMillan Company, 1907), 124.

38. For many Buddhist quotes, see BuddhaQuotes: Resource for Everything Buddha (website), accessed June 18, 2012. While these quotes are from the Buddha, we think it is worth mentioning that citing the Tripitaka directly is complicated and difficult, since there is only one copy surviving and the copy is with monks. Thus, most of the works of the Buddha that are made available online quote the Buddha indirectly.

39. Judith Lief, "Starting on the Path of Fear and Fearlessness," Mountain Hermitage (website). April 28, 2022. Accessed July 31, 2023; excerpted from an article that first appeared in May 25, 2017, issue of *Lion's Roar* magazine.

197

NOTES

40. Jean-Paul Sartre, *The Flies* (Paris: Gallimard, 1947), Act 1.

41. Bertrand Russell, "Outline of Intellectual Rubbish," in *The Basic Writings of Bertrand Russell* (New York: Routledge, 2003), 96.

42. Lars Svendsen, *A Philosophy of Fear*, trans. John Irons (London: Reaktion Books Ltd., 2008), 21.

43. Martin Heidegger, *Being and Time*, trans. Joan Stambaugh (Albany: State University of New York Press, 1996), 313.

44. See, for example, Svendsen, *A Philosophy of Fear*, 102, for a reading of Hobbes's philosophy for this account.

45. Giambattista Vico, *New Science*, 3rd ed. (New York: Penguin Classics, 2000). For a discussion of Vico on this point, see Svendsen, *A Philosophy of Fear*, 102.

46. Kenneth Burke, *Permanence and Change: An Anatomy of Purpose*, 3rd ed. (Berkeley: University of California Press, 1984), 272.

47. For an account of the role of fear in the thinking of Xenophon, Aristotle, and Cicero, see Benedetto Fontana, "'Is It Better to Be Feared Than Loved?': Machiavelli and the Bases of Political Action," Paper Presented at the Rhetoric Society of America Conference. (Philadelphia: May 2012); Marcus Tullius Cicero, *De Officiis: On Duties; or, On Obligations*, trans. Walter Miller (New York: Macmillan, 1817), 191; Niccolo Machiavelli, "The Prince," in *The Portable Machiavelli*, ed. and trans. Peter Bondanella and Mark Musa (New York: Penguin Books, 1979), 131; Robert Frost in his poem "A Hundred Collars," *Poetry and Drama* 1, no. 4 (December 1913): 409; Michel Foucault, *Power/Knowledge: Selected Interviews and Other Writings, 1972–1977* (New York: Pantheon, 1980), 47; Erich Fromm, *The Fear of Freedom* (New York: Routledge, 2004); Brian Massumi, *The Politics of Everyday Fear* (Minneapolis: University of Minnesota Press, 1993).

48. James Madison, "The Meaning of the Maxim, Which Requires a Separation of the Departments of Power, Examined and Ascertained," *The Federalist Papers* (New York: Penguin Books, 1987), 303.

49. Robin, *Fear*, 71.

50. Robin, *Fear*, 252.

Chapter 2

1. Justice Fortas, majority opinion in *Tinker v. Des Moines*, 393 U.S. 503 (1969).

2. Fortas, majority opinion in *Tinker*.

3. John D. Pulliam, *History of Education in America* (Columbus, OH: Charles E. Merrill Publishing Company, 1968), 4–5.

4. Pulliam, *History of Education in America*, 5.

5. Peter S. Hlebowitsh, *Foundations of American Education: Purpose and Promise*, (Belmont, CA: Wadsworth Publishing, 2001), 179.

6. Lawrence A. Cremin, "Educational Configurations in Colonial America,"

NOTES

Education in American History: Readings on Social Issues, ed. Michael B. Katz (New York: Praeger Publishers, 1973), 6.

7. Cremin, "Educational Configurations in Colonial America."

8. Cremin, "Educational Configurations in Colonial America."

9. Pulliam, *History of Education in America*, 34.

10. John Jay, Letter to Benjamin Rush, March 24, 1785. *The Selected Papers of John Jay*, vol. 4, 1785–1788, ed. Elizabeth M. Nuxoll (Charlottesville: University of Virginia Press, 2015), 72–73.

11. James Madison. Letter to W. T. Barry. *The Founders' Constitution* (Chicago: University of Chicago Press, 1987).

12. George Washington, "Eighth Annual Message to the Senate and House of Representative, December 7, 1796," available at Yale Law School's Avalon Project: Documents in Law, History and Diplomacy (website), accessed October 26, 2012.

13. Adolphe E. Meyer, *An Educational History of the American People*, 2nd ed. (New York: McGraw-Hill Book Company, 1967), 127.

14. Meyer, *An Educational History of the American People*, 127.

15. Meyer, *An Educational History of the American People*, 128.

16. Horace Mann, "Seventh Annual Report to the Massachusetts State Board of Education, 1843," in *Readings in Public Education in the United States: A Collection of Sources and Readings to Illustrate the History of Educational Practice and Progress in the United States*, ed. Ellwood Cubberly, 287–88 (Boston: Houghton Mifflin, 1934).

17. Elizabeth Midlarsky and Helen Marie Klain, "A History of Violence in the Schools," in *Violence in Schools: Cross-National and Cross-Cultural Perspectives*, ed. Florence Denmark, Herbert H. Krauss, Robert W. Wesner, Elizabeth Midlarsky, and Uwe P. Gielen, 42 (New York: Springer Science and Business Media, 2005).

18. "1,000 Pupils in Riot Against Gary Plan," *New York Times*, October 17, 1917, 6.

19. David Dixon, *Never Come to Peace Again: Pontiac's Uprising and the Fate of the British Empire in North America*, vol. 7 (Norman: University of Oklahoma Press, 2005).

20. Amanda Kay, "The Agony of Ecstasy: Reconsidering the Punitive Approach to United States Drug Policy," *Fordham Urban Law Journal* 29 (2002): 2148.

21. Kay, "The Agony of Ecstasy," 2147.

22. Juneau School District's Policy, available at Juneau School Board website, accessed April 1, 2013.

23. Chief Justice Roberts, majority opinion, *Morse v. Frederick*, 551 U.S. 393 (2007).

24. Justice Alito with whom Justice Kennedy joins, concurring, *Morse v. Frederick*, 4.

25. Justice Thomas, concurring opinion, *Morse v. Frederick*, 3.

NOTES

26. Paulo Freire, "The 'Banking' Concept of Education," in *Educational Foundations: An Anthology of Critical Readings*, 100 (Menlo Park, CA: Sage Publications, 1970).

27. Freire, "The 'Banking' Concept of Education," 100.

28. Justice Breyer, concurring and dissenting in parts, *Morse v. Frederick*, 3.

29. Elizabeth A. Pawelczyk, "*Frederick v. Morse*: Protecting Student Speech beyond the Schoolhouse Gates," Senior thesis, Department of Communication at Boston College, May 2007, 3–4. Morse is cited from Pawelczyk's thesis because the original source is no longer available in the press release archive of the Juneau School District. The original citation for Morse's words is "Frederick v. Morse," Juneau School District press release, March 14, 2006.

30. Gene Policinski, "Student-Free Speech Case Addresses Post-Columbine Fears and Expectations," *Muskogee Phoenix* (website), March 27, 2007, accessed July 4, 2013.

31. Qtd. in James C. Foster, *BONG HiTS 4 JESUS: A Perfect Constitutional Storm in Alaska's Capital* (Anchorage: University of Alaska Press, 2010), 26.

32. Policinski, "Student-Free Speech Case."

33. Justice Breyer, concurring and dissenting in parts, *Morse v. Frederick*, 5.

34. Foster, *BONG HiTS 4 JESUS*, 17.

35. Jay Braiman, "A New Case, an Old Problem, a Teacher's Perspective: The Constitutional Right of Public-School Students," *Brooklyn Law Review* 74 (2009): 439–76.

36. Charles Chulack, "The First Amendment Does Not Require Schools to Tolerate Student Expression That Contributes to the Dangers of Illegal Drug Use: *Morse v. Frederick*," *Duquesne Law Review* 46 (Spring 2008): 521–38.

37. Joseph Frederick quoted in Foster, *BONG HiTS 4 JESUS*, 28.

38. Joseph Frederick quoted in Foster, *BONG HiTS 4 JESUS*, 30.

39. Foster, *BONG HiTS 4 JESUS*, 19.

40. Justice Stevens, dissenting opinion, *Morse v. Frederick*, 13.

41. Justice Stevens, dissenting opinion, *Morse v. Frederick*, 16.

42. Facts on File News Services, "Student Free Speech Rights," April 27, 2007, accessed July 4, 2013.

43. Kellie Nelson, "The Supreme Court Takes a Fractured Stance on What Students Can Say About Drugs: *Morse v. Frederick*," *Wyoming Law Review* 8 (2008): 292–316.

44. Justice Breyer, majority opinion, *Mahanoy v. B.L.*, 594 U.S. ___ Slip Opinion: 11.

45. Justice Breyer, majority opinion, *Mahanoy v. B.L.*, 11.

46. Naomi Harlin Goodno, "How Public Schools Can Constitutionally Halt Cyberbullying: A Model Cyberbullying Policy That Considers First Amendment, Due Process, and Fourth Amendment Challenges," *Wake Forest Law Review* 46 (2011): 642–43.

NOTES

47. Justice Breyer, majority opinion, *Mahanoy v. B.L.*, 5–6.

48. Quoted in Steven M. Puiszis's extensive review of Internet speech rights of students. See Steven M. Puiszis, "'Tinkering' with the First Amendment's Protection of Student Speech on the Internet," *John Marshall Journal of Computer and Information Law* 29 (2011): 167–229.

49. Jamie L. Williams, "Teens, Sexts, and Cyberspace: The Constitutional Implications of Current Sexting and Cyberbullying Laws," *William and Mary Bill of Rights Journal* 20 (2012): 1018.

50. Puiszis, "'Tinkering' with the First Amendment's Protection of Student Speech on the Internet."

51. Emily McNee, "Disrupting the Pickering Balance: First Amendment Protections for Teachers in the Digital Age," *Minnesota Law Review* 97 (2013): 1841–42.

52. Keith Collins, "Filling the Gaps Left by Morse v. Frederick: Empowering Schools to Discipline Cyberbullies and Gang Members," *Whittier Law Review* 32 (2011): 511.

53. Justice Breyer, majority opinion, *Mahanoy Area School District*, 594 U.S. ____ (2021). Slip Opinion: 11.

54. Quoted in Ben Antonow, "B. L. vs. Mahanoy Could Affect Student Free Speech," *Campanile* (website), June 11, 2021, accessed February 1, 2023.

55. *West Virginia State Board of Education v. Barnette*, 319 U.S. 624 (1943).

56. Chief Justice Warren, *Sweezy v. New Hampshire*, 354 U.S. 234, 250 (1957).

57. Justice Brennan, *Keyishian v. Board of Regents*, 385 U.S. 589 (1966).

CHAPTER 3

1. Mark Hanna had opposed putting Roosevelt on the ticket, referring to him as that "damn cowboy." Hanna became a senator from Ohio and died in 1904.

2. For an examination of the roots of the *Citizens United* ruling in progressive and enlightenment thought, see Steven J. André, "The Transformation of Freedom of Speech: Unsnarling the Twisted Roots of *Citizens United v. FEC*," *John Marshall Law Review* 44 (2010): 69–127.

3. *Newbury v. U.S.*, 256 U.S. 232 (1921).

4. *Burroughs v. U.S.*, 290 U.S. 534 (1934).

5. A contribution of ten dollars or more must be reported by the campaign as received; the name and address of the donor must be provided if he/she gives $100 or more.

6. The title was a takeoff on Ray Bradbury's *Fahrenheit 451*, a futuristic novel about freedom of expression being destroyed. Bradbury's independent research during the mid-1950s period when he was writing the novel indicated that 451°F was the temperature at which paper burns ("Remembering Ray Bradbury," *American Libraries Magazine* [website], July 2, 2013), although that is now scientifically disputed (Brian Palmer, "Does Paper Really Burn at 451 Degrees Fahrenheit?: Fact-Checking the Late Ray Bradbury," *Slate* [website], June 8, 2012).

NOTES

7. "More Money than Ever," *Los Angeles Times* (May 16, 1998): A6.

8. Joseph E. Cantor, *Campaign Financing* (Washington, DC: Congressional Research Service of the Library of Congress, 2002), 5.

9. Kim Geiger and Tom Hamburger reporting on the complication of the Center for Responsive Politics in "Hidden Donors Pour Funds into Campaigns," *Los Angeles Times* (October 24, 2010): A34.

10. Michael W. Toner, "The Impact of Federal Election Laws on the 2008 Presidential Election," in *The Year of Obama: How Barack Obama Won the White House*, ed. Larry J. Sabato, 149–65 (New York: Longman, 2010).

11. Matea Gold, "Obama Closing in on Record $1 Billion," *Los Angeles Times* (October 3, 2012): A13.

12. *NAACP v. Alabama*, 357 U.S. 449 (1958) established that the right to assembly includes the right to assemble privately without disclosure.

13. *McIntyre v. Ohio Elections Commission*, 514 U.S. 334 (1995).

14. *Buckley v. Valeo*, 424 U.S. 1 (1976).

15. He relied on Warren Burger, Potter Stewart, Lewis Powell, and William Rehnquist for different parts of the unsigned ruling. Jeffrey Toobin, *The Oath: The Obama White House and the Supreme Court* (New York: Doubleday, 2012), 149.

16. *Buckley v. Valeo*, 424 U.S. 1, 241 (1976).

17. *FEC v. Massachusetts Citizens for Life*, 479 U.S. 238 (1986).

18. *FEC v. Furgatch*, 484 U.S. 850, 864 (1987).

19. *Colorado Republican Committee v. FEC*, 518 U.S. 604 (1996).

20. R. Briffault, "Campaign Finance, the Parties and the Court: A Comment on *Colorado Republican Campaign Committee v. FEC*," *Constitutional Commentary* 14 (1997): 102–3.

21. This statistic, as cited in the following article, is from Common Cause, which claimed that the Republicans had raised $55.7 million in soft money and the Democrats had raised $34.3 million. "Money: More than Ever," *Los Angeles Times* (May 16, 1998): A6.

22. *FEC v. Colorado Republican Party*, 533 U.S. 431 (2001).

23. *Nixon v. Shrink Missouri Government PAC*, 528 U.S. 377 (2000).

24. "Donors: Survey Sheds Light on Firms that Play Politics," *Los Angeles Times* (September 21, 1997): A24.

25. See both *Colorado Republican Committee v. FEC* rulings (518 U.S. 604, 1996) and (533 U.S. 431, 2001).

26. "Donors," *Los Angeles Times* (September 21, 1997): A22.

27. "Soft Money Dollars," *Time* (September 9, 1999): 42–44.

28. "Soft Money Dollars," *Time* (September 9, 1999): 42–44.

29. See Sec. 441e, FECA.

30. Ruth Marcus, "DNC Official Concedes 'Mistakes of Process,'" *Washington Post* (November 13, 1996): A4.

NOTES

31. Jane Mayer, "Schmooze or Lose: Obama Doesn't Like Cozying Up to Billionaires; Could it Cost Him the Election?" *New Yorker*, August 27, 2012.

32. Joseph E. Cantor, *Campaign Financing: Updated* (Washington, DC: Congressional Research Service; Library of Congress, December 17, 1997), 1.

33. By 2008, the limit on individual giving per person per election had risen to only $2,300.

34. *Miami Herald Co. v. Tornillo*, 418 U.S. 241 (1974). See also *Hurley v. Irish American Gay, Lesbian and Bisexual Group*, 515 U.S. 577 (1995); *Wooley vs. Maynard*, 430 U.S. 705 (1977).

35. *McConnell v. FEC*, 540 U.S. 93 (2003).

36. The prior DC Court of Appeals ruling in this case ran sixteen hundred pages and failed to arrive at a consensus on the issues involved.

37. *FEC v. Wisconsin Right to Life*, 551 U.S. 449 (2007).

38. This case is included in an analysis of commercial speech rights in Richard Dillio's "A Critical Mass: Video Games, Violence, and Ineffective Legislation," *First Amendment Studies* 48 (2014): 110–30.

39. Toobin, *The Oath*, 161.

40. *Citizens United v. FEC*, 558 U.S. 310: Oral arguments from March 24, 2009. There were two rounds of oral arguments and fifty-four amicus briefs filed in the case.

41. Jeffrey Toobin, "Annals of Law: Money Unlimited: How Chief Justice Roberts Orchestrated the Citizens United Decision," *New Yorker* (May 21, 2012): 41–42.

42. In its amicus brief support for Citizens United, the ACLU argued for overturning *McConnell* as well as *Austin*.

43. *Va. Pharmacy Bd. v. Va. Consumer Council*, 425 U.S. 748, 761 (1976).

44. *Virginia State Board of Pharmacy v. Virginia Citizens Consumer Council*, 425 U.S. 748, 762 (1976).

45. *Virginia State Board of Pharmacy v. Virginia Citizens Consumer Council*, 425 U.S. 748, 763 (1976).

46. *44 Liquormart, Inc. v. Rhode Island*, 1996 Lexus 3020 (1996): 52–3.

47. Citing *Buckley v. Valeo*, 424 U.S. 1, 19 (1976).

48. The figures were compiled by the Center for Response Politics as reported by Kim Geiger and Tom Hamburger, "Hidden Donors Pour Funds into Campaign," *Los Angeles Times* (October 24, 2010): A34.

49. See tracking study by Kantar Media/CMAG on the Wesleyan Media Project (website).

50. Morgan Little, "Election Spending Caps Backed in Poll," *Los Angeles Times* (September 17, 2012): A7. The spending rate increased between September 17 and election day.

51. Melanie Mason, "Republicans' Attack," *Los Angeles Times* (October 19, 2012): A12.

NOTES

52. Jean Merl and Richard Simon, "Outside Cash Stoking State House Races," *Los Angeles Times* (October 26, 2012): A1.

53. Merl and Simon, "Outside Cash Stoking State House Races," A1.

54. Cruz was by far the biggest beneficiary of this practice. He also received $11.3 million from hedge fund operator Robert Mercer and $10 million from Toby Neugebauer, who operates a private equity firm.

55. The first significant instance of such a ruling came in *United States v. Cruikshank*, 92 U.S. 542 (1875), in which the Supreme Court asserted that the First Amendment guarantees "the right of the people to assemble peaceably" in order to "petition the government."

56. *McIntyre v. Ohio Elections Comm'n*, 514 U.S. 334, 348 (1995).

57. This was a 6–3 summary ruling issued on June 29, 2010, against an appeal of the law by the Republican National Committee.

58. Richard S. Wheeler, *The Richest Hill on Earth* (New York: Forge Books, 2011).

59. Larry Howell, "Once Upon a Time in the West: Citizens United, Caperton, and the War of the Copper Kings," *Montana Law Review* 73 (2012): 25–59.

60. Howell, "Once Upon a Time in the West."

61. Howell, "Once Upon a Time in the West."

62. We hasten to add that in that presidential election year, candidates endorsed by Rove's American Crossroads lost 90 percent of their races, showing that the correlation between money and results is very low, at least in presidential years; Lisa Miscaro, "Rove Keeps Low Profile for November," *Los Angeles Times* (June 8, 2014): A7.

63. Miscara, "Roves Keeps Low Profile for November," A7.

64. Joseph Tanfani, "Democrats Lost Dark-Money Game," *Los Angeles Times* (November 9, 2014): A14.

65. Sam Sanders, "Five Things to Know About the 2014 Midterm Elections," NPR, *The Two-Way* (blog), November 2, 2014, accessed November 4, 2014.

66. *Citizens United*, 558 U.S. 50, 143–44, 150.

Chapter 4

1. The European tradition is further documented in Smith and Hunsaker, *The Four Freedoms of the First Amendment*.

2. Philip Hamburger, "Church and State: Separation and Interpretation," *Journal of Law and Politics* 18 (2002), 30.

3. Robin, *Fear*, 71.

4. David E. Steinberg. "Thomas Jefferson's Establishment Clause Federalism," *Hastings Constitutional Law Quarterly* 40 (2013): 288.

5. Steinberg, "Thomas Jefferson's Establishment Clause Federalism," 302.

6. Zachary Somers, "The Mythical Wall of Separation: How the Supreme Court has Amended the Constitution," *Georgetown Journal of Law & Public Policy* 2 (2004): 278.

NOTES

7. Carl H. Esbeck, "Uses and Abuses of Textualism and Originalism in Establishment Clause Interpretation," *Utah Law Review* (2011): 523.

8. The religious test clause refers to Article VI, paragraph 3 of the Constitution, stating, "No religious test shall ever be required as a qualification to any office or public trust under the United States." Esbeck, "Uses and Abuses of Textualism and Originalism in Establishment Clause Interpretation," 523.

9. Esbeck, "Uses and Abuses of Textualism and Originalism in Establishment Clause Interpretation," 523.

10. The history described in this and the previous paragraph may be found more extensively in chapter 3 of Smith and Hunsaker, *The Four Freedoms of the First Amendment.*

11. Robert J. Morris, "'What Though Our Rights Have Been Assailed?' Mormons, Politics, Same-Sex Marriage, and Cultural Abuse in the Sandwich Islands (Hawai'i)," *Women's Rights Law Reporter* 18 (1997): 152.

12. See the historical account of the era in Clark B. Lombardi, "Nineteenth-Century Free Exercise Jurisprudence and the Challenge of Polygamy: The Relevance of Nineteenth-Century Cases and Commentaries for Contemporary Debates About Free Exercise Exemptions," *Oregon Law Review* 85 (2006): 435.

13. Lombardi, "Nineteenth-Century Free Exercise Jurisprudence and the Challenge of Polygamy," 435.

14. Chief Justice Waite, majority opinion, *Reynolds v. United States*, 98 U.S. 145, 167 (1879).

15. *Sherbert v. Verner*, 374 U.S. 398 (1963).

16. Douglas Laycock and Oliver S. Thomas, "Interpreting the Religious Freedom Restoration Act," *Texas Law Review* 73 (1994): 226.

17. Laycock and Thomas, "Interpreting the Religious Freedom Restoration Act," 226–27.

18. Jonathan Knapp, "Annual Review of Environmental and Natural Resources Law: Note: Making Snow in the Desert: Defining Substantial Burden under RFRA," *Ecology Law Quarterly* 36 (2009): 271.

19. Nicholas Nugent, "Toward a RFRA That Works," *Vanderbilt Law Review* 61 (2008): 1029.

20. Nugent, "Toward a RFRA That Works," 1030.

21. Nugent, "Toward a RFRA That Works," 1030.

22. Jonathan C. Lipson, "On Balance: Religious Liberty and Third-Party Harms," *Minnesota Law Review* 84 (2000): 594.

23. Bonnie I. Robin-Vergeer, "Disposing of the Red Herring: A Defense of the Religious Freedom Restoration Act," *Southern California Law Review* 69 (1996): 606.

24. 42 USCS Sec. 2000bb.

25. 42 USCS § 2000bb at (b) Purposes.

26. Wendy S. Whitbeck, "Restoring Rites and Rejecting Wrongs: The Religious Freedom Restoration Act," *Seton Hall Legislative Journal* 18 (1994): 853.

NOTES

27. Eric Alan Shumsky, "The Religious Freedom Restoration Act: Postmortem of a Failed Statute," *West Virginia Law Review* 102 (Fall 1999): 88.

28. Justice Sandra Day O'Connor, dissenting opinion, *City of Boerne v. Flores*, 521 U.S. 507 (1997).

29. O'Connor, *City of Boerne v. Flores*.

30. L. Darnell Weeden, "A First Amendment Establishment Clause Analysis of Permanent Displays on Public Property as Government Speech," *Thurgood Marshall Law Review* 35 (2010): 221.

31. Adam F. Sloustcher, "*Arizona v. Winn*: Negative Implications for First Amendment Proponents and Possibly for Our Nation's Schoolchildren," *Hastings Constitutional Law Quarterly* 40 (2013): 972.

32. RSOs are distinct from other groups on a campus in a few ways. In this case, the main differences are that groups granted RSO status have certain benefits including the use of school funds, facilities, and channels of communication and the Hastings name and logo.

33. Justice Ruth Bader Ginsburg, majority opinion, *Christian Legal Society v. Martinez*, 561 U.S. 661 (2010).

34. Ginsburg, *Christian Legal Society v. Martinez*.

35. Ginsburg, *Christian Legal Society v. Martinez*.

36. Justice Ginsburg references "gay persons as a class" from Justice O'Connor's concurrence in *Lawrence v. Texas*. Ginsburg, *Christian Legal Society v. Martinez*.

37. Kevin A. Johnson, "The Kennedy Court: Reflections on the First Amendment Ruling in *Christian Legal Society v. Martinez*," *Free Speech Yearbook* 45 (2011): 31–45.

38. Justice Anthony Kennedy, concurring opinion, *Christian Legal Society v. Martinez*.

39. For more on the importance of the distinction, see Barry Brummett, "A Pentadic Analysis of Ideologies in Two Gay Rights Controversies," *Communication Studies* 30 (1979): 250–61.

40. Justice Samuel Alito, dissenting opinion, *Christian Legal Society v. Martinez*.

41. Alito, *Christian Legal Society v. Martinez*.

42. Pew Research: Religion and Public Life, "In Brief: Christian Legal Society v. Martinez," April 6, 2010, accessed October 16, 2014.

43. Ginsburg, *Christian Legal Society v. Martinez*.

44. Ginsburg, *Christian Legal Society v. Martinez*.

45. Ginsburg, *Christian Legal Society v. Martinez*.

46. John D. Inazu, "Siding with Sameness," *New Observer* (website), July 1, 2010, accessed October 16, 2014.

47. Inazu, "Siding with Sameness."

48. Erica Goldberg, "Amending *Christian Legal Society v. Martinez*: Protecting Expressive Association as an Independent Right in a Limited Public Forum," *Texas Journal on Civil Liberties and Civil Rights* 16 (2011): 133n15.

NOTES

49. John K. Wilson, "Commentary on CLS v. Martinez," *College Freedom* (blog), June 29, 2010, accessed October 16, 2014.

50. Peter M. Bozzo, "Pluralism in Public Education," *Harvard Crimson* (website), November 22, 2010, accessed May 3, 2023.

51. Bozzo, "Pluralism in Public Education."

52. Alito, *Christian Legal Society v. Martinez.*

53. Alito, *Christian Legal Society v. Martinez.*

54. Alito, *Christian Legal Society v. Martinez.*

55. Syllabus, *Burwell v. Hobby Lobby*, 573 U.S. _____ (2014), 1.

56. Syllabus, *Burwell v. Hobby Lobby*, 1–2.

57. This is the phrase commonly used in the case. Syllabus, *Burwell v. Hobby Lobby*, 2.

58. Syllabus, *Burwell v. Hobby Lobby*, 5.

59. Justice Alito's summary of the HHS argument in the majority opinion, *Burwell v. Hobby Lobby*, 2.

60. Alito, *Burwell v. Hobby Lobby*, 2.

61. Alito, *Burwell v. Hobby Lobby*, 2.

62. Alito, *Burwell v. Hobby Lobby*, 3.

63. Ginsburg, *Burwell v. Hobby Lobby*, 1.

64. Alito, *Burwell v. Hobby Lobby*, 3.

65. Ginsburg, *Burwell v. Hobby Lobby*, 34.

66. Ginsburg, *Burwell v. Hobby Lobby*, 34–35.

67. Sam Baker, "Is SCOTUS Already Expanding on the Hobby Lobby Ruling?" National Journal (website), July 7, 2014, accessed April 10, 2015.

68. Justice Sonia Sotomayor, dissenting opinion, denial of injunctive relief, *Wheaton College v. Burwell*, 573 U.S. _____ (2014), 3.

69. Ashley Young, "Why HU [Howard University] Students Need to Know About Burwell vs Hobby Lobby," *Hilltop* (website), September 19, 2014, accessed April 11, 2015.

70. Darcie A. Falsioni and Jeffrey M. Tanenbaum, "Religious Freedom for Corporations? The Hobby Lobby Decision Breaks New Ground." Nixon Peabody (website), July 2, 2014, accessed April 11, 2015.

71. Shadee Ashtari, "Judge Cites Hobby Lobby to Excuse Fundamentalist Mormon From Child Labor Testimony." Huffington Post (website), September 18, 2014, accessed April 10, 2015.

72. Erwin Chemerinsky quoted in Shadee Ashtari, "Judge Cites Hobby Lobby to Excuse Fundamentalist Mormon From Child Labor Testimony."

73. Pema Levy, "Does the Hobby Lobby Decision Threaten Gay Rights?" *Newsweek* (website), July 9, 2014, accessed April 11, 2015.

74. Trial judge as quoted in Chief Justice Warren, majority opinion, *Loving v. Virginia*, 388 U.S. 1 (1967).

75. Jonathan Capehart, "What Hobby Lobby Decision Means for the LGBT

NOTES

Community," *Washington Post* (website), June 30, 2014, accessed April 11, 2015.

76. Molly Ball, "How *Hobby Lobby* Split the Left and Set Back Gay Rights," *Atlantic* (website), July 20, 2014, accessed April 11, 2015.

77. Ball, "How *Hobby Lobby* Split the Left and Set Back Gay Rights."

78. Capehart, "What Hobby Lobby Decision Means for the LGBT Community."

79. Jessica Valenti quoted in John McCormack, "Hobby Lobby Hysteria," *Weekly Standard* (website), 19.41 (July 14, 2014, accessed April 11, 2015).

80. Jessica Valenti, "The Hobby Lobby Ruling Proves Men of the Law Still Can't Get Over 'Immoral' Women Having Sex," *Guardian* (website), June 30, 2014, accessed April 11, 2015.

81. Valenti, "The Hobby Lobby Ruling Proves Men of the Law Still Can't Get Over 'Immoral' Women Having Sex."

82. Randall E. Winn, Executive Director at Veterans and Friends of Puget Sound, Comment in the comment section of Jill Filipovic, "13 Reactions to the Hobby Lobby Case That Are Completely Misinformed," *Cosmopolitan* (website), July 2, 2014, accessed May 2, 2023.

83. Amber Watson-Tardiff, "Jillian Michaels Believes Pregnancy Ruins the Body, Plans to Adopt," NJ (website), April 23, 2010, accessed April 14, 2010.

84. Office on Women's Health (website), US Department of Health and Human Services, "You're Pregnant: Now What?" September 27, 2010, accessed April 14, 2015.

85. Gretchen Livingston, "The Rise of Single Fathers: A Ninefold Increase Since 1960," Pew Research Center: Social and Demographic Trends (website), July 2, 2013, accessed April 14, 2015.

86. Livingston, "The Rise of Single Fathers."

87. Lauren Markoe, "Five Takeaways from the Hobby Lobby Case," Religion News Service (website), June 30, 2014, accessed April 11, 2015.

88. Louis D. Johnston, "Hobby Lobby Ruling: The Crux of the Problem is Employer-Provided Health Insurance," *Minnesota Post* (website), July 1, 2014, accessed April 11, 2015.

89. Johnston, "Hobby Lobby Ruling."

90. W. David Koeninger, "Removing Access to Health Care from Employer and State Control: The ACA as Anti-Subordination Legislation," *University of Baltimore Law Review* 44 (2015): 225–26.

91. Koeninger, "Removing Access to Health Care from Employer and State Control," 226.

92. Alito, *Burwell v. Hobby Lobby*, 18.

93. Alito, *Burwell v. Hobby Lobby*, 18.

94. Alito, *Burwell v. Hobby Lobby*, 18.

NOTES

95. *Kennedy v. Bremerton School District*, 597 U.S. _____ (2022). Slip Opinion: 3.

96. *Kennedy v. Bremerton School District*, 597 U.S. _____ (2022). Slip Opinion: 3.

97. Justice Sotomayor, dissenting opinion, *Kennedy v. Bremerton School District*, 597 U.S. _____ (2022). Slip Opinion: 17.

98. Justice Sotomayor, dissenting opinion, *Kennedy v. Bremerton School District*, 597 U.S. _____ (2022). Slip Opinion: 18.

99. Justice Sotomayor, dissenting opinion, *Kennedy v. Bremerton School District*, 597 U.S. _____ (2022). Slip Opinion: 11.

100. Quoted in Greg Bishop, "When Faith and Football Teamed Up Against American Democracy," *Sports Illustrated* (website), June 13, 2022, accessed February 1, 2023).

101. *The Jim Baker Show* (website), "Washington State High School Coach Vindicated by Supreme Court Ruling in Favor of His Right to Pray," June 22, 2022, accessed February 1, 2023.

102. Quoted in NRB (National Religious Broadcasters), "Supreme Court Sides with 'Praying Coach' Kennedy, Upholding Right to Public Prayer," June 30, 2022, accessed February 1, 2023.

CHAPTER 5

1. Louis Brandeis and Samuel Warren, "The Right to Privacy," *Harvard Law Review* 4 (1890): 193–220.

2. *Frisby v. Schultz*, 487 U.S. 474 (1988).

3. The original version of the law exempted specific labor disputes with homeowners but was wisely revised to omit the exclusion.

4. *Galella v. Onassis*, 353 F. Supp. 196 (S.D. N.Y., 1972).

5. *Galella v. Onassis* II, 487 F. 2d 986 (2d Cir., 1973). Ironically, Galella invaded even this space and was convicted of contempt.

6. *Hill v. Colorado*, 530 U.S. 703 (2000).

7. *Lee v. Weisman*, 505 U.S. 577 (1992).

8. *Moore v. Ingebretsen*, 519 U.S. 965 (1996); *Santa Fe Independent School District v. Doe*, 530 U.S. 290 (2000).

9. *Cantwell v. Connecticut*, 310 U.S. 296, 1940.

10. *Tinker v. Des Moines Independent Community School District*, 393 U.S. 503 (1969).

11. *Texas v. Johnson*, 491 U.S. 397 (1989).

12. *Chaplinsky v. New Hampshire*, 315 U.S. 568 (1942).

13. *Chaplinsky v. New Hampshire*, 315 U.S. 568, 572 (1942).

14. *Terminiello v. The City of Chicago*, 337 U.S. 3 (1948).

15. *Terminiello v. The City of Chicago*, 337 U.S. 3, 4 (1948).

209

NOTES

16. *Brandenburg v. Ohio*, 395 U.S. 446, 47 (1969).

17. *Cohen v. California*, 403 U.S. 15 (1971).

18. Also known as *Smith v. Collin* 436 U.S. 953 (1978) and *Smith v. Collin*, 439 U.S. 916 (1978).

19. *Snyder v. Phelps*, 562 U.S. 443 (2011).

20. *Hustler Magazine v. Falwell*, 485 U.S. 46, 50–51 (1988).

21. We should not be intimidated by the 8–1 ruling, particularly when it comes to First Amendment rulings. In 1940, the Supreme Court ruled 8–1 in *Minersville School District v. Gobitis* (310 U.S. 586) that children who were Jehovah's Witnesses could be forced to say the pledge of allegiance. The lone dissenter was the Republican appointee, Harlan Fisk Stone. The *Gobitis* decision, written for the Court by Felix Frankfurter, a professor at the time, was reversed in *West Virginia State Board of Education v. Barnette* (319 U.S. 624) in 1943, but not before many Jehovah's Witnesses suffered at the hands of intolerant Americans. The 1969 decision in *FCC v. Red Lion* (395 U.S. 367) was unanimous in restricting the rights of broadcasters versus rights given to newspapers. The decision was allowed to lapse with the suspension of the fairness doctrine eighteen years later. Only Justices Black and Douglas dissented in *Dennis v. U.S.* (341 U.S. 494) in 1951, a decision that was not reversed until the *Yates* (354 U.S. 298) ruling in 1957.

22. The Supreme Court has had difficulty in sorting out what is private and, therefore, unprotected speech and what is public and, therefore, protected speech. See, for example, *Connick v. Myers*, 461 U.S. 138 (1983).

23. Justice Black issued a full-scale defense of original meaning and incorporation of the Bill of Rights against the states in his decision in *Adamson v. People of the State of California*, 332 U.S. 46 (1947). (See particularly, 71–72.) Black attached a thirty-page appendix to his decision laying out the history of the Fourteenth Amendment approved in 1868 and the intent of its author, Congressman John Bingham.

24. Chief Justice Roberts, majority opinion, *Snyder v. Phelps*, 562 U.S. 443(2011).

25. Roberts, *Snyder v. Phelps*, citing *Frisby v. Schultz*, 487 U.S. 474, 479 (1988).

26. Roberts, *Snyder v. Phelps*, citing *Frisby v. Shultz*, 487 U.S. 474, 477 (1988).

27. Roberts, *Snyder v. Phelps*, citing *San Diego v. Roe*, 543 U.S. 77, 83 (2004).

28. Roberts, *Snyder v. Phelps*, citing *Dun & Bradstreet, Inc. v. Greenmoss Builders, Inc.* 472 U.S. 749, 761 (1985).

29. Roberts, *Snyder v. Phelps*.

30. Roberts, *Snyder v. Phelps*.

31. Justice Alito, dissent, *Snyder v. Phelps*.

32. Alito, *Snyder v. Phelps*.

33. Alito, *Snyder v. Phelps*.

34. Roberts, *Snyder v. Phelps*.

35. *Connick v. Myers*, 461 US 138, 147–48 (1983).

NOTES

36. On this point, see also M. Lane Bruner and Susan Balter-Reitz, "*Snyder v. Phelps*: The U.S. Supreme Court's Spectacular Erasure of the Tragic Spectacle," *Rhetoric and Public Affairs* 76 (2013): 651–84.

37. *Cohen v. California*, 403 U.S. 15, 21 (1971).

38. See, for example, *Lee v. Weisman*, 505 U.S. 577 (1992), *Santa Fe Independent School District v. Doe*, 530 U.S. 290 (2000).

39. Alito, *Snyder v. Phelps*.

40. *Chaplinsky v. New Hampshire*, 315 U.S. 568, 572 (1942). See also *Cantwell v. Connecticut*, 310 U.S. 296, 310 (1940).

41. Alito, *Snyder v. Phelps*, citing Prosser and Keeton, *Law of Torts*, section 2, 61 (5th ed., 1984), noting *Wilkinson v. Downton* (1897).

42. Roberts, *Snyder v. Phelps*.

43. Roberts, *Snyder v. Phelps*.

44. Roberts, *Snyder v. Phelps*.

45. The Fourth Circuit District Court was one of the first to follow the precedent. Benjamin C. Zipursky, "*Snyder v. Phelps*, Outrageousness, and the Open Texture of Tort Law," *DePaul Law Review* 60, no. 2 (Winter 2011).

46. Chris Megerian, "Governor OKs Funeral Protest Law," *Los Angeles Times* (September 18, 2012) A3.

47. For example, *West Virginia Board of Education v. Barnette*, 319 U.S. 624 (1943) overturned *Minersville School District v. Gobitis*, 310 U.S. 586 (1940), which had upheld a law requiring students to recite the Pledge of Allegiance. Once the United States entered World War II, the context changed regarding what forced salutes meant.

48. See *West Virginia Board of Education v. Barnette*, 319 U.S. 624 (1943); *Lee v. Weisman*, 505 U.S. 577 (1992); *Moore v. Ingebretsen*, 519 U.S. 965 (1996); *Santa Fe Independent School District v. Doe*, 530 U.S. 290 (2000).

CHAPTER 6

1. *Television and Growing Up: The Impact of Televised Violence* (Washington, DC: US Government Printing Office, 1972), 4, 7.

2. *Surgeon General's Report by the Scientific Advisory Committee on Television and Social Behavior: Hearings Before the Subcommittee on Communications of the Senate Comm. on Commerce*, 92nd Congress, 2nd Session, 25, 26 (1972).

3. *Broadcast of Violent, Indecent, and Obscene Material*, 51 F.C.C. 2d 418 (1975), see particularly page 419.

4. See *Writers Guild of America W., Inc. v. FCC*, 423 F. Supp. 1064, 1161 (C.D. Cal. 1976).

5. He was responsible for the Television Violence Act, which was signed into law in 1990 and granted the three major networks a three-year exemption from the Sherman Antitrust Act so they could pursue a joint agreement on curbing and/or rating television violence. The networks did not meet until December

NOTES

1992, when they announced that existing standards "prohibit depicting violence as glamorous or using it to shock or stimulate an audience." These standards also "limit scenes depicting the use of force that are inappropriate for home viewing; unique or ingenious methods of inflicting pain or injury; portrayals of dangerous behavior or weapons that invite imitation by children." First Amendment advocates were shocked that the networks would cave to such pressure.

6. See G. Browning, "Push-Button Violence," *National Journal* 26 (February 1994): 458.

7. Conrad was responding to the pleas of at least twenty advocacy groups. Browning, "Push-Button Violence," 458.

8. Professor of sociology at USC Karen Sternheimer, "Blaming Television and Movies Is Easy and Wrong," *Los Angeles Times* (February 4, 2001), M5. This procedure, claims Sternheimer, negates "the importance of context and meaning."

9. Sternheimer, "Blaming Television and Movies Is Easy and Wrong," M5.

10. *Winters v. New York*, 333 U.S. 507, 510 (1948). See also *Cohen v. California*, 302 U.S. 15, 25 (1970).

11. The best of these studies was written by Jib Fowles, *The Case for Television Violence* (Menlo Park, CA: Sage Publications, 2000).

12. *FCC v. League of Women Voters*, 468 U.S. 364, 378n12.

13. *Fairness Report*, 102 F.C.C. 2d 143, 191 (1985).

14. *Turner Broadcasting System, Inc. v. FCC*, 512 U.S. 622 (1994).

15. *Turner Broadcasting System, Inc. v. FCC*, 512 U.S. 622 (1994). See also *Arkansas Writers' Project v. Ragland*, 481 U.S. 221, 231–32 (1987).

16. Thomas G. Krattenmaker and L. A. Powe Jr., "Converging First Amendment Principles for Converging Media," *Yale Law Journal* 104 (1995): 1720, 1740.

17. See also *Cantwell v. Connecticut*, 310 U.S. 296 (1940); *Lovell v. City of Griffin*, 303 U.S. 444 (1938).

18. For a detailed discussion of this issue, see Joseph W. Slade, *Pornography: A Reference Guide* (Westport, CT: Greenwood Press, 1998).

19. Thomas Krattenmaker and Scott Powe, "Televised Violence: First Amendment Principles and Social Science Theory," *Virginia Law Review* 64 (1978): 1155.

20. *U.S. v. O'Brien*, 391 U.S. 367 (1968).

21. See, for example, *Consolidated Edison Co. v. Public Service Commission*, 447 U.S. 530 (1980).

22. *Ward v. Rock Against Racism*, 491 U.S. 781, 791 (1989), citing *Clark v. Community for Creative Non-Violence*, 468 U.S. 288, 293 (1984).

23. "Media Violence and Free Speech," paper presented to International Conference on Violence in the Media (October 4, 1994). See also Jonathan Freedman, "Television Violence and Aggression: A Rejoinder," *Psychological Bulletin* 100 (1986): 372–78.

24. See, for example, Victor Strassburger, "Television and Adolescents: Sex, Drugs, Rock 'n' Roll," *Adolescent Medicine* 1 (1990): 161–94.

NOTES

25. Marcia Pally, *Sex and Sensibility: Reflections on Forbidden Mirrors and the Will to Censor* (New York: Ecco Press, 1994), 93.

26. Craig R. Smith, "Violence as Indecency: Pacifica's Open Door Policy," *Law Journal of Florida International University* 2 (2007): 75–92; "Violence in Programming: Can It Be Deemed Obscene or Indecent," *Nexus Law Journal* 10 (2005): 135–57. See also Timothy E. Gray, "V-Chip: The Betamax of the '90s," *Broadcasting & Cable* (April 15, 1996): 30. Sternheimer writes, "People who live in violent neighborhoods and families are more likely to become violent (or the victims of violence) than anybody else. [Furthermore], [i]t is likely that people with a propensity for violence are drawn toward violent media, thus creating a correlation" but not a causal relationship." "Blaming Television and Movies Is Easy and Wrong," M5.

27. For a review of these studies, see Judy Foreman, "Violence May Lie in Damaged Brain Cells," *Los Angeles Times* (April 29, 2002): S1, 6. Foreman is on the faculty of the Harvard Medical School.

28. O. Wiegman, M. Kuttschreuter, and B. Barda, "A Longitudinal Study of the Effects of Television Viewing on Aggressive and Pro-Social Behaviours," *British Journal of Social Psychology* 31 (1992): 159.

29. As cited in Krattenmaker and Powe, "Televised Violence," 1149.

30. "No Correlation with Broadcast Violence," *Broadcasting and Cable* (October 30, 2000): 82.

31. Stanley Milgram and R. Lance Shotland, *Television and Antisocial Behavior* (New York: Academic Press, 1973); R. Lynn, S. Hampson and E. Agahi, "Television Violence and Aggression: A Genotype-environment Correlation and Interaction Theory," *Social Behavior and Personality* 17 (1989): 143–64.

32. Andrew Przybylski and Allison Fine Mishkin, "How the Quantity and Quality of Electronic Gaming Relates to Adolescents' Academic Engagement and Psychosocial Adjustment," *Psychology of Popular Media Culture* 5 (2014): 145–56.

33. *Broadcasters Personal Injury Liability*, 20 ALR 4th 327 (1983), cited in Raymond G. Lande, MD, "The Video Violence Debate," *Hospital and Community Psychiatry* 44 (1993): 349.

34. *Zamora v. Columbia Broadcasting System*, 480 F. Supp. 199 (S.D. Fla. 1979); *Olivia N. v. NBC*, 74 Cal. App. 3d 383 (1977); *Walt Disney Productions v. Shannon*, 276 S. E. 2d 580 (GA.1981); *DeFilippo v. NBC*, 446 A. 2d 1036 (R. I. 1982).

35. See *Brandenburg v. Ohio*, 395 U.S. 444, 447 (1969).

36. *James v. Meow Media*, 90 F. Supp 2d 798 (W.D. Ky., 2000), 804. See also *Watters v. TSR, Inc.*, 904 F. 2d 378 (6th Cir. 1990).

37. *Reno v. ACLU*, 521 U.S. 844 (1997).

38. *Brown v. Entertainment Merchants Assn.*, 564 U.S. 768 (2011).

39. *Ashcroft v. Free Speech Coalition*, 535 U.S. 234 (2002); *Ashcroft v. American Civil Liberties Union*, 535 U.S. 564 (2002).

40. Dmitri Williams and M. Skoric, "Internet Fantasy Violence: A Test of

NOTES

Aggression in an Online Game," *Communication Monographs* 22 (2005): 217–33. See also Dmitri Williams, "Groups and Goblins: The Social and Civic Impact of Online Gaming," *Journal of Broadcasting and Electronic Media* 50 (2006): 651–70.

41. Rhoda Baruch, "Why the Fuss about Television Violence?" *Broadcasting & Cable* (August 29, 1994): 40.

42. Gary Selnow, "Prime-Time TV's Rich Lessons," *San Francisco Chronicle* (March 14, 1994): A21.

43. California Civil Code Annual Sections 1746–1746.5.

44. California Civil Code Annual Section 1746 (d) (1) (A).

45. *Video Software Dealers Assn. v. Schwarzenegger*, No. C-05–04188 RMW (2007).

46. *United States v. Stevens*, 557 U.S. 460 (2010).

47. He relied on *Joseph Burstyn, Inc. v. Wilson*, 343 U.S. 495, 503 (1952). It was refreshing to hear this opinion because the Supreme Court still treats broadcasters as second-class citizens when it comes to the issue of indecency, a position that opens the door for government to regulate violence as indecency.

48. *Miller v. California*, 413 U.S. 15, 24 (1973).

49. Jeremiah Hickey, "Death by Adjective: The Supreme Court's Attack on Legislative Regulations of Violence, or How Chief Justice John G. Roberts and Justice Antonin Scalia Stopped Worrying about Symbolic Violence by Employing Aesthetic Claims to Limit Legislative Restrictions on Violence," *First Amendment Studies* 47 (2013): 106–32.

50. Justice Scalia, majority opinion, *Brown v. Entertainment Merchants Assn.* He also relies on *Winters* to reinforce his point.

51. *Ginsberg v. New York*, 390 U.S. 629 (1963).

52. *Erznoznik v. City of Jacksonville*, 422 U.S. 205 (1975); *Tinker v. Des Moines*, 393 U.S. 503, 511 (1969); Scalia argues that Thomas presents no precedent for his opinion. *Brown v. Entertainment Merchants Assn.*

53. Scalia, *Brown v. Entertainment Merchants Assn.*

54. Scalia, *Brown v. Entertainment Merchants Assn.*

55. Scalia, *Brown v. Entertainment Merchants Assn.*

56. Justice Alito, concurring, *Brown v. Entertainment Merchants Assn.*

57. Alito, *Brown v. Entertainment Merchants Assn.*

58. Alito, *Brown v. Entertainment Merchants Assn.*

59. Justice Thomas, dissenting, *Brown v. Entertainment Merchants Assn.*

60. Justice Breyer, dissenting, *Brown v. Entertainment Merchants Assn.* He appends a list of these studies to his opinion.

61. *Ginsberg v. New York*, 390 U.S. 629, 646–47 (1968). (Not to be confused with *Ginzburg v. U.S.* 383 U.S. 463 [1966].)

62. Breyer, *Brown v. Entertainment Merchants Assn.*

63. Though he does acknowledge that "experts debate the conclusions of all these studies." Breyer, *Brown v. Entertainment Merchants Assn.*

NOTES

64. See, for example, *Police Department of the City of Chicago v. Mosley*, 408 U.S. 92, 96 (1972).

65. Steve Shiffrin, *The First Amendment, Democracy, and Romance* (Cambridge, MA: Harvard University Press, 1990), 5.

66. Franklyn Haiman, *Speech and Law in a Free Society* (Chicago: University of Chicago Press, 1981), 174.

CHAPTER 7

1. *United States v. Stevens*, 557 U.S. 460 (2010).

2. Harry A. Jessell, "WDBJ Fine Highlights Broadcast Inequality," TVNews-Check: The Business of Broadcasting (website), March 27, 2015, accessed June 1, 2016.

3. Smith and Hunsaker, *The Four Freedoms of the First Amendment*, 177.

4. Melissa Mohr, *Holy Shi: A Brief History of Swearing* (New York: Oxford University Press, 2013), 15.

5. Smith and Hunsaker. *The Four Freedoms of the First Amendment*, 213.

6. *Roth v. United States*, 354 U.S. 476 (1957).

7. *Roth v. United States*, 354 U.S. 476 (1957).

8. *Roth v. United States*, 354 U.S. 476, 487 (1957).

9. *Roth v. United States*, 354 U.S. 476, 487 (1957).

10. *Roth v. United States*, 354 U.S. 476, 488 (1957).

11. *Roth v. United States*, 354 U.S. 476, 497 (1957).

12. *Roth v. United States*, 354 U.S. 476, 499 (1957).

13. *Roth v. United States*, 354 U.S. 476, 499 (1957).

14. In this quotation, Chief Justice Burger referred specifically to Justice Harlan's writing in *Interstate Circuit, Inc. v. Dallas*. Chief Justice Warren Burger, majority opinion, *Miller v. California*, 413 U.S. 15, 17 (1973).

15. *Miller v. California*, 413 U.S. 15, 16 (1973).

16. Ernest J. Walker, "The Communications Decency Act: A Cyber-Gag to First Amendment Rights on the Internet," *University of Detroit Mercy Law Review* 75 (1997): 201.

17. Christopher S. Yoo, "Constitutional Transformations: The State, the Citizen, and the Changing Role of Government," *William and Mary Law Review* 53 (2011): 769.

18. Adam J. Tutaj, "Intrusion Upon Seclusion: Bringing an Otherwise Valid Cause of Action into the 21st Century," *Marquette Law Review* 82 (1999): 665; Michelle Everson, "Legal Constructions of the Consumer," in *The Making of the Consumer: Knowledge, Power and Identity in the Modern World*, ed. Frank Trentmann, 99 (New York: Berg Publishers, 2006); Kristin L. Rakowski, "Branding as an Antidote to Indecency Regulation," *UCLA Entertainment Law Review* 16 (2009): 8.

19. Justice John Paul Stevens, majority opinion, *Pacifica Radio Foundation v. Federal Communications Commission*, 438 U.S. 726, 733 (1978).

NOTES

20. Stevens, *Pacifica Radio Foundation v. Federal Communications Commission*, 745.

21. Jay A. Gayoso, "The FCC's Regulation of Broadcast Indecency: A Broadened Approach for Removing Immorality from the Airwaves," *University of Miami Law Review* (1989): 892n133.

22. Gayoso, "The FCC's Regulation of Broadcast Indecency," 892n133.

23. Gayoso, "The FCC's Regulation of Broadcast Indecency," 892.

24. Alec Harrell, "Who Cares About Prior Restraint? An Analysis of the FCC's Enforcement of Indecency Forfeiture Orders," *Southern California Law Review* 70 (1996): 242.

25. The First Amendment applies to government censorship (i.e., public communication) and not censorship by private entities (i.e., cable and Internet providers).

26. Justice Breyer, dissenting opinion, *FCC v. Fox Television Stations, Inc. I*, 556 U.S. 502, 558–59 (2009). Justice Breyer cited "Public Stations Fear Indecency Fine Jump Means Premium Hikes," *Public Broadcasting Report*, July 7, 2006.

27. Breyer, *FCC v. Fox Television Stations, Inc. I*, (2009), 559. Justice Breyer cited "Romano, Reporting Live. Very Carefully,' *Broadcasting & Cable* (July 4, 2005): 8.

28. Breyer, *FCC v. Fox Television Stations, Inc. I*, (2009), 559. Quoting Dennis Fisher, news director at WHTM-TV.

29. Breyer, *FCC v. Fox Television Stations, Inc. I*, (2009), 559.

30. Courtney Livingston Quale, "Hear an [Expletive], There an [Expletive], But[t] . . . The Federal Communications Commission Will Not Let You Say an [Expletive]," *Willamette Law Review* 45 (2008): 209.

31. Quale, "Hear an [Expletive], There an [Expletive]," 209.

32. Quale, "Hear an [Expletive], There an [Expletive]," 257.

33. Jim Dyke, "Letter to the FCC—Re: Court Remand of Section III.B of the Commission's March 2006 *Omnibus Order* Resolving Numerous Broadcast Indecency Complaints," FCC (website), September 21, 2006, accessed February 3, 2021.

34. Steven R. Shapiro, Christopher A. Hansen, and Marjorie Heins. Brief Amicus Curiae of the American Civil Liberties Union, the New York Civil Liberties Union, American Booksellers Foundation for Free Expression, American Federation of Television and Radio Artists, Directors Guild of America, First Amendment Project, Minnesota Public Radio/American Public Media, National Alliance for Media Arts and Culture, National Coalition Against Censorship, National Federation of Community Broadcasters, Pen American Center, and Washington Area, Lawyers for the Arts in Support of Respondents. *Federal Communications Commission v. FOX Television Stations, Inc.* Nos. 07–582, (August 8, 2008).

35. Sarah Herman, "The Battle for the Remote Control—Has the FCC Indecency Policy Worn Out Its Welcome in America's Living Room?" *Washington University Journal of Law and Policy* 38 (2012): 365.

36. Stanley Cohen, *Folk Devils and Moral Panics: The Creation of Mods and*

NOTES

Rockers (New York: Routledge Classics, 2011); Erich Goode and Nachman Ben-Yehuda, "Moral Panics: Culture, Politics, and Social Construction," *Annual Review of Sociology* 20 (1994): 149–71; Shahira Fahmy and Thomas J. Johnson, "Mediating the Anthrax Attacks: Media Accuracy and Agenda Setting During a Time of Moral Panic," *Atlantic Journal of Communication* 19 (2007): 19–40; Tom Morton and Eurydice Aroney, "Journalism, Moral Panic and the Public Interest," *Journalism Practice* 10 (2016): 18–34; Clay Calvert, "The FCC and Profane Language: The Lugubrious Legacy of a Moral Panic and a Grossly Offensive Definition the Must be Jettisoned," *First Amendment Law Review* 17 (2018): 147, 161.

37. Calvert, "The FCC and Profane Language," 162–63.

38. Calvert, "The FCC and Profane Language," 161–62.

39. Justice Samuel Alito, Oral Arguments in *FCC v. Fox Television Stations, Inc. II,* 567 US (2012).

40. Justice Clarence Thomas, concurring opinion, *FCC v. Fox Television Stations, Inc. I,* 556 U.S. 502 (2009).

41. Laith Paul Alsarraf, "Statement of Laith Paul Alsarraf," *Legislative Proposals to Protect Children from Inappropriate Materials on the Internet.* Hearing Before the Subcommittee on Telecommunications, Trade, and Consumer Protection of the Committee on Commerce, United States House of Representatives, 105th Congress, Second Session, September 11, 1998, Serial Nos. 105–19, p. 50.

42. Peter Nickerson, "Prepared Statement of Peter Nickerson, CEO, N2H2," *Legislative Proposals to Protect Children from Inappropriate Materials on the Internet.* Hearing Before the Subcommittee on Telecommunications, Trade, and Consumer Protection of the Committee on Commerce, United States House of Representatives, 105th Congress, Second Session, September 11, 1998, Serial Nos. 105–19, p. 63.

43. Lawrence Lessig, "Statement of Lawrence Lessig," *Legislative Proposals to Protect Children from Inappropriate Materials on the Internet.* Hearing Before the Subcommittee on Telecommunications, Trade, and Consumer Protection of the Committee on Commerce, United States House of Representatives, 105th Congress, Second Session, September 11, 1998, Serial No. 105–19, p. 58.

44. Judge Lowell A. Reed Jr., *American Civil Liberties Union v. Reno.* United States District Court, E. D. Pennsylvania, No. CIV. A. 98–5591 (November 23, 1998), 3.

45. Johanna M. Oldenburg, "'Son of CDA': The Constitutionality of the Child Online Protection Act of 1998," *Communication Law and Policy* 6 (2001): 239.

46. Roodenburg, "'Son of CDA,'" 239–40.

47. Roodenburg, "'Son of CDA,'" 240.

48. Kristin Ringeisen, "The Use of Community Standards by the Child Online Protection Act to Determine if Material Is Harmful to Minors Is Not Unconstitutional: Ashcroft v. American Civil Liberties Union," *Duquesne Law Review* 41 (2003): 456.

NOTES

49. Chief Justice Roberts, majority opinion, *United States v. Stevens*, 559 U.S. 460–61 (2010).

50. Roberts, *United States v. Stevens*, 462.

51. Roberts, *United States v. Stevens*, 462.

52. Justice Alito, dissenting opinion, *United States v. Stevens*, 559 U.S. 477–78 (2010).

53. Roberts, *United States v. Stevens*, 462.

54. Roberts, *United States v. Stevens*, 462.

55. Kevin Volkan, "Written Testimony of Kevin Volkan," Hearing Before the Senate Judiciary Committee: "Prohibiting Obscene Animal Crush Videos in the Wake of United States v. Stevens." (September 15, 2010).

56. Senator Gary C. Peters of Michigan, "Statement of Congressman Gary C. Peters," Hearing on United States v. Stevens: The Supreme Court's Decision Invalidating the Crush Videos Statute. Subcommittee on Crime, Terrorism & Homeland Security of the House Committee on the Judiciary (May 26, 2010), 8.

57. William Paul DeBaron, "Prepared Statement of William Paul DeBaron, Detective, Long Beach Police Department Regarding the 'Crush Video' Legislation," Hearing Before the Subcommittee on Crime of the Committee on the Judiciary of the House of Representatives on Punishing Depictions of Animal Cruelty and the Federal Prisoner Health Care Co-payment Act of 1999, September 30, 1999, 63.

58. Gabriela Wolfe, "Anything but Ag-Gag: Ending the Industry-Advocate Cycle," *Syracuse Law Review* 66 (2016): 370–71.

59. Sheldon Rampton and John Stauber, *Mad Cow USA: Could the Nightmare Happen Here?* (Madison, WI: Common Courage Press, 1997), 192.

60. Ronald K. L. Collins, "Free Speech, Food Libel, & the First Amendment," *Ohio Northern University Law Review* 26 (2000): 4.

61. Lloyd, "Crushing Animals and Crashing Funerals," 272–73.

62. United States Supreme Court, "Oral Argument Transcript for *Virginia v. Black*," 538 U.S. 343 (2003).

63. United States Supreme Court, "Oral Argument Transcript for *Virginia v. Black*."

64. John C. Knechtle, "When to Regulate Hate Speech," *Penn State Law Review* 110 (2006): 550.

65. Syllabus, *Elonis v. United States*, 575 U.S. _____. (2015), p. 1.

66. Syllabus, *Elonis v. United States*, 575 U.S. _____. (2015), p. 1.

67. Petition of Writ of Certiorari, *Elonis*, 134 S. Ct. 2819 (No. 13–983).

68. Justice Alito, concurring opinion, *Elonis v. United States*, 575 U.S. _____. (2015), p. 6.

69. 395 U.S. 444 (1969). See also *Watts v. United States* 394 U.S. 705 (1969), decided just before *Brandenburg*. Watts's threat to "get [LBJ] in my sights" was hyperbole and not a true threat.

NOTES

70. *Virginia v. Black*, 538 U.S. 343 (2003).

71. *Virginia v. Black*, 538 U.S. 343, 359 (2003).

72. Here Roberts cited *Staples*, 511 U.S., at 606–7.

73. *Elonis*, at 2013–14.

74. *Walker v. Texas Division, Sons of Confederate Veterans*, 135 U.S. 2239 (2015).

75. *Pleasant Grove City v. Summum*, 555 U.S. 460, 467 (2009).

76. JTA, "French High Court: BDS Activists Guilty of Discrimination," *Times of Israel* (website), October 23, 2015, accessed February 10, 2021.

77. Glenn Greenwald, "Anti-Israeli Activism Criminalized in the Land of Charlie Hebdo and 'Free Speech,'" *Intercept* (website), October 27, 2015, accessed February 10, 2021.

78. Noah Webster, *American Dictionary of the English Language*. Websters Dictionary 1828 (website), accessed May 2, 2023.

79. Jeremy Engels, "Uncivil Speech: Invective and the Rhetorics of Democracy in the Early Republic," *Quarterly Journal of Speech* 95, no. 3 (2009): 328.

80. Engels, "Uncivil Speech," 328.

81. Engels, "Uncivil Speech," 320.

82. Engels, "Uncivil Speech," 320.

83. Engels, "Uncivil Speech," 320–21.

84. Simona A. Popuşoi, Grigore M. Havârneanu, and Corneliu E. Havârneanu, "'Get the F#*k Out of My Way!' Exploring the Cathartic Effect of Swear Words in Coping with Driving Anger," *Transportation Research Part F: Traffic Psychology and Behaviour* 56 (2018): 215.

85. Michael C. Philipp and Laura Lombardo, "Hurt Feelings and Four-Letter Words: Swearing Alleviates the Pain of Social Distress," *European Journal of Social Psychology* 47 (2017): 517.

86. Eun-Ju Lee, Hyun Suk Kim, and Soonwook Choi. "Violent Video Games and Aggression: Stimulation or Catharsis or Both?" *Cyberpsychology, Behavior, and Social Networking* 24 (2021): 41–47.

CHAPTER 8

1. Plato, *Timaeus*, trans. Donald J. Zeyl (Indianapolis: Hackett Publishing, 2000), 69d.

2. Frans de Waal, *Good Natured: The Origins of Right and Wrong in Humans and Other Animals* (Cambridge, MA: Harvard University Press, 1996).

3. Jonathan Haidt, *The Righteous Mind: Why Good People Are Divided by Politics and Religion* (New York: Pantheon Books, 2012), 279.

4. Breyer, *Brown v. Merchants*.

5. Thomas I. Emerson, "Toward a General Theory of the First Amendment," *Yale Law Journal* 72 (1963): 877–87.

6. Engels, "Uncivil Speech," 311–34.

7. To this end, he cites *Ginsberg v. New York*, 390 U.S. 629, 638 (1968).

NOTES

8. Breyer, *Brown v. Merchants*.

9. Thomas, *Brown v. Merchants*.

10. Thomas, *Brown v. Merchants*.

11. Using authorial discretion, we have chosen to bowdlerize the word in this quotation although it is not bowdlerized in the original quotation.

12. James Madison, "Letter to J. G. Jackson. December 27, 1821," in *The Letters and Other Writings of James Madison*, ed. Philip R. Fendall, vol. 3 (Philadelphia: Lippincott, 1865), 244.

13. Thomas Jefferson, "Letter to W. Johnson. June 12, 1823," in *The Complete Jefferson*, ed. Saul K. Padover (New York: Tudor Publishing Company, 1943), 322.

14. Hugo Black, *Adamson v. People of the State of California*, 332 U.S. 46, 71–72 (1947).

15. L. B. Solum and R. W. Bennet, *Constitutional Originalism: A Debate* (Ithaca, NY: Cornell University Press, 2011); Mark Anthony Frassetto, "Judging History: How Judicial Discretion in Applying Originalist Methodology Affects the Outcome of Post-*Heller* Second Amendment Cases," *William and Mary Bill of Rights Journal* 29 (2020): 413–54.

16. Catherine Langford, *Scalia v. Scalia: Opportunistic Textualism in Constitutional Interpretation* (Tuscaloosa: University of Alabama Press, 2017); Joseph J. Ellis, *American Dialogue: The Founders and Us* (New York: Knopf, 2018), 7; R. M. Howard and J. A. Segal, "An Original Look at Originalism," *Law and Society Review* 36 (2002): 113–38; H. J. Powell, "The Original Understanding of Original Intent," *Harvard Law Review* 98 (1995): 885–948.

17. The rhetorical use of history is explored in a more general way in Kathleen Turner's edited volume *Doing Rhetorical History* (Tuscaloosa: University of Alabama Press, 1998), which includes essays by many leading rhetorical theorists.

18. As previously mentioned, Justice Black issued a full-scale defense of original meaning and incorporation of the Bill of Rights against the states in his decision in *Adamson v. People of the State of California*, 332 U.S. 46 (1947).

19. *Elonis*, at 2012.

Bibliography

18 U.S. Code Section 2102

18 U.S. Code Section 2383

42 U.S. Code Section 2000bb.

"1,000 Pupils in Riot Against Gary Plan." *New York Times*, October 17, 1917, 6.

Abrams v. United States, 250 U.S. 616 (1919).

Adamson v. People of the State of California, 332 U.S. 46 (1947).

Alito, Samuel. Oral Arguments in *FCC v. Fox Television Stations*, 556 U.S. 502 (2012).

Alsarraff, Laith Paul. "Statement of Laith Paul Alsarraf." *Legislative Proposals to Protect Children from Inappropriate Materials on the Internet.* Hearing Before the Subcommittee on Telecommunications, Trade, and Consumer Protection of the Committee on Commerce, United States House of Representatives, 105th Congress, Second Session, September 11, 1998, Serial No. 105–19.

André, Steven J. "The Transformation of Freedom of Speech: Unsnarling the Twisted Roots of *Citizens United v. FEC.*" *John Marshall Law Review* 44 (2010): 69–127.

Antonow, Ben. "B. L. vs. Mahanoy Could Affect Student Free Speech." *Campanile* (website). June 11, 2021, accessed February 1, 2023.

Arkansas Writers' Project v. Ragland, 481 U.S. 221 (1987).

Ashcroft v. American Civil Liberties Union, 542 U.S. 656 (2004).

Ashcroft v. Free Speech Coalition, 535 U.S. 234 (2002).

Ashtari, Shadee. "Judge Cites Hobby Lobby to Excuse Fundamentalist Mormon from Child Labor Testimony." Huffington Post (website). September 18, 2014, accessed April 10, 2015.

Austin v. Michigan Chamber of Commerce, 494 U.S. 652 (1990).

Baggett v. Bullitt, 377 U.S. 360 (1964).

Baker, Sam. "Is SCOTUS Already Expanding on the Hobby Lobby Ruling?" National Journal (website). July 7, 2014, accessed April 10, 2015.

Ball, Molly. "How *Hobby Lobby* Split the Left and Set Back Gay Rights." *Atlantic* (website), July 20, 2014, accessed April 11, 2015.

Baruch, Rhoda. "Why the Fuss about Television Violence?" *Broadcasting & Cable*, August 29, 1994, 41–42.

BIBLIOGRAPHY

Bentley, Alicia J. "*Hustler Magazine v. Falwell*: The Application of the Actual Malice Standard to Intentional Infliction of Emotional Distress Claims." *Ohio State Law Journal* 49 (Summer 1988): 825–40.

Bishop, Greg. "When Faith and Football Teamed Up against American Democracy." *Sports Illustrated* (website). June 13, 2022, accessed February 1, 2023.

Bourke, Joanna. *Fear: A Cultural History*. Emeryville, CA: Shoemaker and Hoard, 2006.

Bozzo, Peter M. "Pluralism in Public Education." *Harvard Crimson* (website). November 22, 2010, accessed May 3, 2023.

Braiman, Jay. "A New Case, an Old Problem, a Teacher's Perspective: The Constitutional Right of Public School Students." *Brooklyn Law Review* 74 (2009): 439–76.

Brandenburg v. Ohio, 395 U.S. 444 (1969).

Briffault, R. "Campaign Finance, the Parties and the Court: A Comment on *Colorado Republican Campaign Committee v. FEC*." *Constitutional Commentary* 14 (1997): 91–126.

Broadcast of Violent, Indecent, and Obscene Material, 51 F.C.C. 2d 418 (1975).

Brown v. Entertainment Merchants Association, 564 U.S. 786 (2011).

Browning, G. "Push-Button Violence." *National Journal* 26 (February 1994): 458.

Brummett, Barry. "A Pentadic Analysis of Ideologies in Two Gay Rights Controversies." *Communication Studies* 30 (1979): 250–61.

Bruner, M. Lane, and Susan Balter-Reitz. "*Snyder v. Phelps*: The U.S. Supreme Court's Spectacular Erasure of the Tragic Spectacle." *Rhetoric and Public Affairs* 76 (2013): 651–84.

Buckley v. Valeo, 424 U.S. 1, 241 (1976).

Burke, Kenneth. *Permanence and Change: An Anatomy of Purpose*, 3rd ed. Berkeley: University of California Press, 1984.

Burwell v. Hobby Lobby, 573 U.S. 682 (2014).

Calabrese, Brian. "Fear-Based Standing: Cognizing an Injury-in-Fact." *Washington and Lee Law Review* 68 (Fall 2011): 1445–77.

California Civil Code Annual Section 1746.

Calvert, Clay. "The FCC and Profane Language: The Lugubrious Legacy of a Moral Panic and a Grossly Offensive Definition That Must Be Jettisoned." *First Amendment Law Review* 17 (2018): 161.

Camp v. Board of Public Instruction, 368 U.S. 278 (1961).

Cantor, Joseph E. *Campaign Financing: Updated*. Washington, DC: Congressional Research Service, Library of Congress, December 17, 1997.

Cantwell v. Connecticut, 310 U.S. 296 (1940).

Capehart, Jonathan. "What Hobby Lobby Decision Means for the LGBT Community." *Washington Post* (website). June 30, 2014, accessed April 11, 2015.

Chaplinsky v. New Hampshire, 315 U.S. 568 (1942).

Christian Legal Society v. Martinez, 561 U.S. 661 (2010).

BIBLIOGRAPHY

Chulack, Charles. "The First Amendment Does Not Require Schools to Tolerate Student Expression That Contributes to the Dangers of Illegal Drug Use: Morse v. Frederick." *Duquesne Law Review* 46 (Spring 2008): 521–50.

Cicero, Marcus Tullius. *De Officiis: On Duties; or, On Obligations.* Walter Miller (Trans). New York: Macmillan, 1817.

Citizens United v. Federal Election Commission, 558 U.S. 310 (2010).

City of Boerne v. Flores, 521 U.S. 507 (1997).

Clark v. Community for Creative Non-Violence, 468 U.S. 288 (1984).

Cohen v. California, 403 U.S. 15 (1971).

Cohen, Stanley. *Folk Devils and Moral Panics: The Creation of Mods and Rockers.* London: Routledge Classics, 2011.

Collins, Keith. "Filling the Gaps Left by Morse v. Frederick: Empowering Schools to Discipline Cyberbullies and Gang Members." *Whittier Law Review* 32 (Spring 2011): 509–31.

Collins, Ronald K. L. "Free Speech, Food Libel, & the First Amendment." *Ohio Northern University Law Review* 26 (2000): 1–56.

Colorado Republican Committee v. FEC, 518 U.S. 604 (1996).

Colorado Republican Committee v. FEC, 533 U.S. 431 (2001).

Connick v. Myers, 461 U.S. 138 (1983).

Consolidated Edison Co. v. Public Service Commission, 447 U.S. 530 (1980).

Cremin, Lawrence A. "Educational Configurations in Colonial America." In *Education in American History: Readings on Social Issues*, ed. Michael B. Katz. New York: Praeger, 1973.

De Waal, Frans. *Good Natured: The Origins of Right and Wrong in Humans and Other Animals.* Cambridge, MA: Harvard University Press, 1996.

DeBaron, William Paul. "Prepared Statement of William Paul DeBaron, Detective, Long Beach Police Department Regarding the 'Crush Video' Legislation," Hearing Before the Subcommittee on Crime of the Committee on the Judiciary of the House of Representatives on Punishing Depictions of Animal Cruelty and the Federal Prisoner Health Care Co-payment Act of 1999. September 30, 1999.

DeFilippo v. National Broadcasting Co, Inc., 446 A. 2d 1036 (R.I. 1982).

Dennis v. United States, 341 U.S. 494 (1951).

Dillio, Richard. "A Critical Mass: Video Games, Violence, and Ineffective Legislation." *First Amendment Studies* 48 (2014): 110–30.

Dixon, David. *Never Come to Peace Again: Pontiac's Uprising and the Fate of the British Empire in North America.* Norman: University of Oklahoma Press, 2005.

"Donors: Survey Sheds Light on Firms That Play Politics." *Los Angeles Times* (September 21, 1997): A24.

Dun & Bradstreet, Inc. v. Greenmoss Builders, Inc. 472 U.S. 749 (1985).

Dyke, Jim. "Letter to the FCC—Re: Court Remand of Section III.B of the

BIBLIOGRAPHY

Commission's March 2006 *Omnibus Order* Resolving Numerous Broadcast Indecency Complaints." FCC (website). September 21, 2006, accessed February 3, 2021.

Easton, Eric B. "The Colonel's Finest Campaign: Robert R. McCormick and *Near v. Minnesota.*" *Federal Communications Law Journal* 60 (March 2008): 183–228.

Ellis, Joseph J. *American Dialogue: The Founders and Us.* New York: Vintage Books, 2018.

Elonis v. United States, 575 U.S. 723 (2015).

Emerson, Thomas I. "Toward a General Theory of the First Amendment." *Yale Law Journal* 72 (1963): 877–87.

Engels, Jeremy. "Uncivil Speech: Invective and the Rhetorics of Democracy in the Early Republic." *Quarterly Journal of Speech* 95, no. 3 (2009): 311–34.

Erznoznik v. City of Jacksonville, 422 U.S. 205 (1975).

Esbeck, Carl H. "Uses and Abuses of Textualism and Originalism in Establishment Clause Interpretation." *Utah Law Review* (2011): 489–521.

Everson v. Board of Education, 330 U.S. 1 (1947).

Everson, Michelle. "Legal Constructions of the Consumer." In *The Making of the Consumer: Knowledge, Power and Identity in the Modern World,* ed. Frank Trentmann. New York: Berg Publishers, 2006.

Facts on File News Services. "Student Free Speech Rights." April 27, 2007, accessed July 4, 2013.

Fahmy, Shahira, and Thomas J. Johnson. "Mediating the Anthrax Attacks: Media Accuracy and Agenda Setting During a Time of Moral Panic." *Atlantic Journal of Communication* 19 (2007): 19–40.

Fairness Report, 102 F.C.C. 2d 143, 191 (1985).

Falsioni, Darcie A., and Jeffrey M. Tanenbaum. "Religious Freedom for Corporations? The Hobby Lobby Decision Breaks New Ground." Nixon Peabody (website), July 2, 2014, accessed April 11, 2015.

FCC v. Fox Television Stations, Inc. I, 556 U.S. 502 (2009).

FCC v. Fox Television Stations, Inc. II, 567 U.S. 239 (2012).

FCC v. League of Women Voters, 468 U.S. 364 (1984).

FCC v. Red Lion Broadcasting Co., 395 U.S. 367 (1969).

FEC v. Furgatch, 484 U.S. 850 (1987).

Federal Employees' Compensation Act. Section 441e.

Fontana, Benedetto. "'Is It Better to Be Feared Than Loved?': Machiavelli and the Bases of Political Action." Paper Presented at the Rhetoric Society of America Conference. Philadelphia, May 2012.

Foreman, Judy. "Violence May Lie in Damaged Brain Cells." *Los Angeles Times* (April 29, 2002): S1.

Foster, James C. *BONG HiTS 4 JESUS: A Perfect Constitutional Storm in Alaska's Capital.* Anchorage: University of Alaska Press, 2010.

BIBLIOGRAPHY

Foucault, Michel. *Power/Knowledge: Selected Interviews and Other Writings, 1972–1977*. New York: Pantheon, 1980.

Fowles, Jib. *The Case for Television Violence*. Menlo Park, CA: Sage Publications, 2000.

"Frederick v. Morse." Juneau School District press release. March 14, 2006.

Freedman, Jonathan. "Television Violence and Aggression: A Rejoinder." *Psychological Bulletin* 100 (1986): 372–78.

Freire, Paulo. "The 'Banking' Concept of Education." In *Educational Foundations: An Anthology of Critical Readings*, 105–17. Menlo Park, CA: Sage Publications, 1970.

Frisby v. Schultz. 487 U.S. 474 (1988).

Fromm, Erich. *The Fear of Freedom*. New York: Routledge, 2004.

Frost, Robert. "A Hundred Collars." *Poetry and Drama* 1, no. 4 (December 1913): 409.

Gadamer, Hans Georg. "On the Scope and Function of Hermeneutical Reflection." G. B. Hess and R. E. Palmer, trans. In *Philosophical Hermeneutics*, ed. D. E. Linge, 18–44. Berkeley: University of California Press, 1976.

Gadamer, Hans Georg. *Truth and Method*. 2nd ed., trans. J. Weinsheimer and D. G. Marshall. New York: Crossroad, 1989.

Galella v. Onassis, 353 F. Supp. 196 (S.D. N.Y., 1972).

Galella v. Onassis, 487 F. 2d 986 (2d Cir., 1973).

Gayoso, Jay A. "The FCC's Regulation of Broadcast Indecency: A Broadened Approach for Removing Immorality from the Airwaves." *University of Miami Law Review* 43 (1989): 871–920.

Geiger, Kim, and Tom Hamburger. "Hidden Donors Pour Funds into Campaign." *Los Angeles Times* (October 24, 2010): A34.

Gibson, Katie L., and Amy L. Heyse. "Suppression of the Suffrage Movement." In *Silencing the Opposition*, ed. Craig R. Smith, 151–74. 2nd ed. Albany: SUNY Press, 2011.

Ginsberg v. New York, 390 U.S. 629 (1963).

Gold, Matea. "Obama Closing in on Record $1 billion." *Los Angeles Times* (October 3, 2012): A13.

Goldberg, Erica. "Amending *Christian Legal Society v. Martinez*: Protecting Expressive Association as an Independent Right in a Limited Public Forum." *Texas Journal on Civil Liberties and Civil Rights* 16 (2011): 129–70.

Goode, Erich, and Nachman Ben-Yehuda. "Moral Panics: Culture, Politics, and Social Construction." *Annual Review of Sociology* 20 (1994): 149–71.

Goodno, Naomi Harlin. "How Public Schools Can Constitutionally Halt Cyberbullying: A Model Cyberbullying Policy That Considers First Amendment, Due Process, and Fourth Amendment Challenges." *Wake Forest Law Review* 46 (2011): 641–700.

BIBLIOGRAPHY

Gray, Timothy E. "V-Chip: The Betamax of the '90s." *Broadcasting & Cable* (April 15, 1996): 30.

Greenwald, Glenn. "Anti-Israeli Activism Criminalized in the Land of Charlie Hebdo and 'Free Speech.'" *Intercept* (website). October 27, 2015, accessed February 10, 2021.

Haidt, Jonathan. *The Righteous Mind: Why Good People Are Divided by Politics and Religion.* New York: Pantheon Books, 2012.

Haiman, Franklyn S. *Speech and Law in a Free Society.* Chicago: University of Chicago Press, 1981.

Hamburger, Philip. "Separation and Interpretation." *Journal of Law and Politics* 18 (Winter 2002): 7–64.

———. *Separation of Church and State.* Cambridge, MA: Harvard University Press, 2004.

Harrell, Alec. "Who Cares About Prior Restraint? An Analysis of the FCC's Enforcement of Indecency Forfeiture Orders." *Southern California Law Review* (1996): 239–51.

Heidegger, Martin. *Being and Time.* Trans. Joan Stambaugh. Albany: SUNY Press, 1996.

Heins, Marjorie. "Media Violence and Free Speech." Paper presented to International Conference on Violence in the Media (October 4, 1994).

Herman, Sarah. "The Battle for the Remote Control—Has the FCC Indecency Policy Worn Out Its Welcome in America's Living Room?" *Washington University Journal of Law and Policy* 38 (2012): 287–352.

Hess v. Indiana, 414 U.S. 105 (1973).

Hickey, Jeremiah. "Death by Adjective: The Supreme Court's Attack on Legislative Regulations of Violence, or, How Chief Justice John G. Roberts and Justice Antonin Scalia Stopped Worrying about Symbolic Violence by Employing Aesthetic Claims to Limit Legislative Restrictions on Violence." *First Amendment Studies* 47 (2013): 106–32.

Hill v. Colorado, 530 U.S. 703 (2000).

Hirsch, E. D. "Objective Interpretation." *PMLA* 75 (1960): 463–79.

Hlebowitsh, Peter S. *Foundations of American Education: Purpose and Promise.* Belmont, CA: Wadsworth Publishing, 2001.

Howard, R. M., and J. A. Segal. "An Original Look at Originalism." *Law and Society Review* 36 (2002): 113–38.

Howell, Larry. "Once Upon a Time in the West: Citizens United, Caperton, and the War of the Copper Kings." *Montana Law Review* 73 (2012): 25–35.

Hurley v. Irish-American Gay-Lesbian and Bisexual Group, 515 U.S. 577 (1995).

Hustler Magazine v. Falwell, 485 U.S. 46 (1988).

Hyde, Michael J., and Craig R. Smith. "Heidegger and Aristotle on Emotion: Questions of Time and Space." In *The Critical Turn: Rhetoric and*

BIBLIOGRAPHY

Philosophy in Postmodern Discourse, ed. Ian Angus and Lenore Langsdorf, 68–99. Carbondale: Southern Illinois University Press, 1992.

Inazu, John D. "Siding with Sameness." *New Observer* (website). July 1, 2010, accessed October 16, 2014.

James v. Meow Media, 90 F. Supp 2d 798 (W.D. Ky., 2000).

Japanese Buddhism. (website). Date Unavailable, accessed July 31, 2023.

Jay, John. Letter to Benjamin Rush, March 24, 1785. *The Selected Papers of John Jay*, Vol. 4, 1785–1788, ed. Elizabeth M. Nuxoll, 72–73. Charlottesville: University of Virginia Press, 2015.

Jessell, Harry A. "WDBJ Fine Highlights Broadcast Inequality." TVNewsCheck: The Business of Broadcasting (website). March 27, 2015, accessed June 1, 2016.

The Jim Bakker Show (website). "Washington State High School Coach Vindicated by Supreme Court Ruling in Favor of His Right to Pray," June 22, 2022, accessed February 1, 2023.

Joseph Burstyn, Inc. v. Wilson, 343 U.S. 495, 503 (1952).

Johnson, Kevin A. "The First Amendment and Rhetorical Style: The Politics of School Dress Codes." In *The Politics of Style and the Style of Politics*, ed. Barry Brummett, 173–90. Lanham, MD: Lexington Books, 2011.

Johnson, Kevin A. "The Kennedy Court: Reflections on the First Amendment Ruling in *Christian Legal Society v. Martinez*." *Free Speech Yearbook* 45 (2011): 31–45.

Johnston, Louis D. "Hobby Lobby Ruling: The Crux of the Problem Is Employer-Provided Health Insurance." *Minnesota Post* (website). July 1, 2014, accessed April 11, 2015.

JTA. "French High Court: BDS Activists Guilty of Discrimination." *Times of Israel* (website). October 23, 2015, accessed February 10, 2021.

Juneau School District's Policy. Available at Juneau School Board website, accessed April 1, 2013.

Kantar Media/CMAG. Political Ads Airing Data. Wesleyan Media Project (website). 2023, accessed July 31, 2023.

Kay, Amanda. "The Agony of Ecstasy: Reconsidering the Punitive Approach to United States Drug Policy." *Fordham Urban Law Journal* 29 (2002): 2132–91.

Kennedy v. Bremerton School District, 597 U.S. _____ (2022). Slip Opinion.

Keyishian v. Board of Regents. 385 U.S. 589 (1966).

Kierkegaard, Søren. *Concluding Unscientific Postscript*. Trans. David F. Swenson and Walter Lowrie. Princeton, NJ: Princeton University Press, 1968.

Knapp, Jonathan. "Annual Review of Environmental and Natural Resources Law: Note: Making Snow in the Desert: Defining Substantial Burden under RFRA." *Ecology Law Quarterly* 36 (2009): 259–316.

BIBLIOGRAPHY

Knechtle, John C. "When to Regulate Hate Speech." *Penn State Law Review* 110 (2006): 539–78.

Koeninger, W. David. "Removing Access to Health Care From Employer and State Control: The ACA as Anti-Subordination Legislation." *University of Baltimore Law Review* 44 (2015): 201–35.

Krattenmaker, Thomas G., and L. A. Powe Jr. "Televised Violence: First Amendment Principles and Social Science Theory." *Virginia Law Review* 64 (1978): 1123–297.

———. "Converging First Amendment Principles for Converging Media." *Yale Law Journal* 104 (1995): 1719–41.

Kunich, John Charles. "Natural Born Copycat Killers and the Law of Shock Torts." *Washington University Law Quarterly* 78 (Winter 2000): 1157–270.

Lande, Raymond G. "The Video Violence Debate." *Hospital and Community Psychiatry* 44 (1993): 347–51.

Langford, Catherine L. *Scalia v. Scalia: Opportunistic Textualism in Constitutional Interpretation.* Tuscaloosa: University of Alabama Press, 2018.

Lawrence v. Texas, 539 U.S. 558 (2003).

Laycock, Douglas, and Oliver S. Thomas. "Interpreting the Religious Freedom Restoration Act." *Texas Law Review* 73 (1994): 209–46.

Lee v. Weisman, 505 U.S. 577 (1992).

Lee, Eun-Ju, Hyun Suk Kim, and Soonwook Choi. "Violent Video Games and Aggression: Stimulation or Catharsis or Both?" *Cyberpsychology, Behavior, and Social Networking* 24 (2021): 41–47.

Lessig, Lawrence. "Statement of Lawrence Lessig." *Legislative Proposals to Protect Children from Inappropriate Materials on the Internet*. Hearing Before the Subcommittee on Telecommunications, Trade, and Consumer Protection of the Committee on Commerce, United States House of Representatives, 105th Congress, Second Session, September 11, 1998, Serial No. 105–19.

Levy, Pema. "Does the Hobby Lobby Decision Threaten Gay Rights?" *Newsweek* (website). July 9, 2014, accessed April 11, 2015.

Lief, Judith. "Starting on the Path of Fear and Fearlessness." Mountain Hermitage (website). April 28, 2022. Accessed July 31, 2023; excerpted from an article that first appeared in May 25, 2017, issue of *Lion's Roar* magazine.

Lipson, Jonathan C. "On Balance: Religious Liberty and Third-Party Harms." *Minnesota Law Review* 84 (2000): 589–625.

Little, Morgan. "Election Spending Caps Backed in Poll." *Los Angeles Times* (September 17, 2012): A7.

Livingston, Gretchen. "The Rise of Single Fathers: A Ninefold Increase Since 1960." Pew Research Center: Social and Demographic Trends (website). July 2, 2013, accessed April 14, 2015.

Lloyd, Harold Anthony. "Crushing Animals and Crashing Funerals: The Semiotics of Free Expression." *First Amendment Law Review* 12 (2013): 1–65.

BIBLIOGRAPHY

Lombardi, Clark B. "Nineteenth-Century Free Exercise Jurisprudence and the Challenge of Polygamy: The Relevance of Nineteenth-Century Cases and Commentaries for Contemporary Debates About Free Exercise Exemptions." *Oregon Law Review* 85 (2006): 369–444.

Lovell v. City of Griffin, 303 U.S. 444 (1938).

Loving v. Virginia, 388 U.S. 1 (1967).

Lucas, George, dir. *Star Wars: Episode I—The Phantom Menace*. Los Angeles: Twentieth Century Fox, 1999.

Lynn, Richard, Susan Hampson, and Edwina Agahi. "Television Violence and Aggression: A Genotype-Environment, Correlation and Interaction Theory." *Social Behavior and Personality: An International Journal* 17 (1989): 143–64.

Machiavelli, Niccolo. *The Portable Machiavelli*. Ed. and trans. Peter Bondanella and Mark Musa. New York: Penguin Books, 1979.

Madison, James. *The Letters and Other Writings of James Madison*. Ed. Philip R. Fendall. Volume 3. Philadelphia: Lippincott, 1865.

———. "The Meaning of the Maxim, Which Requires a Separation of the Departments of Power, Examined and Ascertained." In *The Federalist Papers*. New York: Penguin Books, 1987.

———. Letter to W. T. Barry. *The Founders' Constitution*. Chicago: University of Chicago Press, 1987.

Mahanoy Area School District, 594 U.S. _____ (2021). Slip Opinion.

Mann, Horace. "Seventh Annual Report to the Massachusetts State Board of Education, 1843." In *Readings in Public Education in the United States: A Collection of Sources and Readings to Illustrate the History of Educational Practice and Progress in the United States*, ed. Ellwood Cubberly, 287–88. Boston: Houghton Mifflin, 1934.

Mannheimer, Michael J. "The Fighting Words Doctrine." *Columbia Law Review* 93 (1993): 1527–71.

Marcus, Ruth. "DNC Official Concedes 'Mistakes of Process.'" *Washington Post* (November 13, 1996): A4.

Markoe, Lauren. "Five Takeaways from the Hobby Lobby Case," Religion News Service (website). June 30, 2014, accessed April 11, 2015.

Mason, Melanie. "Republicans' Attack." *Los Angeles Times* (October 19, 2012): A12.

Massumi, Brian. "Everywhere You Want to Be." In *The Politics of Everyday Fear*. Minneapolis: University of Minnesota Press, 1993.

Masterpiece Cakeshop v. Colorado Civil Rights Commission, 584 U.S. _____ (2018).

Mayer, Jane. "Schmooze or Lose: Obama Doesn't Like Cozying Up to Billionaires; Could It Cost Him the Election?" *New Yorker* (August 27, 2012).

McCormack, John. "Hobby Lobby Hysteria." *Weekly Standard* (website), July 14, 2014, accessed April 11, 2015.

BIBLIOGRAPHY

McNatt, Glenn. "Larry Flynt Isn't Worthy, but Freedom of Speech Is." *Baltimore Sun* (January 12, 1997).

McNee, Emily. "Disrupting the Pickering Balance: First Amendment Protections for Teachers in the Digital Age." *Minnesota Law Review* 97 (2013): 1818–57.

Megerian, Chris. "Governor OKs Funeral Protest Law." *Los Angeles Times* (September 18, 2012): AA3.

Merl, Jean, and Richard Simon. "Outside Cash Stoking State House Races." *Los Angeles Times* (October 26, 2012): A1.

Meyer, Adolphe E. *An Educational History of the American People.* 2nd ed. New York: McGraw-Hill Book Company, 1967.

Miami Herald Co. v. Tornillo, 418 U.S. 241 (1974).

Midlarsky, Elizabeth, and Helen Marie Klain. "A History of Violence in the Schools." In *Violence in Schools: Cross-National and Cross-Cultural Perspectives,* ed. Florence Denmark, Herbert H. Krauss, Robert W. Wesner, Elizabeth Midlarsky, and Uwe P. Gielen, 37–54. New York: Springer Science and Business Media, 2005.

Milgram, Stanley, and R. Lance Shotland. *Television and Antisocial Behavior: Field Experiments.* New York: Academic Press, 1973.

Miller v. California, 413 U.S. 15 (1973).

Minersville School District v. Gobitis, 310 U.S. 586 (1940).

Miscaro, Lisa. "Rove Keeps Low Profile for November." *Los Angeles Times* (June 8, 2014): A7.

Mohr, Melissa. *Holy Shit: A Brief History of Swearing.* New York: Oxford University Press, 2013.

"Money: More Than Ever." *Los Angeles Times* (May 16, 1998): A6.

Moore v. Ingebretsen, 519 U.S. 965 (1996).

Morris, Robert J. "'What Though Our Rights Have Been Assailed?' Mormons, Politics, Same-Sex Marriage, and Cultural Abuse in the Sandwich Islands (Hawai'i)." *Women's Rights Law Reporter* 18 (1997): 1–78 .

Morton, Tom, and Eurydice Aroney. "Journalism, Moral Panic and the Public Interest." *Journalism Practice* 18 (2016): 18–34.

McConnell v. Federal Election Commission, 540 U.S. 93 (2003).

Moore v. Ingebretsen, 519 U.S. 965 (1996).

Morse v. Frederick, 551 U.S. 393 (2007).

NAACP v. Alabama, 357 U.S. 449 (1958).

Nelson, Kellie. "The Supreme Court Takes a Fractured Stance on What Students Can Say About Drugs: *Morse v. Frederick.*" *Wyoming Law Review* 8 (2008): 293–316.

New York Times Co. v. Sullivan, 376 U.S. 254 (1964).

Nickerson, Peter. "Prepared Statement of Peter Nickerson, CEO, N2H2." *Legislative Proposals to Protect Children from Inappropriate Materials on the*

BIBLIOGRAPHY

Internet. Hearing Before the Subcommittee on Telecommunications, Trade, and Consumer Protection of the Committee on Commerce, United States House of Representatives, 105th Congress, Second Session, September 11, 1998, Serial No. 105–19.

Nietzsche, Friedrich Wilhelm. *Beyond Good and Evil*. Trans. Helen Zimmern. New York: MacMillan Company, 1907.

NRB (National Religious Broadcasters). "Supreme Court Sides with 'Praying Coach' Kennedy, Upholding Right to Public Prayer." June 30, 2022, accessed February 1, 2023.

Nugent, Nicholas. "Toward a RFRA That Works." *Vanderbilt Law Review* 61 (2008): 1027–66.

Office on Women's Health (website), US Department of Health and Human Services. "You're Pregnant: Now What?" September 27, 2010, accessed April 14, 2015.

Olivia N. v. National Broadcasting Co., 74 Cal. App. 3d 383 (1977).

Pacifica Radio Foundation v. Federal Communications Commission, 438 U.S. 726 (1978).

Pally, Marcia. *Sex and Sensibility: Reflections on Forbidden Mirrors and the Will to Censor*. Hopewell, NJ: Ecco Press, 1994.

Palmer, Brian. "Does Paper Really Burn at 451 Degrees Fahrenheit?: Fact-Checking the Late Ray Bradbury." *Slate* (website), June 8, 2012

Pawelczyk, Elizabeth A. "*Frederick v. Morse*: Protecting Student Speech beyond the Schoolhouse Gates." Senior Thesis. Department of Communication at Boston College. May 2007: 3–4.

Peters, Gary C., Senator of Michigan, "Statement of Congressman Gary C. Peters." Hearing on United States v. Stevens: The Supreme Court's Decision Invalidating the Crush Videos Statute. Subcommittee on Crime, Terrorism & Homeland Security of the House Committee on the Judiciary. (May 26, 2010).

Pew Research: Religion and Public Life (website). "In Brief: Christian Legal Society v. Martinez." April 6, 2010, accessed October 16, 2014.

Philipp, Michael C., and Laura Lombardo. "Hurt Feelings and Four Letter Words: Swearing Alleviates the Pain of Social Distress." *European Journal of Social Psychology* 47 (2017): 17–23.

Plato. *Timaeus*. Trans. Donald J. Zeyl. Indianapolis: Hackett Publishing, 2000.

Pleasant Grove City v. Summum, 555 U.S. 460 (2009).

Police Department of the City of Chicago v. Mosley, 408 U.S. 92 (1972).

Policinski, Gene. "Student-Free Speech Case Addresses Post-Columbine Fears and Expectations." *Muskogee Phoenix* (website). March 27, 2007, accessed July 4, 2013.

Popuşoi, Simona A., Grigore M. Havârneanu, and Corneliu E. Havârneanu. "'Get the F#*k Out of My Way!' Exploring the Cathartic Effect of Swear Words

BIBLIOGRAPHY

in Coping with Driving Anger." *Transportation Research Part F: Traffic Psychology and Behaviour* 56 (2018): 215–26.

Powell, H. J. "The Original Understanding of Original Intent." *Harvard Law Review* 98 (1995): 885–948.

Prosser, W. Page, and William Lloyd Keeton. *Law of Torts*. 5th ed. Eagan, MN: West Group Publishing, 1984.

Przybylski, Andrew, and Allison Fine Mishken. "How the Quantity and Quality of Electronic Gaming Relates to Adolescents' Academic Engagement and Psychosocial Adjustment." *Psychology of Popular Media Culture* 5 (2016): 145–56.

Public Stations Fear Indecency Fine Jump Means Premium Hikes. *Public Broadcasting Report*, July 7, 2006.

Puiszis, Steven M. "'Tinkering' with the First Amendment's Protection of Student Speech on the Internet." *John Marshall Journal of Computer and Information Law* 29 (2011): 167–229.

Pulliam, John D. *History of Education in America*. Columbus, OH: Charles E. Merrill Publishing Company, 1968.

Quale, Courtney Livingston. "Hear an [Expletive], There an [Expletive], But[t] . . . The Federal Communications Commission Will Not Let You Say an [Expletive]." *Willamette Law Review* 45 (2008): 207–60.

Rakowski, Kristin L. "Branding as an Antidote to Indecency Regulation." *UCLA Entertainment Law Review* 16 (2009): 2–43.

Rampton, Sheldon, and John Stauber. *Mad Cow USA: Could the Nightmare Happen Here?* Madison, WI: Common Courage Press, 1997.

Reed, Jr., Lowell A. *American Civil Liberties Union v. Reno*. United States District Court, E. D. Pennsylvania, No. CIV. A. 98–5591 (November 23, 1998).

"Remembering Ray Bradbury." *American Libraries Magazine* (website), July 2, 2013.

Reno v. American Civil Liberties Union, 117 S. Ct. 2329 (1997).

Reynolds v. United States, 98 U.S. 145 (1879).

Ringeisen, Kristin. "The Use of Community Standards by the Child Online Protection Act to Determine if Material Is Harmful to Minors Is Not Unconstitutional: Ashcroft v. American Civil Liberties Union." *Duquesne Law Review* 41 (2003): 449–66.

Robin, Corey. *Fear: The History of a Political Idea*. New York: Oxford University Press, 2004.

Robin-Vergeer, Bonnie I. "Disposing of the Red Herring: A Defense of the Religious Freedom Restoration Act." *Southern California Law Review* 69 (1996): 741–85.

Romano, Allison. "Reporting Live. Very Carefully." *Broadcasting & Cable* (July 4, 2005): 8–9.

Roodenburg, Johanna M. "'Son of CDA': The Constitutionality of the Child

BIBLIOGRAPHY

Online Protection Act of 1998." *Communication Law and Policy* 6 (2001): 227–57.

Roth v. United States, 354 U.S. 476 (1957).

Russell, Bertrand. "Outline of Intellectual Rubbish." In *The Basic Writings of Bertrand Russell*, 45–71. New York: Routledge, 2003.

Sachs, Andrew. "Silencing the Union Movement." In *Silencing the Opposition*, ed. Craig R. Smith, 125–50, 2nd ed. Albany: SUNY Press, 2011.

San Diego v. Roe, 543 U.S. 77 (2004).

Sanders, Sam. "Five Things to Know About the 2014 Midterm Elections." NPR, *The Two-Way* (blog). November 2, 2014, accessed November 4, 2014.

Santa Fe Independent School District v. Doe, 530 U.S. 290 (2000).

Sartre, Jean-Paul. *The Flies*. Paris: Gallimard, 1947.

Schenck v. United States, 249 U.S. 41 (1919).

Selnow, Gary. "Prime-Time TV's Rich Lessons." *San Francisco Chronicle* (March 14, 1994): A21.

Shapiro, Steven R., Christopher A. Hansen, and Marjorie Heins. Brief Amicusc Curiae of the American Civil Liberties Union, the New York Civil Liberties Union, American Booksellers Foundation for Free Expression, American Federation of Television And Radio Artists, Directors Guild of America, First Amendment Project, Minnesota Public Radio/American Public Media, National Alliance for Media Arts and Culture, National Coalition Against Censorship, National Federation of Community Broadcasters, Pen American Center, and Washington Area, Lawyers for the Arts in Support of Respondents. *Federal Communications Commission v. FOX Television Stations, Inc.* No. 07–582 (August 8, 2008).

Shiffrin, Steven H. *The First Amendment, Democracy, and Romance*. Cambridge, MA: Harvard University Press, 1990.

Shumsky, Eric Alan. "The Religious Freedom Restoration Act: Post Mortem of a Failed Statute." *West Virginia Law Review* 102 (1999): 81–130.

Slade, Joseph W. *Pornography: A Reference Guide*. Westport, CT: Greenwood Press, 1998.

Sloustcher, Adam F. "Arizona v. Winn: Negative Implications for First Amendment Proponents and Possibly for Our Nation's Schoolchildren." *Hastings Constitutional Law Quarterly* 40 (2013): 967–88.

Smith v. Collin. 436 U.S. 953 (1978).

Smith v. Collin, 439 U.S. 916 (1978).

Smith, Craig R. *Rhetoric and Human Consciousness: A History*. 5th ed. Prospect Heights, IL: Waveland Press, 2017.

———. "Violence in Programming: Can It Be Deemed Obscene or Indecent." *Nexus Law Journal* 10 (2005): 135–57.

———. "Violence as Indecency: Pacifica's Open Door Policy." *Law Journal of Florida International University* 2 (2007): 75–92.

BIBLIOGRAPHY

———. "The Alien and Sedition Crisis." In *Silencing the Opposition: How the U.S. Government Suppressed Freedom of Expression During Major Crises*, ed. Craig R. Smith, 1–26. 2nd ed. Albany: State University of New York Press, 2011.

———. "The Red Scares." In *Silencing the Opposition*, ed. Craig R. Smith, 175–204. 2nd ed. Albany: State University of New York Press, 2011.

Smith, Craig R., and David M. Hunsaker. *The Four Freedoms of the First Amendment*. Prospect Heights, IL: Waveland Press, 2004.

Smith, Craig R., and Stephanie J. Hurst. "Lincoln and Habeas Corpus." In *Silencing the Opposition*, ed. Craig R. Smith, 87–124. 2nd ed. Albany: State University of New York Press, 2011.

Smith, Craig R., and Michael J. Hyde. "Rethinking the Public: The Role of Emotion in Being-with-Others." *Quarterly Journal of Speech* 77 (1991): 446–66.

Snyder v. Phelps, 562 U.S. 443 (2011).

"Soft Money Dollars." *Time* (September 9, 1999): 42–44.

Somers, Zachary. "The Mythical Wall of Separation: How the Supreme Court Has Amended the Constitution." *Georgetown Journal of Law & Public Policy* 2 (2004): 288–342.

Staples v. United States, 511 U.S. 600 (1994).

Steinberg, David E. "Thomas Jefferson's Establishment Clause Federalism." *Hastings Constitutional Law Quarterly* 40 (2013): 277–318.

Sternheimer, Karen. "Blaming Television and Movies Is Easy and Wrong." *Los Angeles Times* (February 4, 2001): M5.

Strassburger, Victor. "Television and Adolescents: Sex, Drugs, Rock 'n' Roll." *Adolescent Medicine* 1 (1990): 161–94.

Surgeon General's Report by the Scientific Advisory Committee on Television and Social Behavior: Hearings Before the Subcomm. on Communications of the Senate Comm. on Commerce, 92nd Congress, 2nd Session, 25, 26 (1972).

Svendsen, Lars. *A Philosophy of Fear*. Trans. John Irons. London: Reaktion Books Ltd., 2008.

Sweezy v. New Hampshire, 354 U.S. 234 (1957).

Tanfani, Joseph. "Democrats Lost Dark-Money Game." *Los Angeles Times* (November 9, 2014): A14.

Television and Growing Up: The Impact of Televised Violence. Washington, DC: US Government Printing Office, 1972.

Terminiello v. The City of Chicago, 337 U.S. 1 (1949).

Texas v. Johnson, 491 U.S. 397 (1989).

Tinker v. Des Moines Independent Community School District, 393 U.S. 503 (1969).

Toner, Michael W. "The Impact of Federal Election Laws on the 2008 Presidential Election." In *The Year of Obama: How Barack Obama Won the White House*, ed. Larry J. Sabato, 149–65. New York: Longman, 2010.

Toobin, Jeffrey. "Annals of Law: Money Unlimited; How Chief Justice Roberts

BIBLIOGRAPHY

Orchestrated the Citizens United Decision." *New Yorker* (May 21, 2012): 41–42.

———. *The Oath: The Obama White House and the Supreme Court.* New York: Doubleday, 2012.

Tutaj, Adam J. "Intrusion Upon Seclusion: Bringing an Otherwise Valid Cause of Action into the 21st Century." *Marquette Law Review* 82 (1999): 665–90.

United States v. Cruikshank, 92 U.S. 542 (1875).

United States v. O'Brien, 391 U.S. 367 (1968).

United States v. Stevens, 559 U.S. 460 (2010).

United States Supreme Court. "Oral Argument Transcript for *Virginia v. Black*." 538 U.S. 343 (2003).

Vico, Giambattista. *New Science.* Trans. Dave Marsh. 3rd ed. New York: Penguin Classics, 2000.

Va. Pharmacy Bd. v. Va. Consumer Council, 425 U.S. 748 (1976).

Valenti, Jessica. "'The Hobby Lobby Ruling Proves Men of the Law Still Can't Get Over 'Immoral' Women Having Sex." *Guardian* (website). June 30, 2014, accessed April 11, 2015).

Video Software Dealers Assn. v. Schwarzenegger, 556 F. 3d. 350 (2007).

Virginia v. Black, 538 U.S. 343 (2003).

Volkan, Kevin. "Written Testimony of Kevin Volkan." Hearing Before the Senate Judiciary Committee: "Prohibiting Obscene Animal Crush Videos in the Wake of United States v. Stevens" (September 15, 2010).

Walker v. Texas Division, Sons of Confederate Veterans, Inc., 135 U.S. 2239 (2015).

Walker, Ernest J. "The Communications Decency Act: A Cyber-Gag to First Amendment Rights on the Internet." *University of Detroit Mercy Law Review* (1997).

Walt Disney Productions v. Shannon, 247 Ga. 402, 276 S. E. 2d 580 (1981).

Ward v. Rock Against Racism, 491 U.S. 781 (1989).

Washington, George. "Eighth Annual Message to the Senate and House of Representative, December 7, 1796." Available at Yale Law School's Avalon Project: Documents in Law, History and Diplomacy (website), accessed October 26, 2012.

Watson-Tardiff, Amber. "Jillian Michaels Believes Pregnancy Ruins the Body, Plans to Adopt." NJ (website). April 23, 2010, accessed April 14, 2010.

Watters v. TSR, Inc., 904 F. 2d 378 (6th Cir. 1990).

Watts v. United States, 394 U.S. 705 (1969).

Webster, Noah. *American Dictionary of the English Language.* Websters Dictionary 1828 (website). Accessed May 2, 2023.

Weeden, L. Darnell. "A First Amendment Establishment Clause Analysis of Permanent Displays on Public Property as Government Speech." *Thurgood Marshall Law Review* 35 (2010): 217–47.

West Virginia State Board of Education v. Barnette, 319 U.S. 624 (1943).

BIBLIOGRAPHY

Wheaton College v. Burwell, 573 U.S. _____ (2014).

Wheeler, Richard S. *The Richest Hill on Earth*. New York: Forge Books, 2011.

Whitbeck, Wendy S. "Restoring Rites and Rejecting Wrongs: The Religious Freedom Restoration Act." *Seton Hall Legislative Journal* 18 (1994): 821–45.

Wiegman, O., M. Kuttschreuter, and B. Baarda. "A Longitudinal Study of the Effects of Television Viewing on Aggressive and Pro-Social Behaviours." *British Journal of Social Psychology* 31 (1992): 147–64.

Wilkinson v. Downton (1897), 2 Q. B. 57.

Williams, Dmitri, and M. Skoric. "Internet Fantasy Violence: A Test of Aggression in an Online Game." *Communication Monographs* 22 (2005): 217–33.

Williams, Dmitri. "Groups and Goblins: The Social and Civic Impact of Online Gaming." *Journal of Broadcasting and Electronic Media* 50 (2006): 651–70.

Williams, Jamie L. "Teens, Sexts, and Cyberspace: The Constitutional Implications of Current Sexting and Cyberbullying Laws." *William and Mary Bill of Rights Journal* 20 (2012): 1017–50.

Wilson, John K. "Commentary on CLS v. Martinez." *College Freedom* (blog). June 29, 2010, accessed October 16, 2014.

Winn, Randall E. Executive Director at Veterans and Friends of Puget Sound, Comment in the comment section of Jill Filipovic. "13 Reactions to the Hobby Lobby Case That Are Completely Misinformed." *Cosmopolitan* (website). July 2, 2014, accessed May 2, 2023.

Winters v. New York, 333 U.S. 507 (1948).

Wolfe, Gabriela. "Anything but Ag-Gag: Ending the Industry-Advocate Cycle." *Syracuse Law Review* 66 (2016): 367–95.

Wooley vs. Maynard, 430 U.S. 705 (1977).

Writers Guild of America W., Inc. v. FCC, 423 F. Supp. 1064, 1161 (C.D. Cal. 1976).

Yates v. United States, 354 U.S. 298 (1957).

Yoo, Christopher S. "Constitutional Transformations: The State, the Citizen, and the Changing Role of Government." *William and Mary Law Review* 53 (2011): 748–76.

Young, Ashley. "Why HU [Howard University] Students Need to Know About Burwell vs Hobby Lobby." *Hilltop* (website). September 19, 2014, accessed April 11, 2015.

Zamora v. Columbia Broadcasting System, 480 F. Supp. 199 (S.D. Fla., 1979).

Zelezny, John D. *Communications Law: Liberties, Restraints, and the Modern Media*. 5th ed. Belmont, CA: Thomson Higher Education, 2007.

Zipursky, Benjamin C. "*Snyder v. Phelps*, Outrageousness, and the Open Texture of Tort Law." *DePaul Law Review* 60, no. 2 (Winter 2011).

Index

abortion, 15, 70–71, 99, 103–5, 115–16, 182

abuse, 38, 45, 88, 92, 133, 136, 149, 170, 180

Adamson v. People of the State of California, 190, 210n23, 220n18

advertisements, 55–56, 63, 66, 69–73, 76–77, 132

Affordable Care Act (ACA; also known as "Obamacare"), 98, 100–102, 104, 107–8, 184

Alito, Samuel 38, 45, 51, 68, 78, 81, 83, 94–95, 97, 99–100, 104, 123–25, 127, 142–49, 160, 165, 170–72, 176, 180, 184–86

Althusser, Louis, 26

American Amusement Machine Association v. Kendrick, 140

American Indians, 36. *See also* Native Americans

American Tradition Partnership v. Bullock, 79

Americans for Prosperity v. Bonta, 78

animals, 24, 97, 152, 164–68, 188

Anti-Federalists, 10, 59, 107

arbitrary, 59, 74, 117–18, 133–36, 145, 149, 190

Aristotle, 20–22, 26, 175, 198n47

artistic freedom, 140, 142–43, 147, 155, 164, 167, 170, 187–88

Ashcroft v. ACLU, 18, 140, 151, 161–64, 188

Ashcroft v. Free Speech Coalition, 18, 140

Austin v. Michigan Chamber of Commerce, 69–70, 72–74, 183, 203n42

B.L. v. Mahanoy, 27, 45–46, 49

banned books, 68

Bethel School District v. Fraser, 18, 49

Biden, Joe, 1–2

Bigelow v. Virginia, 70

Bill of Rights: English, 115; US, 6, 7, 10–11, 42, 91, 183, 187, 190–91, 210n23, 220n18

Black, Hugo, 123, 189, 190–92, 210n21, 210n23, 220n18

Bono (U2), 151, 157, 173

Brandeis, Louis, 28, 115

Brandenburg v. Ohio, 4–5, 15, 120, 171, 218n69

Brennan, William, 50, 60, 76, 89, 118, 153, 154, 202n15

Brown v. Entertainment Merchants Association, 27, 131, 134, 141, 186

Brown v. Socialist Workers '74 Campaign Comm, 96

Buddha, 22–23, 197n38

Buckley v. Valeo, 60–62, 67, 70, 80

Buckley, James, 59–60

Burger, Warren, 60–61, 155, 202n15, 215n14

Burke, Kenneth, 25

Burwell v. Hobby Lobby (abbreviated as

INDEX

Hobby Lobby), 84–85, 92, 98–109, 111, 184–85, 207n57, 207n59
Bush, George H. W., 56
Bush, George W., 56, 64–65, 68–69, 92, 141; *Bush v. Gore*, 68–69
Bush, Jeb, 76

cable television. *See* television
California, 75–76, 78, 81, 129, 140–45, 147–49, 155, 176, 186–88
campaign finance, 27, 67, 69, 202n21; 203n33, 203n36
campaign fundraising, 58, 61, 204n54
campaign spending, 57, 60, 79–81
Cantwell v. Connecticut, 117
captive audience, 116–17, 126, 129, 185
Carlin, George, 156–57
case at bar, 73, 122
case law, 15, 114–15
Catholicism, 19, 86–87, 90, 107, 122, 125–27, 184
censorship, 4, 14, 18, 42, 44, 74, 130–33, 137, 142–43, 148–50, 158–59, 162–63, 173–74, 179–81, 187, 216n25
Chaplinsky v. New Hampshire, 4, 16, 117, 119–21, 123, 127, 186
Cher (performer), 151
chilling effect, 6, 14, 19, 27–28, 44, 77, 155–57, 159, 162–63, 169, 176, 178, 181, 189
Christian Legal Society v. Martinez, 27, 44, 84–85, 92–94, 97, 183, 206n36
Cicero, 26, 198n47
Citizens United v. FEC, 27, 51–53, 57, 67–68, 70–80, 82–83, 109, 171, 182–84, 201n2, 203n40, 203n42
City of Boerne v. Flores, 91
Clinton, Bill, 132, 133
Clinton, Hillary, 67–68, 70, 76
close reading, 123

coaches, sports, 110–11
Cohen v. California, 120, 126
Colonial America, 17, 31–33, 36, 86, 88, 91, 146, 187
colonies, 10, 32–33, 84, 86, 113–14
Colorado Republican Committee v. FEC, 61
commercial speech, 7, 52, 70–73, 82, 182, 203n38
common carrier, 189
compelling government interest, 69–70, 115, 119, 124, 136, 144
Congress, 73–76, 78, 82, 87, 90–91, 99–100, 131–32, 134, 140–41, 161, 166, 168, 184, 189, 191
Connecticut, 85–86, 117
Connick v. Myers, 126, 210n22
conservative, 44, 59, 72, 74–75, 80, 123, 176, 183–84, 189–90
Constitution, US, 6–7, 10–11, 13, 25–26, 29, 33, 42, 59, 68, 81, 87, 91, 111, 115–16, 123, 140, 148, 154, 177, 189, 190–91
context, 10, 37, 51, 66, 94; campaign reform, 52–53; church-state separation, 85, 97; constitutional, 190–91; creating meaning, 6, 123–29, 212n8; economic, 108; equal protection, 105; expression, 134, 156; historical, 31, 35, 52, 119, 165, 191; liability, 40; political, 59, 72, 108; religious, 104, 105, 117; school, 38, 44, 45, 49, 50; threats, 170–71; violence, 133, 180; war, 211n47
contraceptives, 99, 100–102, 104–5
contributions: candidate, 53–57, 59–60, 62, 182, 201n5; corporate, 8, 52–54, 56, 63, 72, 78, 83; foreign, 61, 64; individual, 203n33; union, 8, 54, 56, 78. *See also* campaign finance; campaign fundraising

238

INDEX

corporate speech, 70–73, 81–82, 183
corporation rights, 69, 109
court order, 121, 135
Cox v. New Hampshire, 135
criminal, 5, 12, 15, 47, 115, 162–65, 171, 180, 190–91
crush videos, 142, 145, 165–68
Cruz, Ted, 76, 204n54
cyberbullying, 36, 46–47, 49, 181

Da Vinci, Leonardo, 24
Danbury, Connecticut, 85
Dante's inferno, 22
death, 3, 5, 9, 19, 24, 27, 130, 165, 175, 178, 181
defamation, 7, 18, 22, 121, 126, 134, 183
DeFilippo v. NBC, 139
Democratic (Party), 52, 54–55, 57, 59, 61, 63–64, 67, 75–76, 80
demonstrators, 2, 3, 5, 114–15, 119, 124–25, 129
discipline, 35, 39–40, 45, 47–49, 177, 180
discourse, 57, 123–25, 127–28, 147, 153, 180, 186, 189, 192
discrimination, 93, 94, 98, 102–3, 108, 135, 172, 184
District of Columbia v. Heller, 189
diversity, 86, 122
Doe et al v. Reed, 77
dogfighting, 164, 165, 168
Douglas, William O., 4, 119, 210n21
drug(s), 8, 37, 39, 44–45, 99, 180, 182
due process, 153

economy, 28, 32–34, 107–8, 133, 160, 163, 167, 169
Edenfield v. Fane, 137
Eisenstadt v. Baird, 105
electoral college, 1, 5
Elonis v. United States, 169–71, 192

emotion/al, 20–21, 166, 175; distress, 9, 18, 27, 119, 122–24, 126–29, 178, 185–86; stability, 8
Employment Division v. Smith, 89–90
Epicurus, 24
equal protection, 92–94, 98, 100, 102–5, 107–8, 111, 191
Erznoznik v. City of Jacksonville, 143, 144
establishment clause, 22, 33, 86, 88, 92, 100, 110–12, 192, 197n31

Facebook, 170, 189
Fahrenheit 9/11 (documentary), 56, 201n6; reference to *Fahrenheit 541* (Bradbury), 201n6
fairness doctrine, 134–35, 149, 210n21
faith based organizations, 92
family, 3, 8, 32, 48, 58, 125–26, 129, 131–32, 146, 149, 185
FCC v. League of Women Voters, 135
FCC v. Red Lion, 210n21
fear: Aristotle on, 175; Joanna Bourke on, 197n33; as pathe', 23; *Star Wars* on, 197n35; theoretical orientation 20–26. *See also individual chapters*
Federal Communication Commission (FCC), 19, 54, 131–32, 135, 140–41, 151–52, 156–60, 18889, 210n21
Federal Elections Commission v. Furgatch, 61
Federal Elections Commission v. Massachusetts Citizens for Life, 61
Federal Election Commission v. Wisconsin Right to Life, 67
Federalists, 11, 59, 85, 87, 91, 107. *See also* Anti-Federalists
Federalist Society, 191
fighting words, 4, 16–17, 117, 119, 121, 125, 127, 186

INDEX

First Amendment: assembly, 202n12, 204n55; censorship, 216n25; dress codes, 196n29; establishment clause, 196–97n31; ratification of, 10–11, 59, 87; religion, 210n21; speech, 210n22, 211n5. *See also* Bill of Rights: US; *individual chapters*

First National Bank of Boston v. Bellotti, 70

44 Liquormart, Inc. v. Rhode Island, 71

Foucault, Michel, 26, 35

Fourteenth Amendment, 47, 53, 93–94, 98, 153, 190, 210n23

FOX News, 3

FOX Television, 151, 152, 157–59, 161, 162, 164, 171

Frankfurter, Felix, 123, 210n21

fraud, 28, 162, 169

free exercise clause, 88, 90, 93–94, 109, 184, 192

freedom: of assembly, 81, 201n12; of conscience, 10; of expression, 12, 14, 15, 18, 29, 45–47, 59–60, 94–95, 114–15, 119, 122, 134, 139, 178, 182, 184–85, 201n6; of press, 7, 16–17, 22; of religion, 27, 85, 205n8; of speech, 18, 42, 46, 50, 62, 110, 118, 142, 144, 146, 153–54, 201n48, 211n45

Frisby v. Schultz, 115, 124, 209n3

Fromm, Erich, 26

"fuck" as expletive, 49, 120, 151–52, 157, 173, 195n12. *See also* freedom: of speech

Galella v. Onassis, 116, 209n5

Gideon v. Wainwright, 191

Ginsberg v. New York, 143, 144, 147, 187

Ginsburg, Ruth Bader, 69, 93, 95, 100–102, 142, 206n36

Gonzales v. O Centro Espirita, 91

government: city, 11, 30, 41, 86, 113–15, 121, 139, 158; county, 34, 120–21; federal v. state, 85

Grayned v. City of Rockford, 14

groups, 1, 14–15, 19, 40, 44, 56–57, 59, 61, 64, 75–77, 86–87, 90–98, 103, 111, 145, 160, 169, 184, 212n7; registered student organizations (RSOs), 93, 94, 95, 206n32

guns, 36, 40, 168; gun control, 189. *See also* Second Amendment

Hamilton, Alexander, 91

Hamlet, 130, 141, 145, 150

Hanna, Mark, 52, 53, 201n1

Harlan, John Marshall, 215n14, 120, 153–55

harmful speech, 7, 8, 128

hate speech, 136, 172, 181

Hazelwood School v. Kuhlmeier, 18, 49, 179–80

heckler's veto, 121

Heidegger, Martin, 24

Heins, Marjorie, 137

Hein v. Freedom from Religion Foundation, 92

Hill v. Colorado, 116

historic context, 31, 52

Hobbes, Thomas, 25

Holder v. Humanitarian Law Project, 14

Holmes, Oliver Wendell, 3, 177

hunting, 165, 167–68

Hustler Magazine v. Falwell, 17–18, 123

ideology / ideological, 4–6, 26, 31, 81, 96, 116, 126, 149–50, 172

in loco parentis, 146, 181

incitement, 1, 3–4, 6, 15, 143, 195nn1–2

inclusiveness, 19, 144

indecency, 18–19, 28, 131, 133, 136,

240

INDEX

139–41, 148–49, 151–54, 156–61, 164, 169, 172–74, 178, 188–89
insurrection, 1, 3, 5–6, 195nn1–2
intentional, 9, 18, 128, 160, 164–65, 188
Iraq, 122

Jackson, Andrew, 149
Jackson, Janet, 152, 159
Jackson, Robert, 50
Jefferson, Thomas, 11, 19, 32, 34, 42–43, 73, 85, 88, 146, 177, 179, 190, 192, 196n31
J. S. v. Blue Mountain School District, 47
Juneau, Alaska, 30, 37, 40–41, 43, 50, 181

Kagan, Elena, 69, 100, 142
Kennedy v. Bremerton School District, 85, 109–11
Kennedy, Anthony, 38, 68–70, 72–74, 77–78, 82, 94, 96, 140, 142, 180, 183–84, 189, 192, 199n24
Kierkegaard, Soren, 22, 197n36
King, Martin Luther, Jr., 196n26

Lawrence v. Texas, 206n36
Layshock v. Hermitage School District, 47
Lee v. Weisman, 116
LGBT people, 27, 93, 94, 98, 103–4, 108, 122, 125, 184, 185, 206n36; expletives slurring, 188, 122, 220n11
liability, 40–41, 121, 125, 158–59, 163, 171
libel, 7, 18, 127, 167, 183, 189
liberal, 26, 59, 64, 72, 77, 80, 85, 104, 123, 172, 176, 189, 191
Lincoln, Abraham, 11–12, 149–50, 195n16
living constitution, 81–82

Lockner v. New York, 53
Loving v. Virginia, 103

Machiavellianism, 26, 67
Madison, James, 26, 33–34, 86–87, 177, 190–92
majority rule, 79
Mann, Horace, 35
Mapp v. Ohio, 191
Marbury v. Madison, 191
marches, 121
marijuana, 27, 43, 181
marketplace of ideas, 8, 23–24, 65, 70, 73, 75, 81–82, 94, 120, 135, 176, 182–83
Marshall, Thurgood, 14, 196n21
Maryland, 11–12, 84, 86, 122, 125, 127–29, 186
Massachusetts, 31–32, 35, 61, 70, 84, 86, 105, 170
Masterpiece Cakeshop v. Colorado Civil Rights Commission, 192
McCain-Feingold law, 65, 66–67, 73–74, 77–78
McCain, John, 58, 65, 132
McConnell v. FEC, 66–67, 70, 72, 183, 203n42
McCutcheon v. FEC, 80
McIntyre v. Ohio Elections Commission, 59
Miller v. California, 18, 143, 145, 147, 155–57, 161, 187
Minersville School District v. Gobitis, 210n21, 211n47
minority: opinion, 9, 25, 43; racial: 15; rights: 25, 43, 91–92, 95, 134, 136, 169, 177, 192
money, 32–33, 53, 55, 56–60, 62–67, 70, 72–73, 76, 78–79, 81–82, 182
Montana, 79, 165
Montesquieu (Baron de Montesquieu, Charles-Louis de Secondat), 26, 85

241

INDEX

Moore v. Ingebretsen, 116
Morse v. Frederick, 27, 30–31, 36, 37–50, 90, 118, 147, 179–81, 200n29
movement, 12, 19, 53, 102–3, 105, 108
MySpace, 47–48

NAACP v. Alabama, 77, 96, 202n12
narrow tailoring, 46, 48–49, 54, 137, 147, 161, 166, 168, 187
National Socialist Party of America v. Village of Skokie, 121
Native Americans, 145. *See also* American Indians
Near v. Minnesota, 17–18
New York, 36, 59, 70, 76, 87, 133, 147
New York Times Co. v. Sullivan, 196n26
New York Times v. United States, 16
news, 3, 17–18, 22, 54, 70, 76–77, 113, 122, 134, 138, 148, 152, 156, 158–59, 183, 210n21
Nietzsche, Friedrich, 22
Nixon, Richard, 6, 54–55, 62, 70
Nixon v. Shrink Missouri Government PAC, 62
nondiscrimination policy, 93, 97–98
North Carolina, 80, 87
NYPD Blue (TV series), 151

O'Connor, Sandra Day, 67, 91, 115, 206n36
Obama, Barack, 51–52, 58, 75, 83, 98, 173; *Obama 2016* (documentary), 77
Obamacare. *See* Affordable Care Act (ACA; also known as "Obamacare")
obscenity, 18, 120, 131, 136, 139, 143–44, 148–49, 153–55, 161, 186–87

offensiveness, 16, 19, 75, 119–20, 122, 139, 142, 149, 151, 155–56, 172, 188, 196n30
Ohio, 4, 15, 52, 59, 75, 201n1
Olivia N. v. NBC, 139
organization, 14, 26–27, 56, 58, 60–61, 65, 85, 91, 93, 95–97, 107–9, 160, 184
original meaning, 38, 81, 74, 123, 146, 180, 187, 189–91, 192, 210n23, 220n18

Pacifica v. FCC, 19, 156–57
Pawelczyk, Elizabeth A., 39, 200n29
personal attack, 48, 123–27, 129
Phelps, Fred, 122–28, 185. See also *Snyder v. Phelps*; Westboro Baptist Church.
Plato, 24, 175
Pleasant Grove City v. Summum, 92, 171
Pointer v. Texas, 191
police, 2, 11, 39, 133, 155, 160, 166, 196n26
political action committees (and super PACs), 54, 56, 58, 62–63, 65, 76, 80–82
Powell, Lewis, 60, 70, 71, 202n15
president, 1–6, 11, 13–14, 19, 51–52, 54–58, 64–65, 70, 7576, 79, 85, 92, 98, 131, 141, 149, 191–92, 204n62
principals, school, 18, 30, 36–37, 39–40, 47–48
prior restraint, 159
privacy, 14, 18, 58, 92, 108–9, 114–17, 122, 124–26, 128, 178, 185
private schools, 179
pro-choice advocacy, 105. *See also* abortion
protection from indoctrination, 89, 179

242

INDEX

protest, 4, 8, 14, 16, 29, 36, 55, 77, 114, 117, 122–25, 129, 180, 185

psychological effects, 20, 28, 30, 134, 138, 144–45, 147, 148, 150, 166, 168

public forum, 94, 96, 98, 118, 148

Puiszis, Steven M., 201n48

race and racism, 4–5, 19, 103, 169, 172, 195n10

Reagan, Ronald, 191

"reasonable person" standard, 142, 170–71, 187–88

Regina v. Hicklin, 18

regulation, 15, 27, 36, 38, 48, 57, 71, 73, 86, 88–89, 131–37, 143–44, 149, 152–58, 160–62, 166, 171, 173, 180, 183–84

religion, free exercise of, 88, 90, 93–94, 109, 184, 192, 205n8

Religious Freedom Restoration Act (RFRA), 90–92, 98–99, 102–3, 184–85

renaissance, 22, 84

Reno v. ACLU, 139

Republican (Party), 1, 3, 5, 55, 57–59, 61, 63–64, 66, 75–76, 80, 85, 118, 182, 191, 202n21, 204n57, 210n21

Revolutionary War, 33–34, 177

Rehnquist, William, 16, 60, 71, 202n15

Reynolds v. United States, 88

rhetoric/rhetorical, 8–10, 21, 30, 52, 72, 76, 98, 104, 108–9, 112, 114, 120, 125, 152, 153, 168–69, 172–75, 178, 189, 192, 196–97n31, 220n17

Richie, Nicole, 151–52

rights: civil rights, 102; habeas corpus, 11, 19, 190, 195. *See also* freedom

risk, 29, 33, 39–41, 77, 98, 100, 156–58, 162–64

Roberts, John, 37–38, 68–69, 74, 80, 123–26, 128–29, 142, 144, 165, 171, 192

Roberts Court, 8, 10, 20, 26–28, 30, 52, 85, 92, 111, 114, 152, 169, 172–73, 179–80, 185

Roosevelt, Franklin, 54, 192

Roosevelt, Theodore, 52–53, 79, 201n1

Roth v. United States, 18, 153–55

Rove, Karl, 74, 80, 204n62

Russell, Bertrand, 23

safety, 7, 14–15, 19, 24, 38, 46, 89, 111, 141

Santa Fe Independent School District v. Doe, 116

Sartre, Jean-Paul, 23

Scalia, Antonin, 74, 77, 81, 90, 95, 142–44, 149, 189, 214n52

Schenck v. United States, 3, 15–16

schools; captive audience, 116–17, 126, 129, 185; learning environment, 29, 38, 46, 178–81

schoolhouse, 18, 29, 35–36, 45–49, 110, 118, 181

scientific evidence, 148

Second Amendment, 168, 189

Section 230 of Communication Act, 189

security, 1, 2, 11, 15–16, 26, 33, 85, 115, 178

Senate, 3, 5, 12, 33, 53, 55, 65–66, 76, 79–80, 166

separation of church and state, 19, 26, 51, 84–85, 88, 96, 196–97n31, 204n1

sexual assault/harassment, 142

sexual conduct, 7, 18–19, 36, 93, 105, 108, 131, 140, 148, 151–53, 155–57, 160, 166, 168, 185, 188

Sherbert v. Verner, 88–90

INDEX

"shit," as expletive, 151–52. *See also* freedom: of speech

slander, 7, 183, 189

Snyder v. Phelps, 9, 27, 113–15, 117–19, 122–29, 171, 185–86, 192. See *also* Phelps, Fred; Westboro Baptist Church

social media, 1, 70, 170, 181

Sotomayor, Sonia, 100–101, 110, 142

South Carolina, 11, 53, 89

Spanish Inquisition, 86

stare decisis, 78

states' rights, 85, 91

Stern, Howard, 160

Sternheimer, Karen, 133, 212n8, 213n26

Stevens, John Paul, 16, 43–44, 59, 67, 69–74, 81–83, 139, 163, 181, 189

Stewart, Malcolm, 68, 89

Stewart, Potter, 60, 202n15

Stone, Harlan Fisk, 210n21

strict scrutiny, 90, 144

Sweezy v. New Hampshire, 50

symbolic speech, 59, 117–19, 121, 170, 189

television, 1, 67–68, 70, 77, 134, 158, 160–61, 189, 211n5, 213n26, 214n47, 216n25

Terminiello v. The City of Chicago, 4, 119, 186

terror, 11, 13–14, 19–21, 26–27, 85, 115, 169, 173

Texas, 118, 167, 172, 185

Texas v. Johnson, 16, 118, 186

Thomas, Clarence, 21, 38–39, 77, 78, 81, 140, 142–43, 146–47, 149, 161, 169, 172, 180, 187, 189, 214n52

threats, 3–6, 81, 170–71, 188, 191, 193, 218n69

Tinker v. Des Moines, 18, 29, 37–38,

44–46, 49, 110, 117–18, 121, 143, 180, 186, 187

Trump, Donald, 1–6, 63

Turner Broadcasting System, Inc. v. FCC, 135

Turner, Kathleen, 220n17

Twitter (X), 189

unconstitutionality, 15, 59, 62, 65–66, 71, 79–80, 82, 131, 133, 135–36, 147, 157, 161, 166

United Nations, 14

United States v. Cruikshank, 204n55

United States v. Playboy Entertainment Group, Inc., 18

universities, 34–35, 76, 105, 114, 133, 138, 141, 191

vagueness, 8, 14, 44, 85, 96, 118, 123, 133, 136, 139, 145, 147, 149, 157, 186, 191

veto, 54

Vico, Giambattista, 25

video games, 8, 36, 130, 133–35, 137–49, 176, 186–87, 203n38

Vietnam War, 13, 29, 55, 117–18, 120, 180

viewpoint discrimination, 98

violence, 3, 4, 7, 12–15, 35–36, 40, 45, 114, 119–22, 130–50, 152, 169, 171–72, 176, 180, 186–87, 191, 211n5, 213n26, 214n63

violent speech, 143

Virginia v. Black, 21, 169–71

Virginia State Board of Pharmacy v. Virginia Citizens Consumer Council, 71

Walker v. Texas Division, Sons of Confederate Veterans, 171

Walt Disney Productions v. Shannon, 139